INTRODUCTION TO ADDICTIVE BEHAVIORS

THE GUILFORD SUBSTANCE ABUSE SERIES
HOWARD T. BLANE and THOMAS R. KOSTEN, Editors

Recent Volumes

Introduction to Addictive Behaviors
DENNIS L. THOMBS

Treating Alcohol Problems: Marital and Family Interventions
TIMOTHY J. O'FARRELL, Editor

Clinical Work with Substance-Abusing Clients
SHULAMITH LALA ASHENBERG STRAUSSNER, Editor

Clean Start: An Outpatient Program for Initiating Cocaine Recovery
WILLIAM E. McAULIFFE and JEFFREY ALBERT

Clinician's Guide to Cocaine Addiction:
Theory, Research, and Treatment
THOMAS R. KOSTEN and HERBERT D. KLEBER, Editors

Alcohol Tolerance and Social Drinking: Learning the Consequences
MURIEL VOGEL-SPROTT

Removing the Roadblocks: Group Psychotherapy
with Substance Abusers and Family Members
MARSHA VANNICELLI

Preventing AIDS in Drug Users and Their Sexual Partners
JAMES L. SORENSEN, LAURIE A. WERMUTH, DAVID R. GIBSON,
KYUNG-HEE CHOI, JOSEPH R. GUYDISH, and STEVEN L. BATKI

Alcohol in Human Violence
KAI PERNANEN

Clinical Textbook of Addictive Disorders
RICHARD J. FRANCES and SHELDON I. MILLER, Editors

Drinking and Driving: Advances in Research and Prevention
R. JEAN WILSON and ROBERT E. MANN, Editors

Addiction and the Vulnerable Self:
Modified Dynamic Group Therapy for Substance Abusers
EDWARD J. KHANTZIAN, KURT S. HALLIDAY,
and WILLIAM E. McAULIFFE

Alcohol and the Family: Research and Clinical Perspectives
R. LORRAINE COLLINS, KENNETH E. LEONARD,
and JOHN S. SEARLES, Editors

Introduction
to Addictive Behaviors

DENNIS L. THOMBS, PhD

THE GUILFORD PRESS
New York   London

© 1994 The Guilford Press
A Division of Guilford Publications, Inc.
72 Spring Street, New York, NY 10012

Printed in the United States of America

This book is printed on acid-free paper.

Last digit is print number: 9   8   7   6   5   4   3   2   1

Library of Congress Cataloging-in-Publication Data

Thombs, Dennis L.
    Introduction to addictive behaviors / Dennis L. Thombs.
        p.   cm.
    Includes bibliographical references and index.
    ISBN 0-89862-336-7
    1. Substance abuse—Etiology.   2. Substance
abuse—Treatment.   I. Title
    RC564.T55   1993
    616.86′071—dc20   93-30812
                                                              CIP

To Ken Beck,
whose investment in my professional growth
made this book possible

Acknowledgments

The following publishers have generously given permission to use extended quotations or paraphrases, and/or to reprint or adapt tables or figures, from published works:

From "Alcohol Problems in Adoptees Raised Apart from Alcoholic Biologic Parents" by D. W. Goodwin, F. Schulsinger, L. Hermansen, S. B. Guze, and G. Winokur, 1973, *Archives of General Psychiatry, 28,* 238−243. Copyright 1973 by the American Medical Association.

From *Beyond Freedom and Dignity* by B. F. Skinner, 1975, New York: Bantam. Copyright 1975 by B. F. Skinner. Used by permission of Random House, Inc.

From "Theory in the Practice of Psychotherapy" by M. Bowen, 1976, in P. J. Guerin (Ed.), *Family Therapy: Theory and Practice,* New York: Gardner Press. Copyright 1976 by Gardner Press, Inc.

From *Theories of Personality* (3rd ed.) by C. S. Hall and G. Lindzey, 1978, New York: Wiley. Copyright 1978 by John Wiley & Sons, Inc.

From "Principles of Alcoholism Psychotherapy" by S. Zimberg, 1978, in S. Zimberg, J. Wallace, and S. Blume (Eds.), *Practical Approaches to Alcoholism Psychotherapy,* New York: Plenum Press. Copyright 1978 by Plenum Publishing Corporation.

From "Function of Theory in Counseling" by B. Stefflre and H. M. Burks, 1979, in H. M. Burks and B. Stefflre (Eds.), *Theories of Counseling,* New York: McGraw-Hill. Copyright 1979 by McGraw-Hill, Inc.

From *I'll Quit Tomorrow* (rev. ed.) by V. E. Johnson, 1980, San Francisco: Harper & Row. Copyright 1980 by V. E. Johnson. Used by permission of HarperCollinsPublishers, Inc.

From *Broken Bottles, Broken Dreams: Understanding and Helping the Children of Alcoholics* by C. Deutsch, 1982, New York: Teachers College Press. Copyright 1982 by Teachers College, Columbia University.

Preface

This book was written for the entry-level substance abuse counselor and the practicing mental health professional with no formal training in the addictions. It is intended for students who want to establish careers as substance abuse counselors, and for those professionals currently in practice who have never had the opportunity to learn about the major contemporary perspectives on alcohol and drug dependence. The book has two primary goals. The first is to challenge and strengthen the reader's understanding of addiction by exploring how others in the field have come to know it; I hope that this will enable the reader to create a clear and logically consistent perspective on addiction. The second goal is to show the reader how theory and research are important to clinical practice. This should provide the reader with an array of treatment strategies that are vital to the principle of individualized treatment planning, and help make him or her an effective practitioner.

There are a number of good books currently available on theories of alcoholism and other drug dependencies. For the most part, however, these books are written at an advanced level. They often target advanced graduate students in psychology, sophisticated practitioners, or academics and researchers in the field. The present text is unique in that it attempts to bring contemporary behavioral science theory and research to the front-line practitioner. Those in the "trenches" have often operated in isolation, separated from the research community. Exposure to complex and divergent theories of addictive behavior has often been neglected in the preparation and training of mental health professionals, including substance abuse counselors, social workers, psychologists, nurses, and so forth. Some of these practitioners are familiar with the disease model, but even they have not had the opportunity to examine its propositions critically. This book assumes virtually no pre-existing knowledge in the biological or behavioral sciences. In every case, a careful attempt has been made to explain the concepts upon which each theory is built.

This book is also distinctive in that it emphasizes behavioral science perspectives on addiction. This is purposeful: It may be used in college-based programs that offer a variety of courses on different aspects of addiction. The study of neuroscience, psychopharmacology, and drug metabolism would also be expected to comprise large segments of other courses in such a curriculum, and there are a number of adequate texts already in print in these areas. This text is best suited for use in college courses that examine the behavioral or psychosocial foundations of addiction.

Special thanks are in order to several people for helping me complete this book. I am indebted to Vicky Willis for her assistance in preparing the manuscript; her patience through the many revisions is very much appreciated. I am also grateful to The Guilford Press, and especially to Seymour Weingarten, for his interest in the book. Finally, thanks go to Colleen and Ryan for their love and support.

Dennis L. Thombs
State University of New York at Brockport

Contents

Chapter Six. Family Systems Theory   139

Chapter Seven. Sociocultural Perspectives   190
on Alcohol and Drug Abuse

Chapter Eight. Implications for Clinical Practice   219

Index   227

INTRODUCTION TO ADDICTIVE BEHAVIORS

The Usefulness of Theory and Research in Understanding Addictive Behavior

Historically, alcohol and drug dependencies have been viewed as either sins or diseases. In recent decades, they have also been considered maladaptive behavior patterns (i.e., debilitative habits that have been "overlearned"). Some people today insist that addiction evolves from all three sources—namely, that it is a *disease* in which people *learn* to act in *immoral* ways. This line of reasoning obscures fundamental differences in three visions of addiction. Each of these views suggests different means for controlling the problem of addiction in our society. Let us examine each in turn.

ADDICTION AS SIN

The first position maintains that addiction represents a refusal to abide by some ethical or moral code of conduct. Excessive drinking or drug use is considered freely chosen behavior that is at best irresponsible and at worst evil. By identifying addiction as sin, one does not necessarily ascribe the same level of "evilness" to it as one would to rape, larceny, or murder. Nevertheless, in this view it remains a transgression, a wrong.

Note that this position assumes that alcohol and drug abuse are freely chosen—in other words, that in regard to this sphere of human conduct, people are free agents. Alcoholics and addicts are not considered "out of control"; they choose to use substances in such a way that they create suffering for others (e.g., family members) and for themselves. Thus, they can be justifiably blamed for having the alcohol/drug problem.

Because addiction results from a freely chosen and morally wrong course of action, the logical way to "treat" the problem is to punish the alcoholic or addict. Thus, from this perspective, legal sanctions such as jail sentences, fines, and other punitive actions are seen as most appropriate. The addict is not thought to be deserving of care or help. Rather, punishment is relied upon to rectify past misdeeds and to prevent further chemical use. Relapse is considered evidence of lingering evil in the addict; again, then, punishment is believed to be needed to correct "slipping."

In our society today, this perspective on substance abuse is typically advocated by politically conservative groups, law enforcement organizations, zealous religious factions, and groups of individuals who have been personally harmed by alcoholics/addicts (e.g., Mothers Against Drunk Driving). During political campaigns, candidates frequently appeal to this sentiment by proposing tougher legal penalties for possession and distribution of illicit drugs and for drunken driving. U.S. history is marked by repeated (and failed) government efforts to eliminate addiction with such legal sanctions. The crackdown on Chinese opium smokers in the 1800s and the enactment of Prohibition in the early 20th century stand as two noteworthy examples.

The "addiction as sin" position has several advantages, as well as disadvantages. One advantage is that it is straightforward and clear. There is little ambiguity or murkiness associated with this stance. Furthermore, it is absolute; there is no need for theorizing or philosophizing about the nature of addiction. It is simply misbehavior, and as such needs to be confronted and hence punished. Scientific investigation of the problem is believed to be unnecessary, because that which must be done to correct it (i.e., application of sanctions) is already well understood. In this view, our society's inability to adequately address the problems of alcoholism and addiction reflects widespread moral decay. Proponents of the "addiction as sin" model typically call for a return to "traditional" or "family" values as the way to ameliorate the problem.

There are at least three disadvantages to the "addiction as sin" model as well. First, science suggests that alcoholism and addiction are anything but simple phenomena. They appear to be multifactorial in origin, stemming from pharmcological, biological, psychological, and social factors. The apparent complexity of addiction is underscored by the variety of diverse theories seeking to explain it (many of which are described in this volume). Moreover, as science has begun to shed light on various aspects of compulsive chemical use, it has become clearer that much still remains to be learned. The genetic vulnerability hypothesis, alcohol expectancy theory, and the purported stabilizing effects of alcoholism on family structure are all cases in point.

Another disadvantage with the moral point of view is that it is not at all clear that chemical dependencies are freely chosen. In fact, the disease model (see below) maintains that exactly the opposite is the case. That is, excessive drinking or drugging represents being out of control, or there exists a loss of control; in either case, the substance abuse is not freely chosen by the individual. A further point of departure is offered by the behavioral sciences, where, at least in several theoretical perspectives, a high rate of chemical self-administration is understood to be under the control of social or environmental contingencies. These contingencies are usually external to alcoholics or addicts, and are not under their personal control. Thus, both the disease model and the behavioral sciences challenge the notion that addiction is willful misconduct.

A third disadvantage with the "addiction as sin" position is that history suggests that punishment is an ineffective means of reducing the prevalence of addictive problems in the population. Aside from the issue of inhumane sanctions (a real possibility if a political majority adopts the moral view of addiction), a reasonably strong case can be made, based upon historical precedents, that striking back at substance abusers via governmental authority simply does not work over an extended period of time. In fact, law enforcement crackdowns often have the unintended effects of being an impetus for strengthening organized crime networks, creating underground markets, bolstering disrespect for the law, clogging court dockets, and overloading prisons (at substantial cost to the taxpayer).

ADDICTION AS A DISEASE

In the second view, excessive consumption of alcohol or drugs is the result of an underlying disease process. The disease process is thought to cause compulsive use; in other words, the high rate and volume of use are merely the manifest symptoms of an illness. The exact nature of the illness is not fully understood at this point, but many proponents of the disease model believe that it has genetic origins. For these reasons, it is hypothesized that individuals cannot drink or drug themselves into alcoholism or drug addiction. If the disease (possibly arising from a genetic vulnerability) is not present, then dependencies cannot develop, no matter how much of the substance is consumed.

The "addiction as a disease" model maintains that the alcoholic and addict are victims of an illness. The afflicted individual is not evil or irresponsible, just sick. Thus, the chemical abuse is not freely chosen; rather, the excessive drinking or drugging is seen to be beyond the control of the sufferer. In fact, a chief characteristic of addiction in the disease model is the loss of control over substance use. It is hypothesized that once an addict has consumed a small amount of a drug, intense cravings are triggered via unknown physiological mechanisms, and these cravings lead to compulsive overuse. This mechanism is beyond the personal control of the addict.

Since alcoholics and addicts are seen as suffering from an illness, the logical conclusion is that they deserve compassionate care, help, and treatment. Because the condition is considered a disease, medical treatment is appropriate. Competent treatment, then, especially on an inpatient basis, should be supervised by physicians. Traditionally, treatment based on the disease model has emphasized the management of medical complications (e.g., liver disease, stomach ulcer, anemia), as well as patient education about the disease model and about recovery.

The disease model is strongly advocated by at least three groups in our society today. One of these is the profession of medicine. Critics have indicated that physicians have a vested interest in convincing society that addiction is a disease. As long as it is considered such, they can admit patients to hospitals, bill insurance companies, and collect fees. Another group that has strongly advocated the disease model is the alcohol industry (i.e., the brewers, distillers, and winemakers), which also has a vested interest in viewing alcoholism, specifically, as a disease. As long as it is a disease suffered by only 10% of all drinkers, then our society (i.e., our government) will not take serious steps to restrict the manufacture, distribution, sale, and consumption of alcoholic beverages. In other words, the alcohol industry wants us to believe that the problem lies within the "host" (i.e., the alcoholic), and not with the "agent" (i.e., alcohol). A third group that strongly advocates the disease model is the "recovery movement," which is made up of individuals and families recovering from chemical dependencies. This group can also be considered to have a vested interest in identifying alcoholism and addiction as diseases. First, calling alcoholism or addiction a disease makes it more respectable than labeling it a moral problem or a mental disorder. Second, maintaining that it is a disease can serve to reduce possible guilt or shame about past misdeeds. This may allow recovering individuals to focus on the work that they need to do to maintain a chemical-free life.

There are a number of advantages to the disease model. Most importantly, addiction is taken out of the moral realm, and its victims are helped rather than scorned and punished. In addition, society is more willing to allocate resources to help persons who have a disease than to individuals who are merely wicked. It is also clear that the disease model has helped hundreds of thousands of alcoholics and addicts to return to healthful living. Thus, its utility in assisting at least a large subset of addicts is beyond question.

There are also a number of disadvantages to the disease model; only a few are discussed here. (Chapter Two includes a more extensive discussion of these.) Briefly, several of the key concepts of the disease model have not held up under scientific scrutiny. For example, the loss-of-control hypothesis, the supposedly progressive course of alcoholism, and the belief that a return to controlled drinking is impossible are all propositions that have been seriously challenged by scientific investigations. Within the scientific community, it is widely acknowledged that little empirical evidence supports the disease model. Unfortunately, a large segment of the treatment community appears to be unaware of this literature, or perhaps chooses to ignore it.

ADDICTION AS MALADAPTIVE BEHAVIOR

The third position holds that addiction is a behavioral disorder; as such, it is shaped by the same laws that shape all human behavior. Essentially, then, addiction is learned. It is neither sinful (as the moral model purports) nor out of control (as the disease model purports). Instead, it is seen as a problem behavior that is clearly under the control of environmental, family, social, and/or even cognitive contingencies. The addict, as in the disease model, is seen as a victim—not a victim of a disease, but a victim of destructive learning conditions. For the most part, addictive behavior is not freely chosen, although some behavioral science theories (e.g., social learning theory) do assert that addicts retain some degree of control over their drinking or drugging.

It is important to understand the value placed upon objectivity in the behavioral sciences. When alcoholism (or addiction) is described as a "maladaptive behavior," this is very different from describing the condition as "misbehavior" (a moral perspective). Behavioral scientists avoid passing judgment on the "rightness" or "wrongness" of substance abuse. By "maladaptive," the behavioral scientist means that the behavior pattern has destructive consequences for addicts and/or their families (and possibly society). It does not imply that the addicts are bad or irresponsible.

In the behavioral science view, the most appropriate treatments are based on learning principles. More specifically, "clients" (this term is preferred over "patients") are taught skills to prevent relapse. The medical aspects of treatment are attended to when necessary, but they are generally de-emphasized. The emphasis instead is placed on client training and on experimentation with these procedures. Behavioral scientists are most heavily involved in this treatment approach.

At present, the only strong advocacy groups for this position are professional organizations of scientists and practitioners who work in the area. One example is the Society of Psychologists in Addictive Behaviors. This group, and others like it, are relatively small in number and work without the benefit of much political clout or public recognition. Furthermore, behaviorally oriented treatment is labor-intensive and research-oriented. It is constantly evolving as new data are generated. These characteristics appear to have little appeal to most conventional, community-based treatment programs. However, it should be added that with the growing demand for accountability and positive outcomes, treatment programs may become increasingly interested in behavioral science methods.

THE NEED FOR THEORY

Why a book on *theories* of addictive behavior? As the discussion up to this point has outlined, there exist today three broad perspectives (i.e., sin, disease, maladaptive behavior) on the nature of addiction. The first, the moral model, is not a theory, at least as the term "theory" is understood in science. The disease model is the theoretical base from which most treatment providers operate in the United States today. The behavioral science perspectives, though sharing an emphasis on faulty learning, are represented by an array of distinctive theoretical positions. It is my own belief that the "addiction as sin" position is the only perspective that is clearly understood by the majority of professionals working in the alcohol and drug abuse field today. This is not to say that they rely on it; indeed, the moral model is almost universally rejected by competent practitioners (with good reason, as has been mentioned above). Unfortunately, it appears that critical examination of the disease model and the various behavioral science theories has been largely ignored by many in the alcohol and drug abuse field. All too often, practitioners rigidly cling to their favorite theory, in many cases without fully understanding all its concepts and implications. At the same time, other theories may be callously disregarded. Stefflre and Burks (1979) maintain that because *all* counselors necessarily operate from a theory (it may be informal or personal, but nevertheless exists), it is essential that they hold the theory "explicitly"—that is, that they understand it with great clarity. These authors state:

> Just as the personality defects and emotional problems of the counselor need not preclude the possibility of effective work if they are taken into account and corrected for, so theory may be used better in counseling if we are aware that the theory is held, and if we acknowledge its limitations and some of the sources of its attraction to us. (p. 10)

In my view, the nearly dogmatic stance that some practitioners take today regarding the disease model is slowing the development of the addictions treatment field. Clearly, the disease model has helped a large number of chemically dependent clients. However, as judged by the very large number of addicts who refuse treatment, drop out of treatment, and/or relapse, it can be reasonably asserted that the disease model is not a "good fit" for many (perhaps most) chemically dependent clients. It is imperative that practitioners consider alternative models of recovery for clients who cannot work within the disease model. All too often, such clients are labeled as "being in denial." This tendency to reduce all client resistance to denial can obscure the possibility that the problem may lie in the treatment model, not in the clients. Rather than forcing a model on clients, perhaps we should work to help them discover their own paths to recovery. If these paths include traditional approaches, that is fine. However, as practitioners, we should possess the flexibility to guide clients in different directions as well. The theories outlined in detail in this volume will inform and assist counselors in identifying appropriate options.

WHAT EXACTLY IS A THEORY?

The popular understanding of the term "theory" is usually "a belief that stands in opposition to fact." Many of us have heard someone retort, "Oh, that's just a theory." In other words, theories are commonly thought to be unsubstantiated hypotheses or speculation. Furthermore, there is a tendency to equate theory with things that are impractical or devoid of common sense. However, as Monette, Sullivan, and De Jong (1990) note, all of us necessarily rely on theories to function in our relationships with family members, friends, professional colleagues, and others. In most cases, these theories are crude and not explicit; nonetheless, they exist, if only in our minds. Thus, to dismiss theory as useless is to fail to recognize its universal application, both in science and in everyday life.

Hall and Lindzey (1978) define the term "theory" as a "set of conventions created by the theorist" (p. 10). This straightforward definition underscores the fact that theories are not predetermined by nature or data or any other orderly process. It rests largely on the theorist's prior knowledge and creativity. In the following passage, Hall and Lindzey (1978) insightfully describe it this way:

> Just as the same experiences or observations may lead a poet or novelist to create any one of a multitude of different art forms, so the data of investigation may be incorporated in any of countless different theoretical schemes. The theorist in choosing one particular option to represent the events in which he or she is interested is exercising a free creative choice that is different from the artist's only in the kinds of evidence upon which it focuses and the grounds upon which its fruitfulness will be judged. . . . There is no formula for fruitful theory construction any more than there is a formula for making enduring literary contributions. (p. 10)

The basic function of a theory is to organize data or our observations of some phenomenon (Monette et al., 1990). Theories allow us to impose order and meaning on a collection of isolated observations. Thus, they attempt to make sense of dissimilar findings and to explain relationships among variables of interest.

Because a theory is provisional (i.e., it does not explain in absolute or final terms), it is inappropriate to characterize it as "true" or "false." Instead, it is best described as "useful" or "not useful" (Hall & Lindzey, 1978). A theory's utility, then, can be assessed by its ability to predict events, or by how closely the data generated in research support hypothesized relationships.

FORMAL ATTRIBUTES OF A GOOD THEORY

Stefflre and Burks (1979) have identified five formal attributes of a good theory. They are described below.

1. *Clarity.* A good theory must exhibit clarity in a number of ways. First, there should be agreement among its general assumptions (i.e., its philosophical foundation), as well as agreement between its consequences and generated data or observations (i.e., its scientific foundation). Second, the propositions of a good theory should be clearly described and easily communicated. Third, a good theory should serve as "an easily read map" (Stefflre & Burks, 1979, p. 9)

2. *Comprehensiveness.* A good theory can be applied to many individuals in many different situations. Its ability to explain events should extend across a variety of time periods, geographic areas, sociocultural contexts, and sociodemographic variables (e.g., gender, race, religion, etc.).

3. *Explicitness.* Precision is a chief characteristic of a good theory. Important theoretical concepts must be capable of being defined operationally. That is, concepts must be measurable with a high degree of reliability. Theories that rely on vague, ill-defined, or difficult-to-measure concepts cannot be checked against clear referents in the real world (Stefflre & Burks, 1979).

4. *Parsimony.* A good theory explains phenomena in a relatively simple and straightforward manner. A theory that can explain behavioral events in innumerable ways is suspect. A theory that "overexplains" something may be creative, but it may also be fiction. That is, it may not accurately reflect reality.

5. *Generation of useful research findings.* A good theory has a history of generating research findings (i.e., data) that support its concepts. Theories that have little or no empirical support are less useful than those that have considerable data driving further investigation of its propositions. Stefflre and Burk (1979) summarize these formal attributes by stating: "A theory is always a map that is in the process of being filled in with greater detail. We do not so much ask whether it is true, but whether it is helpful" (p. 9).

SUBSTANTIVE ATTRIBUTES OF THEORIES
OF ADDICTIVE BEHAVIOR

In the section above, the formal attributes of a good theory are identified as value-based standards against which a theory can be compared. In other words, the adequacy or inadequacy of a theory can be gauged by the formal attributes presented above. The substantive attributes, discussed here, possess no such evaluative quality; they are neutral relative to a theory's adequacy or inadequacy. These substantive attributes are the particular assumptions that undergird various theories of addictive behavior (Hall & Lindzey, 1978).

1. *Purposive versus mechanistic nature of the behavior.* This is a very old issue in philosophy and psychology. As it relates to addiction, the question is this: Should the abuse of alcohol or drugs be seen as purposeful and goal-directed? Or, rather, should it be seen as one element in a larger dynamic system of behavior? Typically, those holding to the former position maintain that chemical use has an immediate benefit of some kind for the addict. In the other camp are those who maintain that addiction (e.g., drug-seeking behavior) is instead a symptom of a larger destructive process. The view that drug use is purposive does not necessarily suggest that it is sinful or freely chosen. For example, conditioning theory maintains that compulsive use is goal-directed, but it relies on the concept of reinforcement as an explanation. Examples of mechanistic theories include the disease model and family systems theory.

2. *Conscious versus unconscious determinants.* This is another very old debate. At issue is whether addictive behavior is determined by conscious or by unconscious factors. Some theories on addictive behavior question the very existence of the unconscious. Others assert that it cannot be measured, and therefore is not within the realm of scientific inquiry. Still other theories (e.g., psychoanalysis) give it a central role in the development of alcohol/drug problems. Interestingly, some treatment providers today unwittingly assign little importance to unconscious factors, yet in counseling practice they focus on clients' defense mechanisms. Such an apparent inconsistency suggests an incomplete analysis of the problem.

3. *Degree of emphasis on reward.* Theories of addictive behavior vary as to role of reinforcement in driving compulsive use. This is a central concept in conditioning theory, and in social learning theory as well. However, other theories assign little significance to the rewards derived from chemical use, and instead only emphasize the negative consequences (e.g., the disease model). Other theories stress reward only as it relates to family or social relationships (e.g., family systems theory and sociocultural perspectives).

4. *Learning process versus stable structures.* An important distinction between theories on addictive behavior has to do with those that outline a specific process of behavior change, in contrast to those that

deal primarily with stable structures of the personality, the family, or the society. Those theories that emphasize a learning process usually seek to explain how an individual moves from drug experimentation to drug abuse to drug dependence. Theories emphasizing stable structures do not usually detail such a progression.

5. *Genetic versus environmental factors.* This issue is the center of much contemporary controversy. The disease model has traditionally emphasized (or, as some would say, exaggerated) genetic determinants of alcoholism, and in recent years other drug addictions as well. Most behavioral science theories, by contrast, have de-emphasized hereditary influences. In fact, many of these theories have made no attempt to incorporate genetic susceptibility. Some behavioral or sociocultural theorists acknowledge that heredity may play a small role in the development of addictions; frequently, however, they do not account for this influence in their theorizing (Peele, 1985).

6. *Degree of emphasis on the operation of homeostatic mechanisms.* Some theories of addictive behavior emphasize the need of the individual or the family to maintain "homeostasis" or "balance" (e.g., psychoanalytic theory and family systems theory). This process is seen as a vital, automatic tendency to preserve the unity and integrity of the psyche or the social unit. The homeostatic mechanisms are seen as operating in much the same manner as biological mechanisms. Conditioning theories and other learning theories generally place little emphasis on homeostatic mechanisms. Such theories do not assume that addiction is related to being "in" or "out" of balance.

7. *Degree of emphasis on sociocultural determinants.* Most theories of addictive behavior focus on factors (genetic, physiological, psychological) within the individual. To date, relatively little emphasis has been placed upon such factors as institutional structure and change, cultural beliefs, government actions and policies, tax law, the deterrent effect of criminal law, ethnic and racial identity, subcultures, or the like. In general, those theories that most strongly emphasize genetic determinants of addiction are those that tend to disregard the sociocultural context completely. Theories based on the learning process are usually more sympathetic toward sociocultural perspectives. In this volume, various sociocultural perspectives are presented; none of them can be considered an elegant theory by itself.

CONTEMPORARY PERSPECTIVES AND CLINICAL PRACTICE

One of the fundamental assumptions of science is that virtually all phenomena have multiple causes (Hardyck & Petrinovich, 1975). The implication is that theories on addiction should integrate biological, psychological, and social factors in an effort to explain compulsive substance use. Unfortunately, this is not yet the case in the addictions field. To date, none of the major contemporary theoretical perspectives has adequately accounted for the enormous number of data collected on substance abuse and dependence. Some are best described as "single-factor" theories (Fingarette, 1988); that is, a single factor (such as a genetic predisposition, or the reinforcement value of a drug) is relied upon to explain all compulsive use. Other theories are limited because they narrow themselves to one level of analysis (e.g., biochemical reactions, personality dynamics, family structure, social relations, etc.), and ignore data that does not fit into their conceptual scheme.

The theories to be discussed in this volume can be accurately described as "single-factor" and "one-level-of-analysis" explanations of addiction. Some of them probably fall into both categories. Separately, they represent distinct visions of the problem of substance abuse. In many cases, a theory is built on assumptions that places it squarely at odds with the other theories; thus, it is difficult to imagine how the theories presented here could be integrated. This dilemma poses a special challenge to professionals in the field. Although practitioners need a theoretical framework to work from, they also need to keep in mind that the scientific understanding of addiction is still in its infancy, and that none of the theories presented in this volume can justifiably be discarded with ease. This ambiguity must be tolerated for the foreseeable future. Though this may be uncomfortable, it is preferable to developing a ideology that espouses one theory and rejects all others. Above all, I hope that this book will instill cognitive flexibility based not only on objectivity, but also on an appreciation of the uniqueness of each perspective.

In most conventional addiction treatment programs in the United States today, there is little integration of theory and research into clinical practice (Caldwell, 1991). Knowledge about alcoholism, other addictions, and their treatment grew during the 1970s and 1980s. However, the use of this knowledge base by substance abuse counselors has been minimal. The gap has grown so great that the National Institute on Alcohol Abuse and Alcoholism sponsored a 1990 conference titled "Linking Alcoholism Treatment Research with Clinical Practice" (Gordis, 1991). It was unique in that it allowed researchers and practitioners to address one another. In commenting on the meeting, Enoch Gordis, the director of the National Institute on Alcohol Abuse and Alcoholism, noted:

In theory, alcohol researchers seek knowledge about alcohol-related health conditions, and practitioners use this knowledge to help their patients recover. In practice, however, we often find that alcohol researchers and alcohol practitioners travel in two largely unrelated circles; they speak different languages, attend different meetings, and generally view problems—and their solutions—from very different perspectives. (1991, p. 173)

The origins of this schism between theory-based research and clinical practice are multiple. Historically, alcoholism treatment programs in the United States have been staffed primarily by counselors who are themselves in recovery from alcoholism. This has also often been true of the nurses and physicians who work in alcoholism treatment programs. For many years, the theory and research base in addictions treatment was minimal. Practitioners were therefore forced to rely on what worked for them (i.e., the disease model). Thus, there never evolved a tradition of using theory and research to guide clinical counseling practice. According to Caldwell (1991),

. . . most people entering treatment were considered to fit Jellinek's description of the gamma alcoholic and were treated as such. (The gamma alcoholic is the physiologically addicted alcoholic.) This is somewhat understandable, because the practitioner was, more often than not, himself or herself a recovering gamma alcoholic who had entered the field in response to years of neglect by the professional community. Such practitioners tended to view other alcoholics as fitting this pattern and delivered treatment accordingly. (p. 175)

The division between researchers and practitioners also stems from the fact that multiple disciplines have been involved in alcoholism research and treatment. The professions have included medicine, psychology, nursing, social work, and many others. Each of these disciplines has different views on the relative importance of research versus clinical practice. For instance, whereas some physicians have been heavily involved in research, most are more concerned with the delivery of services, program administration, and other aspects of clinical practice. The reverse can often be said of psychologists who work in the addictions field. Moreover, the relatively distinct training in each of the disciplines often makes it awkward for professionals from different backgrounds to communicate with one another. Physicians are often confused by behavioral science concepts and helping strategies, and nonmedical professionals may be ignorant of biomedical issues.

BARRIERS TO CHANGE IN THE TREATMENT COMMUNITY

Probably the single greatest barrier to the integration of theory, research, and clinical practice is the treatment community's strong tradition of relying on personal experience, clinical anecdotes, and testimonials. These sources of knowledge are limited because they assume that all addicts or alcoholics are alike. The belief here is this: "It worked for me, so it will work for everyone." It has been clear for some time, however, that alcoholism and addictions to other drugs are not unitary disorders (Cloninger, Christiansen, Reich, & Gottesman, 1978; McLellan, Luborksy, Woody, Druley, & O'Brien, 1983). They require different treatment modalities to maximize client outcomes.

It is often asserted that resistance to change is normal and should be expected. Most organizations work to resist innovation, even when science calls for change. Caldwell (1991) notes that this resistance is hardly unique to the addictions treatment community. He cites a statement made by the famous physicist Max Planck more than 50 years ago about the field of physics: "An important scientific innovation rarely makes its way by gradually winning over and converting its opponents. What does happen is that its opponents gradually die out and that growing generation is familiarized with the idea from the beginning" (Planck, 1936, p. 50). This is likely to be the case with the addictions field as well. It is regrettable that change occurs so slowly.

Another barrier to change is the common belief among treatment providers that experimentation with clinical procedures is too risky. The fear, as often expressed, is that some treatment failures will occur with experimentation, so the best course of action is to "stick with what we're doing now." Indeed, it is true that some clients may not respond favorably to a new treatment protocol. However, given the fact that relatively high relapse rates occur in conventional treatment now, this argument seems specious. This position is probably related more simply to a fear of change or of doing something different. Furthermore, experimentation implies that treatment knowledge is incomplete—that there is still more for researchers and treatment providers to learn. This is an uncomfortable position for counselors, who are often faced with convincing clients of the effectiveness of their particular program.

Today, substantial numbers of counselors and other practitioners in the addictions treatment field lack of adequate preparation in terms of formal education, counselor skills, and ongoing training, including effective clinical supervision (Lawson & Lawson, 1990; Milgram, 1990). This is another significant barrier to the collaboration of researchers and treatment providers. Many practitioners today do not understand research reports (Huey, 1991). Others have no access to important research literature; unfortunately, still others do not know that it even exists. This should not be surprising, given that the minimum formal educational requirement for alcoholism counselor certification in several states is the high school diploma.

A final barrier to the synthesis of research and clinical practice deserves mention here. It consists of the often overwhelming caseloads carried by many counselors, and the lack of time and resources necessary for the improvement of skills. The use of theory-based relapse prevention strategies requires not only a highly skilled practitioner, but also a great deal of individual attention to each client. Most conventional treatment programs today are forced to rely almost solely on group counseling because they lack the resources for more individualized care. This is a problem not only in publicly funded programs, but in private ones as well.

PRACTICAL ISSUES IGNORED BY RESEARCHERS

The research community has also been faulted for the gap between treatment research and clinical practice. Let us examine some of the concerns the treatment community has had about research endeavors. First, it has been pointed out that relapse prevention programs are often designed for mildly to moderately impaired clients. These are clients who are typically young, have no biomedical complications, and have a great deal to gain by maintaining abstinence. Huey (1991) notes, however, that practitioners are most interested in learning how to assist severely impaired clients. In some treatment programs, the majority of the client pool can be described as severely impaired. Thus, relapse prevention programs based on learning principles may be inappropriate for use in some programs.

Another practical problem often ignored by researchers also pertains to client characteristics. It is the problem of the client who demonstrates little or no commitment to recovery. Again, some relapse prevention strategies assume that all clients are motivated to change. A small but significant portion of clients may have no intention to change. They sometimes enter treatment simply to escape or avoid some punitive action by a court, an employer, or some other authority. More research is needed about this important issue.

Archer (1991) has stated that researchers have not paid enough attention to marketing new ideas to practitioners. He has suggested that researchers should devise ways to disseminate their research findings to counselors. Archer also notes that the reward structure of universities and grant makers discourages this type of professional activity. Researchers may not earn tenure and promotion or obtain federal grants by writing "how to" manuals.

BRIDGING THE GAP

What can be done to bridge the gap between research and clinical practice? The efforts that are needed are known and are being addressed, but unfortunately only in a piecemeal manner. Progress is slowed largely by insufficient resources.

Three broad initiatives are needed to speed progress in this area, so that the quality of service delivery will be enhanced. First, a coalition of forces from within the addictions field and from related fields (e.g., law enforcement agencies, bar associations, medical groups, mental health organizations, etc.) need to lobby within the appropriate political channels for a shift of federal funds away from drug interdiction to addictions treatment and research. Interdiction is enormously expensive, and its effectiveness has been seriously questioned (Ray & Ksir, 1993).

Second, the educational requirements for certified addiction counselors need to be strengthened. It would be helpful if the National Institute on Alcohol Abuse and Alcoholism or another federal agency were to assume a leadership role in this area. A plan could be developed for the gradual enhancement of counselor preparation and training. Currently, certification requirements vary from state to state; it would also be helpful if this patchwork system could be replaced by national certification standards that were widely supported by both institutions of higher education and employers.

A federal grant program is needed to assist in the dissemination of research findings to the treatment community, and to train existing staff members in relapse prevention strategies. If treatment outcome rates are not improved, the long-term consequences could be dwindling support for treatment, and an intractable public perception that alcoholism and other drug addictions are hopeless conditions.

This book is intended to help bridge the gap between theory and research on one side and clinical practice on the other. I hope that substance abuse counselors will find the review of theory and research in each area to be useful to the improvement of clinical care. Frequently, counselors "in the trenches" adopt an eclectic approach to their practice; this is understandable, given the complex and varied patterns of addictive behavior that they observe. This text should serve to strengthen counselors' understanding of diverse theoretical perspectives on addiction, and to assist them in helping their clients find paths to recovery.

REVIEW QUESTIONS

1. What are the three fundamentally different views of addiction?

2. What are the characteristics of these three views that make them distinctive and logically exclusive of one another?

3. What are the advantages and disadvantages of each view?

4. According to the author of this book, which view is best understood? Which is most utilized by the treatment community?

5. According to the author, what theory-related issue threatens the continuing development of the field?

6. What are the basics of theory?

7. What are the formal attributes of a *good* theory?

8. What are the substantive attributes of theories of addictive behavior?

9. What are "single-factor" and "one-level-of-analysis" theories?

10. What fundamental assumption of science suggests that addiction is a biopsychosocial phenomenon?

11. What dilemma faces the practitioner in applying theory to practice?

12. What are some of the reasons for the gap between treatment research and clinical practice? What are the origins of this schism?

13. What are the barriers to the use of research findings in the treatment community?

14. What practical issues do researchers tend to ignore in regard to the use of their findings?

15. What three initiatives could facilitate the integration of research and practice in the addictions field?

REFERENCES

Archer, L. (1991). Marketing new ideas about treatment. *Alcohol, Health, and Research World, 15*(3), 213–214.

Caldwell, F. (1991). Refining the link between research and practice. *Alcohol, Health, and Research World, 15*(3), 175–177.

Cloninger, C. R., Christiansen, K. O., Reich, T., & Gottesman, I. I. (1978). Implications of sex differences in the prevalence of antisocial personality, alcoholism, and criminality for familial transmission. *Archives of General Psychiatry, 35*, 941–951.

Fingarette, H. (1988). *Heavy drinking: The myth of alcoholism as a disease.* Berkeley: University of California Press.

Gordis, E. (1991). Linking research with practice. *Alcohol, Health, and Research World, 15*(3), 173–174.

Hall, C. S., & Lindzey, G. (1978). *Theories of personality* (3rd ed.). New York: Wiley.

Hardyck, C., & Petrinovich, L. F. (1975). *Understanding research in the social sciences.* Philadelphia: Saunders.

Huey, E. (1991). Finer points about new treatment approaches. *Alcohol, Health, and Research World, 15*(3), 219–220.

Lawson, G. W., & Lawson, A. W. (1990). Quality substance abuse education—To be or not to be. *Psychology of Addictive Behaviors, 4*, 37–39.

McLellan, A. T., Luborsky, L., Woody, G. E., Druley, K. A., & O'Brien, C. P. (1983). Predicting response to alcohol and drug abuse treatments: Role of psychiatric severity. *Archives of General Psychiatry, 40*(6), 620–635.

Milgram, G. G. (1990). Certification of alcoholism/drug counselors. *Psychology of Addictive Behaviors, 4*, 40–42.

Monette, D. R., Sullivan, T. J., & De Jong, C. R. (1990). *Applied social research: Tool for the human services.* Fort Worth, TX: Holt, Rinehart & Winston.

Peele, S. (1985). *The meaning of addiction: Compulsive experience and its interpretation.* Lexington, MA: D. C. Heath.

Planck, M. (1936). *The philosophy of physics.* New York: Norton.

Ray, O., & Ksir, C. (1993). *Drugs, society, and human behavior.* St. Louis: Mosby.

Stefflre, B., & Burks, H. M. (1979). Function of theory in counseling. In H. M. Burks & B. Stefflre (Eds.), *Theories of counseling.* New York: McGraw-Hill.

CHAPTER TWO

The Disease Model

In the United States today, the predominant model for understanding alcoholism and other addictions is the view that these disorders are diseases. This view is particularly strong within the treatment community and within self-help fellowships such as Alcoholics Anonymous (AA) or Narcotics Anonymous (NA). The vast majority of treatment programs rely on the disease (or medical) model for a conceptual base; it shapes selection of treatment options and focuses the content of patient and family education. Thus, most treatment programs in this country employ a supervising physician, require AA or NA attendance, advocate abstinence, teach that the disorder is a chronic condition, and so forth. To the credit of the treatment community, these efforts have lessened the stigma associated with chemical dependency. Compared to 50 years ago, alcoholics and addicts today are less likely to be scorned and more likely to be offered help.

However, it should be recognized that enormous controversy continues to surround the disease concept of addiction. Some legal experts and criminologists insist that the use and abuse of chemical substances are intentional acts that deserve punishment (Wilbanks, 1989). In such a view, substance abuse results from a lack of self-restraint and self-discipline. Herbert Fingarette (1988), a philosopher, maintains that the disease model is a myth that endures because it fulfills economic or personal needs of some groups (i.e., the medical community and recovery groups, respectively). Fingarette (1988) strongly supports helping alcoholics or addicts, but believes that the "disease myth" limits treatment options for many needy individuals. Behavioral science researchers and its proponents also question the validity of the model (Peele, 1985). Some have claimed that it is patently unscientific (Alexander, 1988).

Such disparate views are not likely to be resolved in the near future. In order to evaluate these arguments and counterarguments knowledgeably, it is essential that counselors and other human service professionals understand exactly what is meant by addiction as a disease. Only then can the advantages and disadvantages of this model (i.e., its utility) be intelligently weighed.

DIFFERENT DISEASE CONCEPTUALIZATIONS

Before the core concepts of the disease model are reviewed, it should be noted that there is not just one disease model. A number of proponents of the model, though not necessarily in disagreement, have emphasized different elements. The differences can be striking. For instance, Johnson's (1980) description of the dynamics of alcoholism progression is different from that described by Milam and Ketcham (1983), and Vaillant (1990) provides yet another perspective. The models differ with respect to the importance of physical, psychological, and spiritual factors in the etiology of alcoholism. These different emphases are probably related to the authors' personal experience with alcoholism (i.e., whether or not they are recovering alcoholics) and their professional training (i.e., whether they are physicians, psychiatrists, psychologists, etc.).

It can also be asserted that the disease model of AA differs somewhat from that espoused by the medical community. The disease model as emphasized by AA stresses the importance of spirituality in the etiology of, and recovery from, alcoholism. In fact, many AA members report that they are recovering from a "spiritual disease." Though many outsiders to AA consider this an oxymoron (i.e., a figure of speech that is a contradiction in terms), many recovering persons that feel it accurately describes their drinking problems. AA encourages its members to find a "Higher Power" and to turn their wills and lives over to a supernatural being. These spiritual conversions are considered crucial to recovery.

In contrast, the medical community tends to point to the significance of biological factors in alcoholism. Physicians often emphasize the role of genetic susceptibilities, increasing tolerance, withdrawal symptoms, liver disease, brain abnormalities, and so forth. Of course, this biomedical approach is consistent with their training. It is not that they ignore spiritual elements; rather, they tend to give such factors less weight than, for example, laboratory test results.

There is another difference between the disease model of AA and that of the medical community. It is a subtle difference, and it is closely related to the dichotomy of spirituality versus science. In

AA, members often use the disease concept in a metaphoric sense; that is, they describe their alcohol problems as being "like" a disease. In many cases, recovering individuals do not intend (or perhaps even care) to convey that they *literally* have a disease. They are simply trying to express that the experience of compulsive chemical use *feels* like having a disease. It is characterized by feelings of loss of control and hopelessness, conditions familiar to the victims of other diseases (e.g., cancer, heart disease, emphysema, etc.).

Most often, physicians do not use the term "disease" as a metaphor. They tend to use the term in a literal sense—that is, "Alcoholism *is* a disease." Consider the following statement by a physician who directs a chemical dependency rehabilitation program:

> Whether you become an alcoholic or not depends on genetic predisposition. We know the reason the compulsivity exists is because of a change in the endorphin and cephalin systems in a primitive portion of the brain. The reason for this disturbance in the biochemistry of the primitive brain is a predisposition. Nobody talks any longer about becoming an alcoholic. You don't become an alcoholic—you are born an alcoholic. (Talbott, 1989, p. 57)

As this discussion illustrates, the disease model is not a unitary framework for understanding addiction. However, despite the nuances and ambiguities, there exist certain concepts that have traditionally represented the disease model of addiction. Let us examine these concepts in light of the current scientific literature.

ADDICTION AS A PRIMARY DISEASE

Addiction, especially alcoholism, is often described as a "primary disease"; that is, it is *not* the result of another condition. This is usually taken to mean that the disease is *not* caused by heavy drinking or drug use, stress, or psychiatric disorders; rather, it is thought to be the cause of these very conditions. In other words, heavy drinking/ drug use, stress, psychiatric disorders, and so forth are secondary symptoms or manifestations of an underlying disease process known as addiction. If the drinking or drug use is stopped, it is believed that the symptoms will, for the most part, disappear (Milam & Ketcham, 1983; Talbott, 1989).

This is contrary to popular conceptions of addiction, especially alcoholism. To take alcoholism as an example, many laypeople (even those who view alcoholism as a disease) feel that alcoholism results from abusive drinking, which in turn stems from irresponsibility, stress, or emotional problems. The disease model, properly understood, disputes these ideas (Milam & Ketcham, 1983). The model proposes that alcoholics are not responsible for contracting their disease; the disease itself causes or drives the heavy drinking. Furthermore, it is maintained that those drinkers who lack genetic susceptibility to the disease cannot drink themselves into alcoholism (Milam & Ketcham, 1983).

In recent years, however, various lines of research have developed data that contradict the primary-disease concept for all alcoholics. For example, researchers note that there may be multiple types of alcoholisms (National Institute on Alcohol Abuse and Alcoholism, 1990). Some forms may be more sensitive to genetic factors, while others are influenced by environmental conditions (Cloninger, 1987). Environmental factors (stress, marital and family problems, depression, anxiety, etc.) may cause some forms of alcoholism. Schuckit (1989) has reported that a proportion of alcoholics "fulfill criteria for a clearly preexisting antisocial personality disorder (ASPD)" (p. 2). This suggests that severe antisocial life problems may cause alcoholism in some. Cox (1985) has noted that certain psychological traits predispose individuals to substance abuse in general:

> Specifically, future substance abusers are characterized by disregard for social mores, independence, impulsivity, and affinity for adventure. These are enduring personality characteristics that appear to be biologically mediated (Eysenck, 1981; Zuckerman, 1983). Persons exhibiting these personality characteristics are able to satisfy their psychological needs through substance use, and they appear to be especially susceptible to environmental influences promoting substance use. (p. 233)

This passage cogently describes how genetics and environment interact to promote alcohol and drug abuse. It also suggests that a "sensation-seeking" alcoholic personality will not disappear upon cessation of alcohol use. Successful recovery may often depend upon the alcoholic's finding alternative (i.e., nonchemical) ways to fulfill psychological needs for excitement and risk taking.

Findings such as these suggest that the causes of alcoholism (and probably other addictions as well) are multiple and mediated by both genetic and environmental factors. For each alcoholic, there is probably a relatively unique combination of forces that led to the development of the drinking problem. Some cases may be strongly influenced by genetic factors; others may be mediated solely by environmental ones. In the future, the concept of "primary" alcoholism is likely to be further and further restricted as various types of the disorder continue to be identified.

GENETIC ORIGINS OF ALCOHOLISM

In this section, a thorough examination of the evidence for a genetic predisposition to alcoholism is presented. The discussion is limited to alcoholism, because there is no empirical evidence to date for a genetic predisposition to other drug dependencies in humans (Alexander, 1988; Crabbe, McSwigan, & Belknap, 1985; Nunes & Klein, 1987). Virtually no studies of this kind have been conducted. There exists the possibility that some humans may be genetically susceptible to dependencies on illicit drugs, such as cocaine and heroin addiction; however, such present-day claims are entirely speculative and are not based on existing science.

The study of genetics deals with characteristics that are transmitted from parents to their offspring via biological mechanisms. These characteristics are not acquired as a result of learning, modeling, socialization, or other postnatal experiences; they are hereditary or inborn. Such human characteristics as eye color and blood type are determined by genetic factors.

"Genes" are the basic structural units of heredity. Each person shares 50% of the genes of each parent in a unique arrangement that is different from both parents. This assemblage of genes is the person's "genotype." During both pre- and postnatal development, the individual is exposed to a variety of environmental influences. This interaction between genotype and environment generates an enormous number of individual traits and characteristics, which are referred to as the person's "phenotype." The phenotype, then, is the outcome of the interaction between genes and environment.

In plants (and some animals), a genotype can be isolated, reproduced, and regulated. Such experiments with humans, even if they were possible, would be unethical. Thus, research on human genetic issues is restricted to relatively simple designs (e.g., adoption and twin studies) that do not require manipulation of the genotype or the environment. According to Lester (1988),

> For concepts like intelligence, or schizophrenia, or alcoholism, there is no evidence that simple relationships exist; indeed, there is every reason to believe that the highest levels of organismic function are involved, embracing the most complex developing and evolving relationships of humans as social beings. (p. 2)

Lester (1988), a biochemist, argues that the current state of knowledge is inadequate for the assignment of values to the respective contributions of "nature" and "nurture" in alcoholism. Despite such a cautionary warning from a respected biochemist and alcoholism researcher, many in the treatment community have widely proclaimed that scientific evidence unequivocally supports a genetic basis for alcoholism. The following discussion features those studies that are often cited as "proof" of the genetic foundation of alcoholism.

Goodwin's Work

Donald Goodwin, a psychiatrist and widely respected alcoholism researcher, was among the first to establish a link between genetics and alcoholism. His well-known adoption study is usually cited as the basis for the claim often made that children of alcoholics are four times more likely to develop alcoholism than children of nonalcoholics (Goodwin, Schulsinger, Hermansen, Guze, & Winokur, 1973). This pivotal work involved a pool of Danish children ($n = 5,483$) who were given up for adoption shortly after birth during the period from 1924 to 1947. The pool of adoptees was originally created for a study on schizophrenia. The study was conducted in Denmark because that country maintains national adoption registries, which are available for scientific investigations. Also, its citizenry is much less geographically mobile; thus, locating individuals many years after their birth and subsequent adoption is much easier in Denmark than in the United States or some other countries.

   The design of an adoption study is relatively simple. It is based on the principle that children born to alcoholic parents but adopted and raised by others (probably by nonalcoholic adoptive parents) may have a greater likelihood of developing alcohol problems than adopted children born to nonalcoholic parents (and most likely raised by nonalcoholic adoptive parents). Any differences in the rates of problem drinking or alcoholism between the two groups of adoptees can then be attributed to heredity rather than to family rearing practices. Furthermore, because both groups of children are adoptees, any relationships between being adopted and later alcoholism should be the same for both groups.

   Goodwin et al. (1973) identified a group of 67 male adoptees who had an alcoholic parent (85% of these were fathers), who were adopted by nonrelatives before the seventh week of life, and who had no known contact with biological relatives. These subjects were referred to as "probands." In addition, two control groups (adoptees born to nonalcoholic parents) were identified. One of these consisted of 70 adoptees who were matched to the probands on age, sex, and time of adoption. The biological parents of these control group adoptees had no hospital record of problem drinking, alcoholism, or psychiatric disorder. The second group of controls was comprised of 37 adoptees who were born to nonalcoholic parents but "had a biological parent hospitalized for a psychiatric condition other than alcoholism" (Goodwin et al., 1973, p. 238).

Thus, the study's total sample consisted of 174 adoptees (i.e., 67 probands plus 70 controls plus 37 controls). This is a far smaller number than supporters of the disease model, including the federal government, have cited in their reviews of Goodwin's work (National Institute on Alcohol Abuse and Alcoholism, 1985, 1986). It has been frequently claimed that Goodwin and his colleagues studied all 5,483 adoptees of the original pool; this was not the case.

Of the sample of 174 adoptees (who by the time of the study were adults), 41 could not be found or refused to be interviewed for the study. Of this group, 14 were probands. All of the remaining subjects were interviewed by a Danish psychiatrist (in Danish; the responses were later translated into English). In a structured interview, information was obtained on demographic variables, parents, drinking practices, and other relevant factors. Later, it was found that the two control groups did not differ substantially from each other, so they were combined (Goodwin et al., 1973). Also, one adoptee was excluded from the data analysis because it could not be determined which of two possible biological fathers was his actual one. It was not reported whether this adoptee was a proband or a control subject.

Table 2.1 shows the drinking problems and patterns in the two adoptee groups. As can be seen, the two groups differed significantly on five variables. One was "hallucinations"; according to Goodwin (1988), this referred to "auditory or visual perceptual distortions associated with withdrawal from alcohol" (pp. 102–103). The second variable on which there was a significant difference, "lost control," referred to the experience of wanting not to use alcohol on an occasion but being unable to do so. The variable "morning drinking" assessed repeated drinking in the morning, rather than just one or two drinks on an occasion. The other two variables on which there were significant differences—"alcoholic, ever" and "treated for drinking, ever"—are self-explanatory. On each of these five variables, the probands were overrepresented, compared to controls. Notice that

TABLE 2.1. Drinking Problems and Patterns in Two Adoptive Groups

	Probands (n = 55)	Controls (n = 78)
Problems		
Hallucinations*	6%	0%
Lost control*	35%	17%
Amnesia	53%	41%
Tremor	24%	22%
Morning drinking*	29%	11%
Delirium tremens	6%	1%
Rum fits (seizures after withdrawal)	2%	0%
Social disapproval	6%	8%
Marital trouble	18%	9%
Job trouble	7%	3%
Drunken-driving arrests	7%	4%
Police trouble, other	15%	8%
Treated for drinking, ever*	9%	1%
Hospitalized for drinking	11%	0%
Patterns		
Moderate drinker	51%	45%
Heavy drinker, ever	22%	36%
Problem drinker, ever	9%	14%
Alcoholic, ever*	18%	5%

Note. From Goodwin, Schulsinger, Hermansen, Guze, and Winokur (1973). Copyright 1973 by the American Medical Association. Reprinted by permission.
* Indicates statistically significant differences between groups.

on most of the remaining drinking problems (i.e., those not followed by an asterisk), the probands also reported greater levels of alcohol problems than controls. However, these differences did not reach statistical significance (as determined by chi-square analyses and Student's *t* tests). Thus, they could have occurred by chance.

For a full understanding of the findings in Table 2.1, it is important to consider the classification criteria for the four drinking patterns. Outlined in Table 2.2 are the criteria employed by Goodwin et al. (1973). According to the criteria described in Table 2.2, 18% of the probands were alcoholic, compared to 5% of the controls. In other words, the rate of alcoholism among adopted sons with an alcoholic biological parent was 3.6 times greater than that among adopted sons whose biological parents were not alcoholic. This find-

TABLE 2.2. Criteria for Drinking Categories

Moderate drinker	Neither a teetotaler nor heavy drinker
Heavy drinker	For at least one year drank daily and had six or more drinks at least two or three times a month; or drank six or more drinks at least once a week for more than a year, but reported no problems
Problem drinker	(A) Meets criteria for heavy drinker (B) Had problems from drinking but insufficient in number to meet alcoholism criteria
Alcoholic	(A) Meets criteria for heavy drinker (B) Must have had alcohol problems in at least three of the following four groups: Group 1: Social disapproval of drinking by friends or parents Marital problems from drinking Group 2: Job trouble from drinking Traffic arrests from drinking Other police trouble from drinking Group 3: Frequent blackouts Tremor Withdrawal hallucinations Withdrawal convulsions Delirium tremens Group 4: Loss of control Morning drinking

Note. From Goodwin et al. (1973). Copyright 1973 by the American Medical Association. Reprinted by permission.

ing has been widely used by Goodwin and many in the treatment community to support the claim that alcoholism is genetically determined (Goodwin, 1988; Milam & Ketcham, 1983).

Unfortunately, as evidence for a genetic basis of alcoholism, the importance of these findings has been grossly exaggerated (Fingarette, 1988; Lester, 1988; Murray, Clifford, & Gurling, 1983; Peele, 1985). Consider, for example, the fact that relatively small proportions of both groups (i.e., proband and control) actually became alcoholic later in life. As Fingarette (1988) notes,

> In Goodwin's study, about 18 percent of the sons who had an alcoholic parent became alcoholics, compared to 5 percent of the sons of nonalcoholic parents. The hypothesis is that the difference between these groups is attributable to heredity. But to see the full picture, let's turn the numbers around: 82 percent of the sons who had an alcoholic parent—more than four out of five—did not become alcoholics. So if we generalize from Goodwin's results, we must say that about 80 percent

of persons with an alcoholic parent will not become alcoholics. Either the relevant genes are usually not transmitted or the genes are transmitted but are usually out-weighed by other factors. (pp. 52–53)

Moreover, if alcoholism is always determined by genetic factors, how is it that 5% of the control group (i.e., sons of nonalcoholic parents) developed alcoholism in later life? The reluctance to acknowledge the potent influence of environmental factors is highlighted by Goodwin's (1988) painful admission that the genetic hypothesis "certainly may not apply to all alcoholics. Even the possibility of environmental influence cannot be entirely ruled out" (p. 107). This comment (and others like it) seems to suggest that environmental explanations are nearly inconceivable!

Other serious problems also exist with the Goodwin et al. (1973) study. Extensive reviews of the study's limitations and errors have been conducted by Murray et al. (1983) and Lester (1988). However, two points bear mentioning here. Aside from a half dozen errors in calculating different tests (Lester, 1988), Goodwin et al. (1973) failed to reduce the level of statistical significance (alpha) in accordance with the relatively large number of univariate analyses that were conducted. Whenever a study relies on a large number of univariate analyses (i.e., tests that assess single relationships involving two variables only, such as adoptee group and "hallucinations"), it is customary to divide the alpha level by the number of conducted tests. If this is not done, it becomes likely that one or more findings believed to be statistically significant are actually the results of chance instead. For example, the results in Table 2.1 required 18 separate univariate statistical tests. If one divides the .05 level of significance by 18, the result (with rounding) is .003. None of Goodwin et al.'s (1973) findings reached this level of significance. It is entirely possible that at least one of the five statistically significant findings in the study actually occurred by chance.

The other serious data-analytic problem in the Goodwin et al. (1973) study rests with the distinction made between problem drinkers and alcoholics. Goodwin (1988) himself admits that the criteria employed were "arbitrary" (p. 105). This being the case, it is important to consider the results of combining the problem drinkers and the alcoholics into one group. Lester (1988) and Murray et al. (1983), using Goodwin et al.'s (1973) data, did just this. The result was that there was no statistically significant difference between the proband and control groups in regard to number of problem drinkers/alcoholics. Murray et al. (1983) have noted:

If the cut-off point for abnormality is widened to include not just alco-holism but also problem drinking, then evidence for any genetic predis-position vanishes. . . . Could it be that Goodwin's findings are simply an artifact produced by the threshold for alcoholism accidentally divid-ing heavy drinkers in the index and control groups unevenly? (p. 42)

Twin Studies

Before several of the well-known twin studies are examined, let us examine the logic, design, and limitations of a twin study. There are two types of twins: "monozygotic" (MZ) and "dizygotic" (DZ). MZ twins develop from a single ovum and sperm, whereas DZ twins develop from separate ova and sperm. MZ twins share identical geno-types; however, DZ twins share only half of their genes. MZ twins are usually referred to as "identical" twins, while DZ twins are often known as "fraternal" twins. Of course, MZ twins are always of the same gender. DZ twins may be of different genders, and are no more alike (in terms of genetic makeup) than any two siblings.

In twin studies, concordance rates are determined for a specific characteristic or trait. A "concordance rate" is the degree of similarity between the twins in each pair in a series on any given characteristic. The greater the concordance between MZ twins, as compared to DZ twins, is taken as evidence of the degree of genetic determination for a characteristic. Stated in another way, the concordance rate of the DZ twins serves as a baseline representing environmental input on a characteristic. The greater the degree to which the MZ twins' concor-dance rate exceeds that of the DZ twins, the greater the role heredity plays in determining that characteristic.

Lester (1988) points out that twin studies are based on some questionable assumptions. He lists the following problems that can affect the validity of such studies:

1. Twin studies assume that mating of the parents is random. That is, there exists no conscious preference for marriage partners possessing similar obvious traits (such as drinking habits).
2. [It is assumed that] no dominance or other genetic effects are in-volved in the particular trait (e.g., alcohol use).
3. The within-pair environmental variance is the same in DZ twins as in MZ twins. That is, the post-natal experience of the identical twin pairs is roughly equivalent to that of fraternal twins. It is assumed that fraternal twins have the same degree of social contact with each other as do identical twins. (p. 6)

This last assumption is particularly problematic. It is quite probable that the "twin experience" of MZ twins is significantly different from that of DZ twins. Lester (1988) describes this threat to the validity of twin studies in the following passage:

> MZ twins are frequently confused with one another and treated as the same person. Because they share fewer traits, DZ twins are not only more likely to be differentiated by others but also more likely to differ in their talents, interests, friends, and occupations, and share far fewer common experiences; their greater genetic dissimilarity ensures that the sets of environments that they experience will be more dissimilar than the sets encountered by MZ pairs. The fact that intrapair environmental variances are unequal means that the ostensible heritability calculated will perforce include these unequal variances. (p. 6)

The first twin study of alcoholism, and one that is still frequently cited as evidence of the genetic basis of alcoholism, was conducted by Kaij (1960). A recent report from the National Institute on Alcohol Abuse and Alcoholism to the U.S. Congress includes this work in its review. The seventh *Alcohol and Health* report states:

> One of the earliest studies of alcoholism in twins was Kaij (1960), who found 74 percent concordance of alcoholism between identical twins. That is, if one member of a pair of genetically identical twins was alcoholic, the probability of the other member's also being an alcoholic was 74 percent. In contrast, the concordance of alcoholism between fraternal twins was only 32 percent. (National Institute on Alcohol Abuse and Alcoholism, 1990, p. 44)

It is indeed very curious that the federal government agency directly responsible for alcoholism treatment research and information dissemination would cite a study that has been essentially discredited in two separate reviews of alcoholism twin studies (Lester, 1988; Murray et al., 1983). After an extensive review of the Kaij (1960) study, Lester (1988) has remarked, "I can only conclude that Kaij's study is so flawed that no conclusion, least of all about the hereditary nature of alcoholism, can be drawn" (p. 9). Here is a brief overview of the deficiencies of Kaij's (1960) work.

1. *The study was not "blind."* Kaij interviewed the twins himself and classified them on a 5-point scale ranging from "abstainer" (scored as 0) to "chronic alcoholic" (scored as 4). Though his method is not explicitly stated, it appears that Kaij decided how to classify a co-twin (i.e., one twin in a pair) on the basis of an interview with

the other twin. That is, with possibly a few exceptions, Kaij only interviewed one twin from each pair, and used information from that twin to classify the other.

2. *The MZ twins received much lengthier and more detailed interviews than DZ twins.* This creates the possibility that the DZ twins, who were less thoroughly investigated, may have appeared discordant when they actually were not.

3. *Kaij's method of calculating the concordance rate was unorthodox.* When Lester (1988) applied a traditional rule for measuring concordance, the differences between the MZ group and the DZ group (within each classification level—abstainer to chronic alcoholic) were *not* statistically significant.

4. *Kaij misapplied a rule for rectifying incomplete sibling information.* This resulted in 16 of the 48 MZ pairs of twins' being counted twice (Lester, 1988). Similar data on the DZ twins were not reported. According to Lester's (1988) recalculation using the correct MZ data, the difference between the two twin groups on alcoholism concordance was not statistically significant. Of course, Lester's recalculation could also be in error, because the degree of "double-counting" in the DZ group is unknown.

More recent and better-designed twin studies have established that both environmental and genetic factors play a role in the development of alcoholism. A close examination of the evidence suggests that the environment may play a somewhat more important role than heredity. Kaprio et al. (1987) conducted a twin study involving 2,800 male pairs from Finland. The subjects responded to a questionnaire that assessed quantity and frequency of drinking, density of drinking (i.e., regularity of drinking at particular times, such as weekends), frequency of passing out from drinking, and frequency of social contact between twins (including cohabitation). Kaprio et al. (1987) found that (1) identical twins had more social contact with each other (as adults) than fraternal twins; (2) frequent social contact between twins was significantly correlated with concordance rates in drinking patterns; (3) the concordance rate among the identical twins was somewhat higher than that for the fraternal twins; and (4) the higher concordance rate among the identical twins was explained by both social contact (an environmental factor) and genetic variables. It was estimated that for measures of quantity, frequency, and density of drinking, "environment" accounted for 60–64% of the variance in these three variables (Kaprio et al., 1987). Frequency of drinking to unconsciousness was completely explained by environmental factors.

Insight into how genetic and environmental factors interact has emerged from a twin study conducted by Heath, Jardine, and Martin (1989). This is one of the few studies that has relied on female twins. The sample was obtained through the Australian National Twin Register; it consisted of 1,200 identical twin pairs and 750 fraternal twin pairs (all twins were female). The most important finding of this study was that marital status was a major modifier of genetically influenced drinking patterns. Among both younger and older adult women, being married (or living with a man but not actually being married) suppressed the emergence of genetically influenced drinking patterns. Women who were not married (or not in a similar relationship) tended to drink more heavily (Heath et al., 1989). This supports the notion that both environment and genetics are important, and that they interact in a variety of complex ways to spur the development of alcoholism. In other words, genetics set the stage for vulnerability to later environmental influences.

Further support for the interactive influence of both genetics and environment comes from a recent twin study (McGue, Pickens, & Svikis, 1992). The investigation located cotwins of probands (i.e., patients) from alcohol and drug abuse treatment programs in Minnesota. About 57% of the same-sex twin pairs had their zygosity (MZ vs. DZ status) determined by blood test, while the remainder were determined by self-report questionnaire administered to both the probands and their co-twins. Approximately 8% of the pairs were eliminated from the data analyses because the questionnaire method could not confirm their zygosity. The sample of twin pairs was then broken down by gender and age of first symptom of alcoholism. Within each gender, "early-onset" twin pairs were identified as those where the probands reported a symptom of alcoholism prior to the age of 20. Otherwise, the pairs were classified as "late-onset" (McGue et al., 1992). A summary of the results of the investigation appears in Table 2.3.

As shown in Table 2.3, .725 (or 73%) of the variance in alcoholism among the male early-onset twin pairs could be accounted for by genetic factors. This compared to about 30% of the variance in the male late-onset pairs, and to about 54% of the variance among the total number of male twin pairs. In contrast, the data provided no evidence of genetic influence in female alcoholism for either age group (McGue et al., 1992). These data suggest that genetic factors play a strong role in male alcoholism that appears prior to the age of 20. Genetic variables seem to have only a moderate influence on male alcoholism that begins later in life, and inheritance may play no role in the development of female alcoholism (McGue et al., 1992).

TABLE 2.3. Sex and Age Effects on the Inheritance of Alcohol Problems: A Twin Study

Group	Monozygotic		Dizygotic		Proportion of variance		
	Number of pairs	Concordance rate	Number of pairs	Concordance rate	Genetic	Shared environmental	Unshared environmental
			Males				
Early onset	52	.865	44	.568	.725	.232	.043
Late onset	33	.606	52	.509	.295	.372	.333
Total	85	.765	96	.536	.543	.331	.126
			Females				
Early onset	20	.500	22	.500	.000	.732	.268
Late onset	24	.292	21	.333	.000	.525	.475
Total	44	.386	43	.419	.000	.633	.367

Note. Adapted from McGue, Pickens, and Svikis (1992). Copyright 1992 by the American Psychological Association. Adapted by permission.

Areas of scientific inquiry that are in formative stages, such as the role of genetics in alcoholism, often include investigations that yield inconsistent or contradictory results. Another recent twin study is a case in point. Directly contradicting the work of McGue et al. (1992), an investigation by Kendler, Heath, Neale, Kessler, and Eaves (1992) found evidence supporting a genetic basis for female alcoholism. In this study, data analyses used 1,030 female–female twin pairs of known zygosity from the Virginia Twin Registry. The data were collected from structured psychiatric interviews. The interviewer was "blinded" as to the psychopathological status of each cotwin. The feature of this study that distinguishes it from the McGue et al. (1992) study is that it did not use a cotwin's admission to an alcoholism treatment facility as the basis for selecting the twin pair for the study. The Kendler et al. (1992) study was a population-based study in which twin pairs were identified through a registry. The proportion of the twins who had received treatment for a drinking problem was not reported.

Kendler et al. (1992) used four different definitions of alcoholism. They found that genetics accounts for 50–60% of the variance in female alcoholism. However, these estimates assumed that the environmental experiences of the MZ and DZ twins were equal. When this factor was controlled for, the heritability of liability to alcoholism in women was in the range of 40–50% (Kendler et al., 1992).

Why are the findings of McGue et al. (1992) and Kendler et al. (1992) so contradictory with respect to the role of genetics in female alcoholism? The authors of the second study state it best:

> One plausible hypothesis is that the genetic loading for alcoholism in the modest proportion of women who seek treatment may not be typical of that found in the entire population of women with alcoholism. It is possible, for example, that patients seen in treatment settings may have been particularly influenced by social or environmental factors. (Kendler et al., 1992, p. 1881)

Following this line of reasoning, it would also then be plausible to conclude that males who seek treatment for alcoholism tend to have a stronger genetic loading than their female counterparts. The reasons for this difference are not clear. Age may play a role: Women entering treatment facilities for the first time may tend to be older than the men who do so. Perhaps women are more likely to have a form of alcoholism caused primarily by social/environmental factors. Further research is needed before firm conclusions can be reached about the role of genetics in alcoholism, and about any possible differences in its etiology in women and men.

Metabolic Studies

During the 1970s, several medical researchers published studies purporting to show that alcoholics and relatives of alcoholics tend to metabolize (i.e., to break down) alcohol in abnormal ways (Fingarette, 1988). In most of these studies, the alcohol metabolite of concern was acetaldehyde. Acetaldehyde is a rather toxic breakdown product; it was postulated to be responsible for the increasing tolerance and physical dependency that are sometimes part of alcoholism. Some studies that measured blood levels of acetaldehyde found higher levels in alcoholics and relatives of alcoholics than in individuals with no positive family history of alcoholism (Schuckit, 1984). However, as the National Institute on Alcohol Abuse and Alcoholism (1987) has observed, the hypothesis that acetaldehyde is a genetic marker for alcoholism predisposition is largely speculative. The National Institute on Alcohol Abuse and Alcoholism (1987) concludes:

> On balance, these studies suggest a probable increase in acetaldehyde in alcoholics, but the measurement of acetaldehyde in biological fluids is fraught with technical difficulties and is subject to significant errors. In any case, the positive studies provide no information as to whether

this tendency is antecedent to the development of alcoholism or is a consequence of it. (p. 36)

This highlights two serious problems with this line of research—that is, measurement of acetaldehyde in body fluids, and uncertainty about whether acetaldehyde is a cause or a consequence of years of heavy drinking. For a technical review of the problems with these studies, readers should see Lester (1988).

Another set of studies has examined alcohol elimination in certain ethnic groups (e.g., Japanese and Native Americans) (Okada & Mizoi, 1982; Tsukamoto, Sudo, Karasawa, Kajiwara, & Endo, 1982). The hypothesis here is that rates of alcoholism among an ethnic group are determined by an inborn reaction to ethanol, called a "flushing response." Members of some groups, such as Japanese, tend to flush (reddening of the face, warm sensations, dizziness) when they drink. It is believed that this may be a result of a deficiency in an enzyme that breaks down acetaldehyde. As a result of this deficiency, acetaldehyde is metabolized more slowly, allowing the toxic substance to accumulate in body fluids (and cause flushing).

Here, the hypothesis becomes contradictory, or at the very least it branches into two inconsistent ones. One hypothesis is that ethnic groups that eliminate alcohol slowly and tend to flush (e.g., Japanese) will have lower rates of alcoholism, because the flushing is an aversive consequence that discourages heavy drinking. As a result, members of these groups will not abuse alcohol because of this uncomfortable reaction when ethanol is consumed. However, others put forth the hypothesis that those groups that eliminate alcohol slowly and tend to flush (e.g., Native Americans) will be very susceptible to alcoholism, because the high levels of acetaldehyde cause tolerance to alcohol to increase. Obviously, alcohol elimination cannot be used to explain alcoholism etiology in opposite directions!

The studies examining alcohol metabolism among ethnic groups are also seriously flawed (Lester, 1988). They possess the same flaws as those mentioned earlier: inability to measure acetaldehyde in body fluids accurately, and confusion about cause-and-effect relationships. Schwitters, Johnson, McClearn, and Wilson (1982) comment on these studies that "once persons drink at all, whether flushing occurs following the use of alcohol has only a trivial effect on drinking behavior" (p. 1262).

Finally, it is important to note that these studies ignore important differences among ethnic subgroups. This is particularly true of such ethnic groups as "Orientals" (who include Chinese, Japanese, Koreans, Vietnamese, etc.) and "Native Americans" (who come from dozens of different tribes) (National Institute on Alcohol Abuse and Alcoholism, 1990). For example, Christian, Dufour, and Bertolucci (1989) have found that among 11 Native American tribal groups in Oklahoma, the alcohol-related death rate ranged from less than 1% to 24%. Such a finding suggests that abuse of alcohol among Native Americans is much more closely related to the norms and customs of specific tribes than it is to any supposed metabolic abnormalities of genetic origin.

P3 Wave Studies

During the 1980s, a series of studies examining the brain waves (specifically the P3 wave) of persons at risk for developing alcoholism were conducted (Begleiter, Porjesz, Bihari, & Kissin, 1984; Porjesz & Begleiter, 1985). The strength of the P3 wave is measured by its amplitude on an electroencephalogram (EEG). In a study of young sons of alcoholics who had never themselves drunk alcohol, it was found that their P3 wave amplitude was generally reduced, compared to that of boys of similar ages who were not sons of alcoholics (Begleiter et al., 1984). Because the subjects had never consumed alcohol, the findings indicate that the P3 wave deficit precedes the development of alcoholism. In other words, it cannot be construed to be a consequence of alcohol abuse (National Institute on Alcohol Abuse and Alcoholism, 1990). Rather, it may be evidence of a biological marker for susceptibility to alcoholism. Unfortunately, a more recent study by Polich and Bloom (1988) failed to replicate P3 wave differences among boys of alcoholics versus controls. Thus, much further research is needed in this area before definitive conclusions can be drawn. Longitudinal studies (i.e., studies following individuals over a period of many years) would be especially helpful to determine the rate at which boys with P3 wave deficits later develop alcoholism themselves.

LOSS OF CONTROL

Loss of control is a central premise of the disease model of alcoholism. Indeed, Step One of AA's "Twelve Steps" is an admission that alcoholics are "powerless over alcohol" (AA, 1981). It is asserted that the alcoholics' loss of control stems from some unknown abnormality.

Though the exact nature of this abnormality is not claimed to be understood, the "Big Book" of AA teaches:

> We are equally positive that once he takes any alcohol whatever into his system, something happens, both in the bodily and mental sense, which makes it virtually impossible for him to stop. The experience of any alcoholic will abundantly confirm this. (AA, 1976, pp. 22–23)

As this passage indicates, the notion of loss of control is consistent with the subjective experience of many alcoholics. Why, then, do so many of the leading alcoholism researchers reject the concept?

Logical Inconsistency

Fingarette (1988), a philosopher, has pointed out that the classic loss-of-control concept is illogical. It maintains that *after* a minimal amount of alcohol enters the body, all ability to control drinking disappears. If this were actually the case, then an alcoholic would have no desire, cravings, or compulsion to drink when sober. Abstention from drinking and recovery from alcoholism would actually by quite easy! Fingarette (1988) observes:

> If the loss of control is triggered by the first drink, then the only hope for an alcoholic is to refrain from that first drink, that is, total abstention. But if loss of control is triggered only after the first drink, and not before, why should the alcoholic have any special difficulty mustering the self-control to simply avoid that first drink? Why should abstinence pose any special problem? (p. 34)

Why is the hypothesis maintained that control is lost after consumption has begun? One can only speculate, but it may be related to the alcoholic's need to blame the drug (alcohol) or some unknown biological mechanism. If the hypothesis did not first require alcohol to be introduced into the body, then the only possible explanations would be psychological or behavioral in nature. Proponents of the traditional disease model typically prefer to avoid nonbiological explanations.

Laboratory Experiments

There exists conclusive evidence that chronic alcoholics (including those who have previously experienced alcohol withdrawal sickness) can drink in a controlled manner in laboratory settings (Pattison, Sobell, & Sobell, 1977). A 1977 review of the alcoholism research literature found that in almost 60 laboratory studies, some involving experiments lasting as long as 2 months, alcoholics demonstrated no loss of control (Pattison et al., 1977). Fingarette (1988) points out that the amount of alcohol consumed by alcoholics is a function of the "costs and benefits perceived by the drinker—an observation that radically contradicts the idea of some overpowering inner drive that completely overwhelms all reason or choice" (p. 36). The contingencies (i.e., rewards and punishers) attached to drinking (as perceived by the drinker) appear to control the amount consumed. The arrangement of contingencies in three different studies involving alcoholics are concisely described by Fingarette (1988):

> One research team was able, by offering small payments, to get alcoholics to voluntarily abstain from drink even though drink was available, or to moderate their drinking voluntarily even after an initial "priming dose" of liquor had been consumed. (The larger the "priming dose," the less moderate the subsequent drinking, until a modest increase in the amount of payment offered prompted a resumption of moderation.)
>
> In another experiment, drinkers were willing to do a limited amount of boring work (pushing a lever) in order to earn a drink, but when the "cost" of a drink rose (that is, more lever pushing was asked of them) they were unwilling to "pay" the higher price. Still another experiment allowed alcoholic patients access to up to a fifth of liquor, but subjects were told that if they drank more than five ounces they would be removed from the pleasant social environment they were in. Result: Most of the time subjects limited themselves to moderate drinking. (p. 36)

(Readers should note that the three studies cited here are as follows, respectively, in the reference list: Cohen, Liebson, Fallace, & Speers, 1971; Bigelow & Liebson, 1972; and Cohen, Liebson, Fallace, & Allen, 1971.)

A common counterargument to these findings is that the drinking occurred in artificial or unnatural drinking environments (i.e., hospital units or laboratories), and that because of this fact, the data have little relevance for understanding typical alcoholic drinking. In other words, drinking in a clinic under the observation of investigators radically affects alcoholics' self-control and drinking behavior. This counterargument is faulty and does not adequately address deficiencies in the loss-of-control hypothesis. If it is argued that the social setting and/or observation by others affects alcoholic drinking, then it cannot be argued that loss of control stems from the effects of alcohol or some biological abnormality. Thus, even though the experimental settings may have been anomalous, the findings indicate that frequency and quantity of drinking among alcoholics are not determined solely, or even in a significant way, by ethanol or endogenous mechanisms.

ADDICTION AS A PROGRESSIVE DISEASE

In the classic disease model, addiction is believed to follow a "progressive" course (Talbott, 1989). That is, if alcoholics or addicts continue to abuse chemicals, their condition will deteriorate further and further. Marital, family, work, and medical problems only worsen over time; they do not get better with continued use. Life becomes increasingly unmanageable.

Johnson (1980) has described the progression of alcoholism in terms of the alcoholic's emotional relationship to the drug. His scheme has four phases. The first two phases represent "normal" drinking, while the third and fourth are typical of alcoholic drinking. Johnson identifies these four phases as (1) learning the mood swing, (2) seeking the mood swing, (3) harmful dependence, and (4) drinking to feel normal.

In phase 1, learning the mood swing, the drinker is initiated into the use of alcohol. In our culture, it usually occurs at a relatively young age. The drinking is associated with pleasant feelings. There are no emotional "costs" as a result of the consumption. In phase 2, seeking the mood swing, the drinker purposely drinks to obtain euphoria. The amount of alcohol increases as intoxication becomes desired; however, in this phase, there are still no significant emotional costs or adverse consequences. In phase 3, harmful dependence, an "invisible line" is crossed (Johnson, 1980, p. 15). In this first stage of alcoholic drinking, the individual still finds euphoria in excessive consumption, but there is a price to pay. Following each drinking episode, there are consequences (e.g., hangovers, damaged relationships, arrests for driving while intoxicated). Despite such problems, the alcoholic continues to drink excessively. In the last phase, the alcoholic's condition has deteriorated to the point that he/she must drink just to feel "normal." When the alcoholic is sober, he/she is overwhelmed by feelings of remorse, guilt, shame, and anxiety (Johnson, 1980); the natural tendency is to drink to block out these feelings.

Johnson (1980) describes the alcoholic in this last phase as at risk for premature death.

Milam and Ketcham (1983) describe the progression of alcoholism in somewhat different terms. Their scheme focuses more on physiological deterioration than on the emotional relationship with the chemical. It consists of three stages: (1) the adaptive stage, (2) the dependent stage, and (3) deterioration.

In the adaptive stage, the chief characteristic is increasing tolerance to the drug. Alcoholics believe they are blessed by having such a capacity for alcohol because they experience no negative symptoms. They typically do not appear to others to be grossly intoxicated; thus, there is no apparent behavioral impairment. However, physiological changes associated with increasing tolerance are occurring. The drinker is not aware of these changes (Milam & Ketcham, 1983).

The chief characteristic of the dependent stage is physical withdrawal. These symptoms build gradually during this stage. Initially, they are not recognized as withdrawal symptoms, but are confused with symptoms of a hangover. In order to manage these symptoms "effectively," many alcoholics fall into a "maintenance drinking" pattern in which they drink relatively small amounts at frequent intervals to avoid withdrawal sickness. They usually avoid gross intoxication out of a fear of having their problem exposed to others (Milam & Ketcham, 1983).

The last stage, deterioration, is characterized by major medical problems. Various organs are damaged as a result of long-term heavy drinking. In addition to the liver, the brain, the gastrointestinal tract, the pancreas, and even the heart may be affected. These pathological organ changes will cause death if an alcoholic does not receive treatment (Milam & Ketcham, 1983).

Johnson (1980) and Milam and Ketcham's (1983) cogent descriptions of the progression of alcoholism (and possibly other addictions) are not consistent with epidemiological findings, however. Studies that examine large populations, rather than just those alcoholics who present themselves for treatment, indicate that alcoholism and other addictions do not follow a predictable sequence of stages in which the user inevitably deteriorates (National Institute on Alcohol Abuse and Alcoholism, 1990). On the contrary, spontaneous remission (disappearance of an alcohol problem without treatment) is not uncommon among men as they move into older age categories (Fillmore, 1987a). Furthermore, it appears that among males there is a relationship between dependence problems and alcohol-related social problems on the one hand, and age on the other. Generally, by the time men reach their 40s, alcohol problems have declined; in many cases, such men still drink, but more moderately (Fillmore & Midanik, 1984). In women, alcohol problems appear to peak in the 30s (compared to the 20s for men). Also, women are more likely than men to display considerably higher rates of remission across all decades of life (Fillmore, 1987b).

Peele (1985) has advanced a concept called "maturing out" to explain how many alcoholics and addicts give up substance abuse without the benefit of treatment or self-help programs. This "natural" remission is thought to be related to developmental issues. Peele (1985) suggests that addiction is a maladaptive method of coping with the challenges and problems of young adulthood. Such challenges may include establishing intimate relationships, learning to manage one's emotions, finding rewarding work, and separating from one's family of origin. Abuse of alcohol or drugs is a way to evade or postpone dealing with these challenges. Peele (1985) contends that as addicts tire of the "night life" and the "fast lane," and become more confident in their ability to take on life challenges (i.e., responsibilities), they will *gradually* (in most cases) give up substance abuse.

How is it that the disease model has emphasized that the course of addiction is invariably progressive (a notion supported by many in recovery), and yet empirical data indicate that natural remission increases with age? This discrepancy can probably be traced to the fact that the disease model emerged from recovering alcoholics' first-person accounts and from clinical anecdotes. All of these were given by alcoholics who recovered through AA or presented themselves for treatment. Such individuals probably represent just a subgroup of all those persons with addiction problems. So although the concept of addiction as a progressive disease may fit some alcoholics and addicts, it does not apply to most with these problems.

ADDICTION AS A CHRONIC DISEASE

Questions about the "chronicity" of addiction constitute one of the most controversial issues in the field, and have become a source of great tension between the treatment and research communities (Marion & Coleman, 1990; Peele, 1985). The disease model maintains that addiction is a chronic disorder, meaning that it never disappears (e.g., "Once an alcoholic, always an alcoholic"). The disease can be readily treated with sustained abstinence and growth within AA or NA, but it is never "cured." For this reason, most individuals in AA or NA refer to themselves as "recovering," rather than "recovered." In this way, chemical dependence is likened to other chronic diseases, such as cancer, diabetes, or heart disease.

Abstinence from all mood-altering substances, then, is the goal of virtually all treatment programs in the United States (it should be noted, however, that caffeine and nicotine are not prohibited). Marion and Coleman (1990) admit that the basis for this treatment goal is not based on science, but rather on folklore. They write:

> . . . abstinence in recovery is supported by the knowledge gained by the experience of drug addicts and alcoholics in their attempts to recover. Through A.A./N.A. "leads" and testimonials, alcoholics and drug abusers daily report their inability to recover while using any mood- and mind-altering chemicals. (p. 103)

In contrast, the research community has produced a relatively large body of data indicating that controlled drinking is a viable treatment strategy for many alcoholics, particularly those of younger ages (Heather & Robertson, 1981; Miller, 1982). In addition, it appears that it may produce better posttreatment outcomes than abstinence-oriented treatment (Sobell & Sobell, 1976). However, more comparative research is needed. Unfortunately, in the United States today there are very few grant providers willing to fund such investigations. In Chapter Four of this volume, the controlled-drinking controvesy is discussed in greater detail.

DENIAL

Denial is another central feature of the disease model. According to Massella (1990), it is the "primary symptom of chemical dependence" (p. 79). Denial is best characterized as an inability to perceive an unacceptable reality; the unacceptable reality is being an "alcoholic" or an "addict." Denial is not lying. It is actually a perceptual incapacity—the most primitive of the psychological defenses. Denial protects the ego from the threat of inadequacy. George (1990) recognizes that it also "protects the option to continue to use, which for the addicted individual is the essence of life" (p. 36).

Stories of alcoholic denial are legendary. I have personally consulted with so-called "end-stage" alcoholics, who were gravely ill (e.g., pancreatitis, gastrointestinal bleeding, liver cirrhosis) and hospitalized, and have heard them deny that alcohol had any role in causing their medical crises. Certainly, denial is a common aspect of alcoholism and other addictions. However, instead of narrowly defining it as a symptom of a disease, it is useful to take a broader view and to consider how other forces, in combination, foster its use. For instance, the general social stigma attached to addiction is responsible in part for the frequent emergence of the defense. There are few labels today worse than that of "alcoholic" or "addict." With this moral condemnation, it is no wonder that individuals unconsciously react the way they do when initially offered help. Another contributing factor is that increasingly coercive methods are used to force clients into treatment today (Peele, 1988). The use of confrontative procedures (e.g., family interventions, employee assistance program efforts, group confrontation) to break down the denial may in many situations have the unintended effect of actually strengthening it.

This is not to say that chemical abuse should be ignored or "enabled." However, it should be kept in mind that at least in some cases, denial is a product of well-intentioned coercion by "concerned others" or treatment personnel. To describe it as a disease symptom is to ignore its social origins and the universality of its use by almost all humans, addicted as well as nonaddicted.

STRENGTHS OF THE DISEASE MODEL

The enduring value of the disease model is that it removes alcohol and other drug addictions from the moral realm. It proposes that addiction sufferers should be treated and helped, rather than scorned and ridiculed. Though the moral model of addiction has by no means disappeared in the United States, today more resources are directed toward rehabilitation, rather than just toward punishment. The emergence of the disease model is largely responsible for this shift in resources. Increasingly, it is being recognized that harsh penal sentences do little to curb substance abuse in our society.

Another strength of the disease model rests in its simplicity. Recall from Chapter One that a good theory is one that is parsimonious. This applies to the disease model: It is straightforward and relatively easy to teach to newly recovering clients. Clients, in turn, are often comfortable with the disease concept because it is familiar. Most clients have known someone with a disease (e.g., heart disease, diabetes), so it is somewhat less foreign.

Lastly, the disease model provides the individual who is new to recovery with a mechanism for coping with any guilt and shame stemming from past misdeeds. The disease model teachers that problem behaviors are symptoms of the disease process. The alcoholic or addict is not to blame; the fault rests with the disease process. As one alcoholic with many years in recovery shared with me, "Calling it [alcoholism] a disease allows us to put the guilt aside so that we can do the work that we need to do."

WEAKNESSES OF THE DISEASE MODEL

The weaknesses of the disease model have been identified throughout this chapter; they are not repeated here in detail. Simply put, the disease model is not well supported by empirical data. In fact, most of its major hypotheses are disputed by research findings. It either ignores or underemphasizes the impact of environmental forces and the role of learning as etiological bases. Furthermore, since virtually all treatment programs in the United States are based on the disease model and since their effectiveness is generally poor (as judged by high relapse rates), it must be concluded that the model does not adequately explain compulsive substance abuse. It apparently does not account for the enormous complexity of the problem. Subsequent chapters in this volume explore some alternatives to the disease model. None of them is without significant limitations either, as we will see.

REVIEW QUESTIONS

1. Why is the disease model of alcoholism/addiction controversial in many quarters?

2. Along which dimensions and among which groups do different conceptualizations of the disease model emerge?

3. What is meant by addiction as a "primary disease"?

4. In what ways do research data restrict the applicability of the primary-disease concept?

5. Is there evidence of genetic susceptibilities to commonly abused "street" drugs?

6. What is meant by the terms "genes," "genotype," and "phenotype"?

7. How is an adoption study designed?

8. Why is Donald Goodwin a significant figure in the work on the hereditability of alcoholism? What commonly cited statistic stems from his work?

9. What are the weaknesses of Goodwin et al.'s (1973) study?

10. How are MZ and DZ twin pairs different?

11. How is a twin study designed?

12. What are the three questionable assumptions upon which twin studies rest?

13. According to the twin study research, what are the respective roles of genetics and environment in the etiology of alcoholism?

14. What is the metabolite of alcohol that many metabolic studies of alcoholism focus upon? What is the major limitation of these studies?

15. Is there strong evidence that Native Americans metabolize alcohol differently than do whites?

16. Why might the P3 wave findings be evidence of a true biological marker for alcoholism?

17. What is meant by "loss of control" in the disease model? Why does Fingarette maintain that it is illogical?

18. Does laboratory research support the loss-of-control concept?

19. How do Johnson's and Milam and Ketcham's descriptions of the progression of alcoholism differ?

20. In what ways do research findings dispute the concept of alcoholism as a "progressive disease"?

21. What is "maturing out"? Is it consistent with the progressive-disease concept?

22. What is meant by addiction as a "chronic disease"?

23. Do research data support the use of controlled drinking as a treatment for alcoholism?

24. How is denial different from lying? What are the problems with calling it a "symptom" of a disease?

25. What are three major strengths of the disease model?

26. What are three major weaknesses of the disease model?

REFERENCES

Alcoholics Anonymous (AA). (1976). *The story of how many thousands of men and women have recovered from alcoholism* [the "Big Book"]. New York: AA World Services.

Alcoholics Anonymous (AA). (1981). *Twelve steps and twelve traditions.* New York: AA World Services.

Alexander, B. K. (1988). The disease and adaptive models of addiction: A framework evaluation. In S. Peele (Ed.), *Visions of addiction: Major contemporary perspectives on addiction and alcoholism.* Lexington, MA: D. C. Heath.

Begleiter, H., Porjesz, B., Bihari, B., & Kissin, B. (1984). Event-related potentials in boys at risk for alcoholism. *Science, 225,* 1493–1496.

Bigelow, W., & Liebson, J. (1972). Cost factors controlling alcoholic drinking. *Psychological Record, 22,* 305–314.

Christian, C. M., Dufour, M., & Bertolucci, D. (1989). Differential alcohol-related mortality among American Indian tribes in Oklahoma. *Social Science and Medicine, 28,* 275–284.

Cloninger, C. R. (1987). Neurogenetic adaptive mechanisms in alcoholism. *Science, 236,* 410–416.

Cohen, M., Liebson, J., Fallace, L., & Allen, R. (1971). Moderate drinking by chronic alcoholics: A schedule-dependent phenomenon. *Journal of Nervous and Mental Disease, 153,* 434–444.

Cohen, M., Liebson, J., Fallace, L., & Speers, W. (1971). Alcoholism: Controlled drinking and incentives for abstinence. *Psychological Reports, 28,* 575–580.

Cox, W. M. (1985). Personality correlates of substance abuse. In M. Galizio & S. A. Maisto (Eds.), *Determinants of substance abuse.* New York: Plenum Press.

Crabbe, J. C., McSwigan, J. D., & Belknap, J. K. (1985). The role of genetics in substance abuse. In M. Galizio & S. A. Maisto (Eds.), *Determinants of substance abuse.* New York: Plenum Press.

Eysenck, H. J. (1981). *A model for personality.* Berlin: Springer-Verlag.

Fillmore, K. M. (1987a). Prevalence, incidence and chronicity of drinking patterns and problems among men as a function of age: A longitudinal and cohort analysis. *British Journal of Addiction, 82,* 77–83.

Fillmore, K. M. (1987b). Women's drinking across the adult life course as compared to men's. *British Journal of Addiction, 82,* 801–811.

Fillmore, K. M., & Midanik, L. (1984). Chronicity of drinking prolems among men: A longitudinal study. *Journal of Studies on Alcohol, 45,* 228–236.

Fingarette, H. (1988). *Heavy drinking: The myth of alcoholism as a disease.* Berkeley: University of California Press.

George, R. L. (1990). *Counseling the chemically dependent: Theory and practice.* Englewood Cliffs, NJ: Prentice-Hall.

Goodwin, D. W. (1988). *Is alcoholism hereditary?* New York: Ballantine.
Goodwin, D. W., Schulsinger, F., Hermansen, L., Guze, S. B., & Winokur, G. (1973). Alcohol problems in adoptees raised apart from alcoholic biological parents. *Archives of General Psychiatry, 28,* 238–243.
Heath, A. C., Jardine, R., & Martin, N. G. (1989). Interactive effects of genotype and social environment of alcohol consumption in female twins. *Journal of Studies on Alcohol, 50*(1), 38–48.
Heather, N., & Robertson, I. (1981). *Controlled drinking.* London: Methuen.
Johnson, V. E. (1980). *I'll quit tomorrow* (rev. ed.). San Francisco: Harper & Row.
Kaij, L. (1960). *Alcoholism in twins: Studies on the etiology and sequels of abuse of alcohol.* Stockholm: Almquist & Wiksell.
Kaprio, J., Koskenvuo, M., Langinvaino, H., Romanov, K., Sarna, S., & Rose, R. J. (1987). Genetic influences on use and abuse of alcohol: A study of 5638 adult Finnish twin brothers. *Alcoholism, 11*(4), 349–356.
Kendler, K. S., Heath, A. C., Neale, M. C., Kessler, R. C., & Eaves, L. J. (1992). A population-based twin study of alcoholism in women. *Journal of the American Medical Association, 268*(14), 1877–1882.
Lester, D. (1988). Genetic theory: An assessment of the heritability of alcoholism. In C. D. Chaudron & D. A. Wilkinson (Eds.), *Theories on alcoholism.* Toronto: Addiction Research Foundation.
Marion, T. R., & Coleman, K. (1990). Recovery issues and treatment resources. In D. C. Daley & M. S. Raskin (Eds.), *Treating the chemically dependent and their families.* Newbury Park, CA: Sage.
Massella, J. D. (1990). Intervention: Breaking the addiction cycle. In D. C. Daley & M. S. Raskin (Eds.), *Treating the chemically dependent and their families.* Newbury Park, CA: Sage.
McGue, M., Pickens, R. W., & Svikis, D. S. (1992). Sex and age effects on the inheritance of alcohol problems: A twin study. *Journal of Abnormal Psychology, 101,* 3–17.
Milam, J. R., & Ketcham, K. (1983). *Under the influence.* New York: Bantam.
Miller, W. R. (1982). Treating problem drinkers: What works. *The Behavior Therapist, 5,* 15–19.
Murray, R. M., Clifford, C. M., & Gurling, H. M. D. (1983). Twin and adoption studies: How good is the evidence for a genetic role? In M. Galanter (Ed.), *Recent developments in alcoholism* (Vol. 1). New York: Plenum Press.
National Institute on Alcohol Abuse and Alcoholism. (1985). *Alcoholism: An inherited disease* (DHHS Publication No. ADM 85-1426). Washington, DC: U.S. Government Printing Office.
National Institute on Alcohol Abuse and Alcoholism. (1986). *Alcohol and health: Sixth special report to the U.S. Congress* (DHHS Publication No. ADM 87-1519). Washington, DC: U.S. Government Printing Office.
National Institute on Alcohol Abuse and Alcoholism. (1990). *Alcohol and*

health: Seventh special report to the U.S. Congress (DHHS Publication No. ADM 90-1656). Washington, DC: U.S. Government Printing Office.

Nunes, E. V., & Klein, D. F. (1987). Research issues in cocaine abuse: Future directions. In H. I. Spitz & J. S. Rosecan (Eds.), *Cocaine abuse: New directions in treatment and research.* New York: Brunner/Mazel.

Okada, T., & Mizoi, Y. (1982). Studies on the problem of blood acetaldehyde determination in man and level after alcohol intake. *Japanese Journal of Alcohol and Drug Dependence, 17,* 141–159.

Pattison, E. M., Sobell, M. B., & Sobell, L. C. (1977). *Emerging concepts of alcohol dependence.* New York: Springer.

Peele, S. (1985). *The meaning of addiction: Compulsive experience and its interpretation.* Lexington, MA: D. C. Heath.

Polich, J., & Bloom, F. E. (1988). Event-related brain potentials in individuals at high and low risk for developing alcoholism: Failure to replicate. *Alcoholism, 12*(3), 368–373.

Porjesz, B., & Begleiter, H. (1985). Human brain electrophysiology and alcoholism. In R. E. Tartar & D. H. van Thiel (Eds.), *Alcohol and the brain.* New York: Plenum Press.

Schuckit, M. A. (1984). Biochemical markers of a predisposition to alcoholism. In S. B. Rosalki (Ed.), *Clinical biochemistry of alcoholism.* Edinburgh: Churchill Livingston.

Schuckit, M. A. (1989). Familial alcoholism. *Drug Abuse and Alcoholism Newsletter, 18*(9), 1–3.

Schwitters, S. Y., Johnson, R. C. McClearn, G. E., & Wilson, J. R. (1982). Alcohol use and the flushing response in different racial–ethnic groups. *Journal of Studies on Alcohol, 43,* 1259–1262.

Sobell, M. B., & Sobell, L. C. (1976). Second year treatment outcome of alcoholics treated by individualized behavior therapy: Results. *Behaviour Research and Therapy, 14,* 195–215.

Talbott, G. D. (1989). Alcoholism should be treated as a disease. In B. Leone (Ed.), *Chemical dependency: Opposing viewpoints.* San Diego: Greenhaven.

Tsukamoto, S., Sudo, T., Karasawa, S., Kajiwara, M., & Endo, T. (1982). Quantitative recovery of acetaldehyde in biological samples. *Nihon University Journal of Medicine, 24,* 313–331.

Vaillant, G. E. (1990). We should retain the disease concept of alcoholism. *Harvard Medical School Mental Health Letter, 6*(9), 4–6.

Wilbanks, W. L. (1989). Drug addiction should be treated as a lack of self-discipline. In B. Leone (Ed.), *Chemical dependency: Opposing viewpoints.* San Diego: Greenhaven.

Zuckerman, M. (1983). *Biological bases of sensation seeking, impulsivity, and anxiety.* Hillsdale, NJ: Erlbaum.

Psychoanalytic Formulations of Chemical Dependence

The first systematic attempt to explain the origins of mental disorders was made by Sigmund Freud (1885–1939). His theory is known as "psychoanalysis." Freud derived psychoanalytic concepts from his clinical practice. His patients were predominantly white female residents of Vienna, Austria, from the 1890s to the 1930s. Psychoanalytic considerations regarding the origin of substance abuse continue to be influential today, particularly in psychiatry, clinical psychology, and clinical social work.

FREUD

As Peter Gay's (1988) biography of Freud attests, the Viennese physician was indeed a remarkable man. His ideas have had a lasting impact on our culture in ways that are sometimes no longer traced to Freud. For example, he originated the notion of defense mechanisms (e.g., denial, rationalization, etc.). He brought attention to the significance of anxiety in the human experience. He was the first to give an extensive description of unconscious mind. He pointed to the importance of early childhood experience, and he was the first to insist that human sexual behavior is an appropriate subject for scientific scrutiny. These achievements suggest that Freud's contributions to our understanding of human behavior have been unmatched by any other single person in the 20th century, with the possible exception of B. F. Skinner.

PSYCHOANALYSIS: A TYPE OF PSYCHOTHERAPY

The terms "psychoanalysis" and "psychotherapy" are not synonymous, though they are sometimes mistakenly thought to be. "Psycho-

49

therapy" is a more general term describing professional services aimed at helping individuals or groups overcome emotional, behavioral, or relationship problems. There are at least several dozen different methods of psychotherapy. Psychoanalysis is one of these approaches.

Traditional psychoanalysis involves an "analyst" and an "analysand" (i.e., the client). Typically, the analysand lies comfortably on a couch while the analyst sits behind him/her, out of view. Often, the analyst takes notes while the analysand describes whatever comes into his/her mind. Interestingly, Freud discouraged analysts from taking notes; he cautioned that doing so would distract their attention (Gay, 1988).

Interpretation

Psychoanalysis relies heavily on the analyst's interpretation of the analysand's concerns. To this end, the analyst encourages the analysand to say absolutely everything that comes to mind. By contrast, the analyst remains as silent as possible, hoping that this will stimulate uninhibited verbal activity on the part of the analysand. Gay (1988) describes the process in this way:

> In the strange enterprise that is psychoanalysis, half the battle and half alliance, the analysand will cooperate as much as his neurosis lets him. The analyst for his part is, one hopes, not hampered by his own neurosis; in any event, he is required to deploy a highly specialized sort of tact, some of it acquired in his training analysis, the rest drawn from his experience with analytic patients. It calls for restraint, for silence at most of the analysand's productions and comments on a few. Much of the time patients will experience their analyst's interpretations as precious gifts that he doles out with far too stingy a hand. (p. 298)

Free Association

According to Freud, the fundamental principle of psychoanalysis is that "free association" should be encouraged. The analysand should be free to reveal the most sensitive things that come to mind, so that the analyst can interpret them. For this reason, the analyst positions himself/herself behind the analysand. The analyst's reactions to shocking disclosures could cause the analysand to be distracted and inhibit the free flow of associations.

Dream Interpretation

Another feature of psychoanalysis is dream interpretation. Its purpose is to uncover unconscious material, which the analysand typically represses. The task of the analyst is to study the symbols presented in the dreams and to interpret their disguised meanings. Psychoanalysts believe that dreams have two types of content: "manifest" and "latent." The manifest content is the dream as it appears to the dreamer, while latent content is what is disguised to the dreamer. The latent content is comprised of the analysand's actual motives that are seeking expression, but that are very painful or personally unacceptable (Coleman, Butcher, & Carson, 1980).

Resistance

In *The Interpretation of Dreams*, Freud (1900/1953) defined resistance as simply "whatever interrupts the progress of analytic work" (p. 555). According to Gay (1988), Freud warned: "Resistance accompanies the treatment at every step; every single association, every act of the patient's must reckon with this resistance, represents a compromise between the forces aiming at cure and those opposing it" (p. 299).

For the psychoanalyst, resistance arises because the analysand becomes threatened by the uncovering of unconscious material. At such times, the analysand may attempt to change the subject, dismiss its importance, become silent, forget dreams, hold back essential information, be consistently late for appointments, become hostile, or employ other defensive mechanisms. Gay (1988) describes resistance as a "peculiarly irrational" but universal human tendency. The contradictory nature of resistance is underscored by the pointlessness of voluntarily seeking help (and paying for it), and then fighting against it.

Transference

In the process of psychoanalysis, the relationship between analyst and analysand becomes emotionally charged. In this situation, the analysand frequently applies to the analyst particular feelings, thoughts, attributes, and motives that he/she had in a past relationship with a parent or other significant person (e.g., a teacher, coach, clergyman, etc.). As a result, the analysand may respond to the analyst as he/she did to that particular person in the past. If the past relationship was characterized by hostility or indifference, the analysand may feel the same way about the analyst. The tasks of the analyst, then, are to help the analysand (1) "work through" these feelings, (2) recognize that the analyst is not the parent or significant other figure, and (3) stop living within the confines of past relationships.

PERSONALITY STRUCTURE

In the psychoanalytic perspective, human behavior is thought to result from the interaction of three major subsystems within the personality: the "id," "ego," and "superego." Although each of these structures possesses unique functions and operating principles, they interact so closely with one another that it is often impossible to separate their distinct effects on behavior. In most cases, behavior is the result of the dynamic interaction among the id, ego, and superego. Each subsystem does not typically function in the absence of the other two (Hall & Lindzey, 1978).

The id is the original source of the personality and consists largely of instinctual drives. Psychoanalytic theorists have a specific understanding of the term "instinct." It is defined as an "inborn psychological representation of an inner somatic source of excitation" (Hall & Lindzey, 1978, p. 39). The psychological representation is more commonly referred to as a "wish," "internal urge," or "craving." The bodily excitations that give rise to wishes or urges are called "needs." Thus, the sensation of hunger represents the physiological need of the body for nutrients. Psychologically, this need is expressed as a wish or craving for food. In addiction, drugs become sources of bodily excitation, which in turn give rise to cravings for that chemical. The chemical craving serves to motivate the addict to seek out the drug of choice. Psychoanalysts note that addicts' instinctual drives make them hypersensitive to environmental stimuli (e.g., offers from friends to "get high," the smell of a burning match, advertisements for alcohol, etc.). These stimuli elicit cravings and make them vulnerable to "slips" and relapses.

The id is present from birth. It is the basic life force from which the ego and superego begin to differentiate themselves. It supplies the psychic energy necessary for the operation of the ego and superego. "Psychic energy" is defined as mental activity, such as thinking and remembering. Freud believed that the id is a bridge that connects the energy of the body to that of the personality. Interestingly, Freud noted that this psychic energy is not bound by logic and reality. It allows us to do such impossible things as to be in two places at once, or to move backward in time.

Some of the instinctual drives of the id are constructive (e.g., sex). However, others are destructive (e.g., aggression, destruction, death). Because the id cannot tolerate increases in psychic energy (they are experienced as uncomfortable states of tension), it is identified as the component of personality that is completely selfish. The id is only concerned with immediate gratification (i.e., discharge of tension). It has no consideration for reality demands or moral concerns.

The id is said to operate via the "pleasure principle." That is, high tension levels (e.g., sexual urges or drug cravings) prompt the id to act to reduce the tension immediately and return the individual to a comfortably constant level of low energy. Thus, the id's aim is to avoid pain (e.g., the discomfort of abstinence) and to increase pleasure (e.g., drug-induced euphoria). (Table 3.1 outlines the effects of intoxication on the id and the other personality subsystems of both nonalcoholics and alcoholics.) The operation of the pleasure principle makes frustration and deprivation difficult to tolerate. Obviously, both frustration and deprivation are common in early recovery, and they make the addict susceptible to relapse.

The ego emerges from the id in order to satisfy the needs of the individual that require transactions with the external world (i.e., reality). Survival requires the individual to seek food, water, shelter, sex, and other basic needs. The ego assists in this effort by distinguishing between subjective needs of the mind (an id function) and the resources available in the external world.

TABLE 3.1. The Effects of Intoxication on the Personality Subsystems of Nonalcoholic and Alcoholic Drinkers

Subsystem	Nonalcoholics		Alcoholics	
	Sober	Intoxicated	Sober	Intoxicated
Id	Striving	Disinhibited	Craving	Triumphant
Ego	Controlling	Exhilarated	Anxious	Overwhelmed
Superego	Restraining	Weakened	Punishing	Disrupted

Note. Adapted from Berry (1988). Copyright 1988 by the Addiction Research Foundation. Adapted by permission.

Ultimately, the ego must answer to the demands of the id. However, it does so in such a way as to ensure the survival and health of the individual. This requires the use of reason, planning, delay of immediate gratification, and other rational resources in dealing with the external world. In "normal" individuals, the ego is able, to some degree, to control the primitive impulses of the id. As a result, the ego is said to operate via the "reality principle." The aim of the ego is to suspend the pleasure principle temporarily, until a time when an appropriate place and object can be found for the release of tension. In this way, the ego is the component of personality that mediates between the demands of the id and the realities of the external world.

The third subsystem of the personality is the superego, which is the moral component of the personality. It emerges from the learning of moral values and social taboos. The superego is essentially that which is referred to as the "conscience"; it is concerned with "right" and "wrong." The superego develops during childhood and adolescence, as a result of reward and punishment. It has three main functions. One is to suppress impulses of the id, particularly sexual and aggressive urges. The second function is to press the ego to abandon realistic goals in exchange for moralistic ones. The third is to impel the individual to strive for perfection.

Hall and Lindzey (1978) aptly describe the nature of the superego in the following passage:

> That is, the superego is inclined to oppose both the id and the ego, and to make the world over into its own image. However, it is like the id in being nonrational and like the ego in attempting to exercise control over the instincts. Unlike the ego, the superego does not merely postpone instinctual gratification; it tries to block it permanently. (p. 39)

Though the three subsystems of personality operate as a whole, each represents distinct influences on human behavior (see Figure 3.1). The id is the biological force that influences human behavior. The ego represents the psychological origins of behavior, while the superego reflects the impact of social and moral forces.

ANXIETY, DEFENSE MECHANISMS, AND THE UNCONSCIOUS

Anxiety plays a prominent role in psychoanalytic theory. The purpose of anxiety is to warn the individual that there is impending danger (i.e., pain). It is also a signal to the ego to take some preventive measure to reduce the threat. According to Hall and Lindzey (1978),

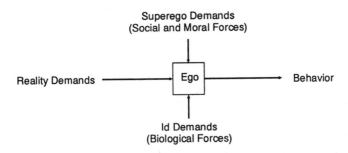

FIGURE 3.1. Influences of the id, ego, and superego and of reality demands on human behavior.

Anxiety is a state of tension; it is a drive like hunger or sex but instead of arising from internal tissue conditions it is produced originally by external causes. When anxiety is aroused it motivates the person to do something. He or she may flee from the threatening region, inhibit the dangerous impulse, or obey the voice of conscience. (p. 48)

Often the ego can cope with anxiety by rational measures. For example, a nervous student with an upcoming exam can spend extra time studying. A "stressed-out" employee can exercise, meditate, or turn to other constructive diversions. A parent can begin to save money now for a child's college education in 15 years. A recovering alcoholic who has cravings can call his/her AA sponsor. Such actions require reason, the ability to plan, and the delay of immediate gratification for long-term gain.

Frequently, the ego is overcome by anxiety that it cannot control. In such situations, rational measures fail and the ego resorts to irrational protective mechanisms, which are often referred to as "defense mechanisms." The defense mechanisms, such as denial and rationalization, alleviate the anxiety. However, they do so by distorting reality instead of dealing directly with the problem. This creates a discrepancy or gap between actual reality and the individual's perception of it. As a consequence, the ego's ability to cope with reality demands becomes increasingly diminished. Such is the case with alcoholics, who, upon being confronted with their problematic drinking, rely on denial and rationalization. These defenses, in turn, allow the abusive drinking to continue and become increasingly dysfunctional.

Typical ego defense mechanisms among the chemically dependent include the following:

1. *Compensation*: making up for the deprivation of abstinence by overindulging in another pleasure. (Example: A recovering drug addict becomes compulsive about gambling, work, eating, etc.)

2. *Denial*: inability to perceive an unacceptable reality. (Example: An employee denies he is suffering from alcoholism when confronted about the bottle he keeps hidden in his desk.)

3. *Displacement*: directing pent-up feelings of hostility toward objects less dangerous than those that initially aroused the anger. (Example: An addict in treatment comes home from a group counseling session and screams at his wife. In group, he had received feedback from the faciliator indicating that he was not actively participating.)

4. *Fantasy*: gaining gratification from the loss of intoxicants by imagining the euphoria and fun of one's past drug abuse. (Example: While in rehabilitation, a group of addicts experience cravings as they reminisce about the "good ol' times.")

5. *Isolation*: withdrawing into a passive state in order to avoid further hurt. (Example: A depressed alcoholic in early recovery refuses to share her problems in group.)

6. *Projection*: assuming that others think badly of one even though they have never communicated this in any way. (Example: An addict unexpectedly blurts out to a counselor, "I know you think I'm a worthless piece of _____ ."

7. *Rationalization*: attempting to justify one's mistakes or misdeeds by presenting rationales and explanations for the misconduct. (Example: An addict reports that he missed an NA meeting because he had to make a very important telephone call to his attorney.)

8. *Regression*: retreating to an earlier developmental level involving less mature responses. (Example: In a therapeutic community, an adult resident "blows up" and makes a huge scene when she learns that iced tea is not available for lunch that day.)

9. *Undoing*: atoning for or making up for an unacceptable act. (Example: An alcoholic goes to a bar after work and gets "smashed." He doesn't get home until 4:00 A.M. His wife is furious. The next day he brings her flowers and cooks dinner.)

The defense mechanisms and other processes operate on an unconscious level. The unconscious, according to Freud, represents the largest part of the human mind. The individual is generally unaware of the content and process of this part of mind. The conscious mind, by contrast, is a function of the ego that has often been likened to the "tip of an iceberg" (see Figure 3.2).

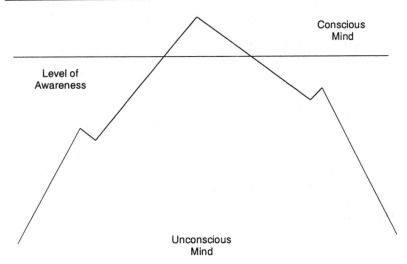

FIGURE 3.2. The "iceberg" view of the conscious versus the unconscious mind.

In the unconscious mind are forbidden desires, painful memories, and unacceptable experiences that have been "repressed," or pushed out of consciousness. Although individuals are unaware of unconscious material, it possesses energy and seeks expression. Thus, at times, unconscious material successfully penetrates into the conscious mind. Typical examples of this are so-called "Freudian slips" (e.g., using the word "sex" when the word "stress" would have been appropriate). Unconscious material also surfaces during fantasies, dreams, and hypnosis. In each case, ego controls are lowered, allowing the unconscious to appear. Psychoanalysts believe that as long as unconscious material is repressed and not integrated into the ego (presumably through psychoanalysis), maladaptive behavior (e.g., addictions) will be maintained.

PSYCHOSEXUAL DEVELOPMENT

Freud believed that the early childhood years are critical to the development of a person's personality—in fact, that one's state of mental health as an adult is largely determined by the degree to which one resolves conflicts at each childhood stage.

According to Freud, children pass through three stages in the first 5 years of life. Together, these are referred to as the "pregenital stages."

Then, at about the age of 5, children enter the "latent stage," a relatively quiet and uneventful period of about 5–6 years. As adolescence nears, the dynamics again become less stabilized; impulses, particularly sexual ones, reappear at this time. This is called the "genital stage."

Freud made sharp distinctions between the dynamics of each of the stages. However, he did not believe that there are abrupt transitions as a person moves from one stage to the next; rather, passage from stage to stage is gradual and often incomplete. According to Hall and Lindzey (1978), "The final organization of personality represents contributions from all four stages" (p. 58).

Freud described each stage of psychosexual development in terms of libidinal drives that are associated with specific zones of the body (Arlow, 1979). The stages are summarized below.

Oral Stage

The oral stage covers the period from birth to about 18 months. During this phase, the infant's main source of libidinal gratification is derived from sucking, which, of course, involves the mouth, lips, and tongue. As the infant's needs for oral gratification are fulfilled, he/she is freed from a state of tension and frustration. This satisfied state induces calm in the infant and allows him/her to sleep. The theory of psychoanalysis asserts that these dynamics form one's basic orientation to frustration. Persons who never had their oral needs met during infancy tend to anticipate disappointment at every turn, and adopt a pessimistic outlook on life.

Alcoholism is thought to be the result of these very dynamics. It is considered an ineffective and destructive attempt at resolving conflicts from the oral period (Blume, 1966). Thus, it has been described as an "oral fixation" (Kinney & Leaton, 1987). That is, alcoholics are persons with unmet oral needs who are easily frustrated, and thus turn to the bottle for relief. The act of drinking, especially from a bottle, is thought to be symbolic of a desire to return to the security and comfort of suckling from the mother's breast.

According to Blume (1966), the infantile behavior exhibited by alcoholics (e.g., narcissism, demandingness, passivity, etc.) results from their being "stuck" in the oral stage. The fixation stems from parental deprivation during this period of childhood. Anxiety and compensatory needs for control, power, and achievement manifest themselves during adulthood. Alcohol abuse is thought of as an attempt to find relief from anxiety, as well as an effort to boost one's feelings of strength and invulnerability. This is referred to as "false courage" (Blume, 1966).

Anal Stage

The anal covers the period from about 18 months to 3 years of age. Libidinal gratification is obtained chiefly through activities associated with the retaining and elimination of feces. During this phase, the child believes that feces are an extruded portion of the self; he/she considers the feces to be a valuable and highly prized possession. Typically, the child's caretakers attempt to shame him/her for such attitudes, which often leads to feelings of low self-worth. This has been described as the "anal retentive" personality. According to Arlow (1979), it is characterized by "stubborn assertiveness, contrary rebelliousness, and by the determination to be in control of whatever happens to him" (p. 13).

Phallic Phase

From the ages of 3 to 5, self-manipulation of the genitals is assumed to be the primary source of libidinal gratification. The dynamics of the phallic phase are thought to be extremely complicated, though subtle. Among boys, the "Oedipus complex" is played out; among girls, essentially the same dynamics occur, but they are referred to as the "Electra complex." Each represents a myth of ancient Greek origin. Boys and girls, during this phase, are thought to symbolically relive these Greek dramas. In each case, the child desires to overthrow the same-sex parent and to possess the opposite-sex parent. For children of both genders, resolution of this conflict is considered essential for the later development of satisfactory heterosexual relationships. Homosexual tendencies are thought to stem from an unsatisfactory resolution of this conflict during the phallic phase.

Under propitious conditions, the child puts aside the hostility of the Oedipus or Electra complex and establishes an identification with the parent of the same gender. Part of this identification process includes the adoption of the parent's moral standards and prohibitions. This results in the emergence of the superego.

Though Freud is not known to have addressed the possibility, the presence of a chemically dependent parent of the same gender could be the origin of addiction in many people. A male child, for example, may incorporate his father's values and attitudes toward drinking during the identification process. Yet the identification process may remain incomplete, so that the son maintains that he despises his father for drinking heavily. Later, during late adolescence, the son also develops a drinking problem, just like his father. Thus, the son's troubles may be seen as an incomplete resolution of the Oedipus complex (i.e., hostility toward his father), coupled with an identification with his father's alcohol-related values. In such a case, introspective psychotherapy focusing on the problem drinker's relationship with his father would perhaps be appropriate. Such therapy should probably not be initiated until after the client establishes a stable sobriety over a significant period of time.

Latency Stage

The latency stage extends from the age of 5 or 6 to about the age of 12. It ends with the onset of adolescence. Presumably, during this period, the child's sexual urges recede as the child develops talents and directs energies toward the outside world. Thus, it is thought of as a relatively quiet period during which the child is socialized.

Genital Stage

The genital stage appears after puberty. The young teen supposedly experiences a "sexual reawakening." From this point on, the greatest pleasure is derived from the genitals. Freud described this period as one of great turbulence. The adolescent makes second attempts to master the conflicts arising from desires of the oral, anal, and phallic phases. Successful resolution of these conflicts results in a consolidation of one's identity in terms of sexual orientation, moral standards, and choice of work or profession. However, in most persons, the resolution of at least some of these conflicts remains incomplete. Many individuals are thought to pass into adulthood with a variety of neurotic tendencies. Thus, it becomes the ego's obligation to mediate between the urges of the id and the demands of the superego.

INSIGHTS INTO COMPULSIVE SUBSTANCE USE

Early psychoanalytic formulations insisted that chemical dependency stems from unconscious death wishes and self-destructive tendencies of the id. It was believed that among alcoholics and drug addicts, the id is oriented toward death instincts, rather than constructive (e.g., sexual) instincts. Thus, many early psychoanalysts viewed compulsive substance abuse as a form of "slow suicide" (Khantzian, 1980). The focus in treatment was on the tendencies of the id. Contemporary psychoanalysts, on the other hand, tend to view chemical dependency as a *symptom* of a deficient ego. Essentially, they believe that substance abuse is only the obvious and outward manifestation of deeper personality problems. The goal of treatment in such cases is to build ego strength, so that the demands of the id can be better managed.

Two Necessary Conditions

According to Wurmser (1974), two general factors are always present in the development of compulsive substance use. The first is described as the "addictive search." This internal urge is a psychological hunger or craving for an entire group of activities; the urge precedes the onset of chemical dependency, but accompanies it and follows it, even after abstinence has been established. The activities may include compulsive gambling, overeating, indiscriminate sexual activity, irresistible violence, compulsive shoplifting, endless television viewing, and/or running away. All of these activities can be used to provide external relief from overpowering internal drives.

The second necessary factor is referred to as the "adventitious entrance" of chemicals (Wurmser, 1974). This is the random introduction (in terms of accessibility and seductiveness) of alcohol or drugs into a person's life. They are typically introduced by peers, or perhaps by drug pushers in the case of illicit drugs. Without access to and experimentation with these substances, addiction is obviously not possible.

Together, these two predisposing factors (i.e., the addictive search and the adventitious entrance) set the stage for the development of chemical dependency. Both must be present for the disorder to appear. According to Wurmser (1974), some people are driven by an addictive search, but they have not been exposed to the world of drug or alcohol abuse. In such cases, "there is no compulsive drug use without this trigger factor; but there is still an overriding emotional compulsiveness directed toward other activities and objects" (Wurmser, 1974, p. 829). This may also be the case for many chemically dependent persons in recovery. That is, they have removed themselves from the drinking/ drugging scene and are abstinent, but they may continue old compulsions or develop new ones. They may be said to be continuing an addictive search even though they are abstinent.

These two predisposing factors may also explain why some people who gain access to the world of drug or alcohol abuse never become dependent upon chemicals. Despite the availability, they may not possess the psychological hunger that is necessary to initiate or maintain compulsive drug or alcohol abuse. In other words, they may not need external relief from internal cravings or urges.

Abuse as Affect Defense

Contemporary psychoanalytic thinking maintains that substance abuse itself is a defense mechanism (Khantzian, 1980; Wurmser, 1980). Addicts abuse alcohol or drugs to protect themselves from overwhelming anxiety, depression, boredom, guilt, shame, and other negative emotions. Wurmser (1974) has stated that compulsive drug use is *"an attempt at self-treatment"* (p. 829). That is, it represents an attempt at self-medication, a way to relieve psychic pain.

For the most part, contemporary psychoanalysts do not view negative affective states (e.g., anxiety, depression) as consequences of substance abuse, but rather as its causes. According to Khantzian (1980):

> I have become convinced, as has Wurmser, that becoming and remaining addicted to drugs is in most instances associated with severe and significant psychopathology. Necessarily, some of the deserved pathology evident in addicts is the result of drug use and its attendant interpersonal involvements. However, it is my opinion that drug-dependent individuals are predisposed to use and become dependent upon their substances mainly as a result of severe ego impairments and disturbances in the sense of self. . . . (p. 29)

Specific Drugs to Correct Different Affects

Psychoanalysts generally dispute the notion that an addict's drug of choice is determined by economic, environmental, or sociocultural factors. Instead, they maintain that addicts become dependent upon the drug that will correct or counteract the specific negative emotional state from which they want relief. For example, Wurmser, (1980) puts it this way:

The choice of drugs shows some fairly typical correlations with otherwise unmanageable affects (moods): narcotics and hypnotics are de-
ployed against rage, shame, and jealously, and particularly the anxiety
related to these feelings; stimulants against depression and weakness;
psychedelics against boredom and disillusionment; alcohol against guilt,
loneliness, and related anxiety. (p. 72)

Khantzian, Halliday, and McAuliffe (1990) have recently outlined the differing types of emotional pain that they believe lead to
dependence on opiates, sedative–hypnotics, or cocaine. They propose
that opiate or narcotic addicts are typically the victims of traumatic
abuse and violence. As a result, they eventually become perpetrators
of violence themselves. This history causes them to suffer with acute
and chronic feelings of hostility and anger. According to Khantzian
et al. (1990),

Narcotic addicts make the powerful discovery that both the distress
they suffer, and the threat they pose with their intense aggression are
significantly reduced or contained when they first use opiates. Thus
addicts have repeatedly described the anti-rage, anti-aggression action
of opiates as "calming—feeling mellow—safe—or, normal for the first
time." (p. 35)

In contrast, these authors propose that sedative–hypnotics, including alcohol, are abused by individuals who are anxious and inhibited. This class of drugs is used to overcome deep-seated defenses
and fears about interpersonal intimacy. Sedative–hypnotic addicts
(alcoholics, tranquilizer addicts, etc.) select these drugs in order to
dissolve their defenses, thereby allowing brief and safe expressions
of love or anger to emerge. Essentially, these addicts feel separate,
lonely, or cut off from others when not intoxicated (Khantzian et
al., 1990).
    Cocaine addicts are thought to select cocaine for its energizing
qualities. These addicts are seeking relief from depression, boredom,
or emptiness. In addition, cocaine is found to be appealing because
it bolsters feelings self-esteem and assertiveness. Its use may also be
thought of as a means of augmenting an already "hyperactive, restless
lifestyle" (Khantzian et al., 1990).

Ego Deficiency

In the psychoanalytic view, addicts are thought to have weak or
impaired egos (Khantzian, 1980; Wurmser, 1980). They have failed

to develop adequate internal controls for coping with the internal drives of the id. This makes addicts dependent upon their external environment (i.e., alcohol and drugs) for the satiation of their psychic needs. Over time, addicts become more and more dependent on these external controls (i.e., alcohol and drugs), and their egos become increasingly dysfunctional.

In addition, a weakened ego does not recognize the ever-increasing dangers of continued alcohol and drug abuse. The perception of risk becomes distorted. This is commonly seen among chemically dependent people when they demonstrate an indifference to others' concerns for their physical and mental health or personal safety. It may also explain why factual and rational messages (i.e., education) about the risks of substance abuse often fail to impress alcoholics and addicts.

Wurmser (1974) believes that deficiencies in both the ego and superego result from faulty parenting:

> Parents who did not provide a minimum of consistency, of reliability, of trustworthiness, of responsiveness to the child, especially during his developmental crises, are not useable as inner beacons; instead they become targets of rebellious rage and disdain. Parents who vacillate between temper tantrums and indulgence, who allow themselves to live out their most primitive demands, parents who are more interested in their careers and their clubs and travels than in their children's needs to have them available, or parents who are absent for economic reasons and cannot impart the important combination of love and firmness—all these parents, unless replaced in their crucial functions by capable substitutes, make it very difficult for their children to accept them as secure models. (p. 147)

Concretization

Substance abuse counselors have noted that many chemically dependent clients do not articulate or label feelings. It is as if they have not language for their emotions or inner life. This condition has been referred to as "concretization." Among children and young adolescents, this is a normal developmental state. However, many chemically dependent adults exhibit it, and in such cases it can be considered a developmental lag.

Wurmser (1974) believes that the condition of concretization predisposes persons to compulsive drug use. He argues that such persons are unable to find pleasure in everyday life. Because they lack the inner controls to create pleasure, they find the world empty, boring, meaningless, and unstimulating. A vague sense of discomfort and low-level tension fills this emotionless void. To find relief, they turn to alcohol and drugs.

CONTEMPORARY TREATMENT OF ADDICTION

Contemporary psychoanalytically oriented practitioners have outlined a practical approach to the treatment of alcoholism and other addictions (Zimberg, Wallace, & Blume, 1978). First, it is believed that alcohol and drug use must stop completely for treatment to be effective (Zimberg, 1978); if abstinence is not initiated, a power struggle will ensue between client and therapist. Second, the development of transference and countertransference must be understood and properly dealt with in the therapeutic process. Transference will appear when the alcoholic or addict applies unresolved past conflicts to the therapist. Typically, the chemically dependent client will "test" the therapist in manipulative ways, and will display paradoxical feelings of hostility and dependency. Countertransference, a primitive "parental" reaction by the therapist, is to be avoided (Zimberg, 1978). It is important that therapists understand these tendencies, and not allow themselves to be drawn into dysfunctional relationships with addicted clients. The therapists must remain objective, not take the hostility personally, and avoid becoming discouraged or disgusted with such clients. Therapists must also keep in mind that they cannot stop determined alcoholics from drinking or addicts from using drugs. Progress in treatment is largely the alcoholics' or addicts' responsibility (Zimberg, 1978).

The Preferred Defense Structure of Alcoholics

Wallace (1978) has identified a "preferred defense structure" among alcoholics. (It may apply to those addicted to other drugs as well.) The concept evolved from his own professional experience in treating alcoholics. He states that this "preferred defense structure (PDS) need not be cast in negative terms" (p. 20). It is comprised of a set of tactics and strategies that alcoholics use to protect the ego. Furthermore, Wallace (1978) asserts that therapy should not attempt to remove an alcoholic's PDS, but should utilize it to help the client maintain abstinence. In the early stages of treatment, confrontation should be avoided. He recommends that the emphasis should be on sobriety rather than insight. According to Wallace (1978), "therapeutic efforts that confront the alcoholic PDS prematurely and too heavily will increase rather than reduce the probability of further drinking" (p. 20). In this perspective, it is believed that eventually the PDS must be given up for long-term sobriety to be achieved. However, Wallace (1978) suggests that the PDS may be useful in maintaining sobriety for 2 to 5 years. Beyond this period, presence of the PDS signifies a lack of personal growth in recovery, and may leave the alcoholic vulnerable to relapse.

Denial is one of the major defenses in the PDS profile (Wallace, 1978). It is believed that denial can actually be used to benefit the alcoholic in early stages of treatment. Alcoholics have a need to "save face" and preserve some self-worth. Rather than making clients face their irresponsible past behavior, therapists should "allow" denial in order to help them cope with overwhelming anxiety. Wallace (1978) acknowledges that alcoholics must believe in the early stages of treatment that they can no longer drink. However, he does not believe that it is desirable, or even possible, to root out all other vestiges of denial in their personality and behavior.

Another defense in the PDS profile is "all-or-nothing thinking" (Wallace, 1978). Alcoholics tend to exhibit a need for certainty; their personal judgments about people, situations, and events are many times extreme. Wallace (1978) notes: "Decision-making does not often seem to take into account the realistically possible. Decision rules are often inflexible, narrow in scope, and simplistic. Perceived alternatives are few, consisting largely of yes–no, go–no go, black–white dichotomized categories" (p. 23). This tendency leads a recovering alcoholic to prefer predictability and structure. AA meetings certainly provide this condition, and most treatment programs apply these principles as well.

"Conflict minimization and avoidance" constitute another component of Wallace's (1978) PDS profile. He indicates that recovering alcoholics do not like interpersonal conflict and seek to avoid it if at all possible. For this reason, confrontation, especially hostile confrontation, is seen as antitherapeutic. Wallace (1978) recommends that counselors use extreme caution when considering whether to use confrontation in the therapeutic process.

A fourth defense of the PDS is described as "self-centered selective attention." Wallace (1978) claims that alcoholics are usually obsessed with self, and they tend to evaluate events unfolding before them in terms of how they will affect them personally. Furthermore, they tend to screen out information that is inconsistent with how they view themselves. This "screening out" is linked to low self-worth, guilt, shame, and fear. This is why feedback is often difficult for alcoholics to accept and utilize in future action. For this reason, it is not imperative that clients in recovery learn the "truth" about themselves immediately. Wallace (1978) maintains the some "truths" may need to be invented to help clients stay sober. In essence, some personal myths may be useful in early recovery.

Still another defense of the PDS is described as "preference for nonanalytical modes of thinking and perceiving" (Wallace, 1978). Alcoholics tend to be persuaded by "warm" emotional or inspirational appeals, rather than by "cool" logic. In other words, a charismatic, spiritual mode is preferred over reason. Wallace (1978) notes that "the alcoholic is more drawn to the warmth of magic rather than the cold objectivity of science" (p. 25). This has obvious implications for counselor–client relationships. Alcoholics may not want experts for counselors as much as they may want advocates and supporters.

The last defense to be mentioned here is described as "obsessional focusing" (Wallace, 1978). Alcoholics are by nature intense people, and they tend to obsess about things. Wallace (1978) reports that alcoholics obsess while actively drinking and when sober as well. He notes that many recovering alcoholics become even more compulsive about work, cigarette smoking, and coffee drinking once they stop drinking alcohol. Furthermore, he states that the goal of therapy should not be to reduce this high intensity level, but rather to redirect it into productive pursuits. A good example would be ritualistic atten-dance of AA meetings. Though some frown on what they see as a substitute addiction (i.e., AA meetings), Wallace (1978) asserts that this is a good use of obsessional energy because it keeps an alco-holic sober.

Three Stages to Recovery

In the psychoanalytic perspective, there are three stages to complete recovery, as shown in Table 3.2 (Zimberg, 1978). Stage I is character-ized by the self-statement "I can't drink or drug." In this stage, exter-nal control (e.g., detoxification, Antabuse) is important. In essence, the clients need protection from their own impulses. The second stage is characterized by the self-statement "I won't drink or drug." Here, the control becomes internalized. Many AA/NA members remain at this level indefinitely. The third stage is represented by "I don't have

TABLE 3.2. A Contemporary Psychoanalytic View of Treatment Stages

Stages	Client status	Treatment
Stage I	"I can't drink or drug" (need for external controls)	Detoxification, directive psychotherapy, Antabuse, drug testing, AA/NA, family therapy
Stage II	"I won't drink or drug" (control becomes internalized)	Directive psychotherapy, supportive psychotherapy, AA/NA; Antabuse and drug testing may be discontinued
Stage III	"I don't have to drink or drug" (conflict over abstinence is resolved)	Psychoanalytic psychotherapy

Note. Adapted from Zimberg (1978). Copyright 1978 by Plenum Publishing Corporation. Adapted by permission.

to drink or drug." Many recovering persons never complete this stage, nor do they necessarily relapse. In the psychoanalytic perspective, insight-oriented therapy is appropriate at this stage (Zimberg, 1978). However, since a recovering client's perception of the need for change is usually diminished at this point (life is relatively "normal" or "manageable"), few recovering persons will pursue insight-oriented therapy.

THE IMPORTANCE OF PSYCHOANALYTIC CONCEPTS IN SUBSTANCE ABUSE COUNSELING

Psychoanalytic concepts are widely employed in the practice of substance abuse counseling. However, many counselors are not aware the concepts are derived from psychoanalytic theory. For example, many counselors make attempts to identify clients' defense mechanisms in an effort to help the clients recognize their perceptual distortions. Denial, rationalization, and fantasy are typical protection mechanisms employed by chemically dependent clients. Closely intertwined with them is the unconscious, an indisputable influence on at least some classes of human behavior.

Psychoanalytic thinking should sensitize substance abuse counselors to the importance of early childhood development and parental influences as possible origins of addictive behavior. Though counselors need not necessarily believe that alcoholics or addicts are "orally fixated" or have unresolved Oedipal conflicts, they should recognize that dysfunctional dynamics in an individual's family of origin often play a role in the development of chemical dependency. Furthermore, the slow progress or frequent relapses that characterize some clients may reflect deep-seated disturbances of personality that originated in childhood.

Psychoanalysts like Khantzian and Wurmser should be credited with making penetrating insights into the personality dynamics of addicts. Wurmser's (1974) notion of an individual's proneness (i.e., the "addictive search") coupled with drug or alcohol availability (i.e., the "adventitious entrance") provides an intriguing explanation for predicting vulnerability to addiction. Likewise, the conceptualization of drug taking as "affect defense" (i.e., a form of self-treatment) is also revealing, particularly when consideration is given to the possibility that an addict's drug of choice is selected in order to provide relief from specific dysphoric moods. The addict's distorted perception of risk, as a function of a weakened ego, sheds light on the weakness of educational approaches (i.e., dissemination of facts) in ameliorating abuse and addiction. Lastly, the developmental lag described as "concretization" helps substance abuse counselors to understand the dynamics that underlie the blunted emotional repertoire of many chemically dependent clients.

GENERAL CRITICISMS OF PSYCHOANALYSIS

The theory of psychoanalysis has come under strong attack from many directions. The theory has been criticized for overemphasizing sexual factors. While acknowledging that sexual issues are frequent sources of conflict for many people, critics contend that Freud and his colleagues gave them too central a role in the development of emotional and behavioral disorders (Coleman, Butcher, & Carson, 1980; Horney, 1967). It has been suggested that a variety of disorders do not stem from unresolved sexual conflicts (e.g., depression, anxiety, cocaine addiction, etc.).

Another general criticism of the theory is that it is unduly pessimistic about human nature. That is, psychoanalysis fails to consider positive human motivations for growth and development. Freud perceived humans as being in a constant state of conflict. This is best illustrated by the conflicting tendencies attributed to the id, ego, and superego. Critics maintain that altruism, love, serenity, and personal growth, among other human qualities, are not readily explained by the theory.

A third important criticism involves the unconscious. Freud asserted that the conscious mind comprises a relatively small part of the mind, and that unconscious processes are, for the most part, the determinants of personality and behavior. Critics of psychoanalysis contend that the opposite is true—that most human functioning is under the control of rational, conscious processes. Moreover, many have contended that what Freud considered inaccessibly buried in the unconscious is nothing of the sort; they believe that so-called "unconscious" thoughts can be brought to awareness with relative ease (i.e., with self-reflection or self-examination).

A fourth criticism is that the theory neglects cultural differences. Freud conceived of psychoanalysis while working with middle- and upper-class white residents of Vienna, Austria, during the last decade of the 19th century and the first three decades of the 20th. In addition, the majority of his clients were female and neurotic. Thus, it can be questioned whether the theory can adequately account for the experience of diverse peoples. For example, it is difficult to believe that the Oedipus complex is relevant to the development of all humans, including those of non-Western nations.

There is also little or no empirical evidence to support many of the assumptions of psychoanalysis. The very structure of the personality (id, ego, and superego) may simply be an illusory, though creative, product of Freud's mind. After all, no one has ever seen an ego, measured the unconscious, or found a defense mechanism in the brain. Yet it is interesting that we ascribe much power to these constructs and refer to them as if they have concrete reality.

Lastly, it has been pointed out that the penetrating insights offered by psychoanalysts may be of little help to clients suffering from affective or behavioral disorders. Mental health professionals have long recognized that learning *why* one acts a certain way often does not lead to changes in one's behavior. Some have even gone so far as to say that a cognitive understanding of the past origins of one's problems is irrelevant to the process of change in the present. This may be particularly the case with substance abuse problems.

CRITICISM OF THE PSYCHOANALYTIC VIEW OF ADDICTION

Contemporary psychoanalysts have pointed out that the chemically dependent suffer from poor ego controls. This makes them poor candidates for psychoanalysis, a process that requires significant ego strength. Wurmser (1974), himself a leading psychoanalyst, states that most compulsive drug users are relatively inaccessible by psychoanalysis. There are various reasons for this poor match. Many chemically dependent persons enter treatment with little initial motivation for personal change. Many others require assistance with the ordinary, mundane challenges of staying sober and "straight" a day at a time (e.g., remembering to take Antabuse, finding a ride to an AA meeting). Still others need strong guidance and structure to avoid relapse. These pressing reality-based concerns are not readily addressed in traditional psychoanalysis, with its emphasis on the intellect, the origins of problems, and protracted self-analysis.

In addition, the psychoanalytic belief that individuals are predisposed to addiction by negative affective states is not supported by existing research findings. According to Cox's (1985) review of the personality correlates of substance abuse, there is little evidence that psychological distress (e.g., anxiety, depression, low self-esteem) leads to addiction. Rather, studies of young people indicate that future substance abusers tend to show three *character* traits: independence, nonconformity, and impulsivity (Cox, 1985). It appears that negative affective states are usually the consequences of years of substance abuse, not the precursors, as claimed by psychoanalysts.

In recent years, several psychoanalytically oriented clinicians have recommended that traditional psychoanalytic practice be modified for the treatment of chemical dependency (Yalisove, 1989). The following modifications have been recommended:

1. The initial stage of treatment should be supportive and didactic in nature.
2. Management issues must be emphasized in early phases of treatment (i.e., hospitalization, dangerous behavior, withdrawal symptoms).
3. Sessions should be held once or twice a week.
4. The "couch" should not be used.
5. Interpretation should be minimized.
6. Abstinence should be encouraged.
7. AA attendance should be emphasized.

A consideration of these "modifications" gives rise to this question: Is it still psychoanalysis? The extent of the modifications eliminates most (possibly all) of the distinctive features of traditional psychoanalysis. That which is left appears to be conventional psychotherapy.

REVIEW QUESTIONS

1. What are the origins of psychoanalysis?
2. How are psychotherapy and psychoanalysis distinguished from each other?
3. What are the five chief characteristics of psychoanalysis?
4. What are the chief characteristics of the id, ego, and superego? How do they interact with one another?
5. What is a defense mechanism? How are defense mechanisms related to anxiety and the unconscious?
6. What are the chief characteristics of the oral, anal, phallic, latency, and genital stages of psychosexual development? Which stages have special significance for the problem of substance abuse?
7. Pertaining to the personality functioning of the addict, how do the interpretations of the traditional and contemporary psychoanalysts differ?
8. What are the "addictive search" and the "adventitious entrance"?
9. What is meant by "abuse as affect defense"?
10. What specific affects are different drugs thought to correct?
11. Why do addicts not recognize the risks associated with their compulsive use?
12. What is "concretization"?
13. What are the primary features of contemporary psychoanalytically oriented treatment?
14. What defenses comprise Wallace's preferred defense structure (PDS)?
15. What are the three stages of contemporary psychoanalytic treatment?
16. What are the general criticisms of psychoanalysis?
17. What are the criticisms of psychoanalysis as a treatment of addiction?

REFERENCES

Arlow, J. A. (1979). Psychoanalysis. In R. J. Corsini (Ed.), *Current psychotherapies*. Itasca, IL: F. E. Peacock.

Berry, H., III. (1988). Psychoanalytic theory of alcoholism. In C. D. Chaudron & D. A. Wilkinson (Eds.), *Theories on alcoholism.* Toronto: Addiction Research Foundation.

Blume, E. M. (1966). Psychoanalytic views of alcoholism: A review. *Quarterly Journal of Studies on Alcohol, 27,* 259–299.

Coleman, J. C., Butcher, J. N., & Carson, R. C. (1980). *Abnormal psychology and modern life.* Glenview, IL: Scott, Foresman.

Cox, W. M. (1985). Personality correlates of substance abuse. In M. Galizio & S. A. Maisto (Eds.), *Determinants of substance abuse.* New York: Plenum Press.

Freud, S. (1953). The interpretation of dreams. In J. Strachey (Ed. and Trans.), *The standard edition of the complete psychological works of Sigmund Freud* (Vols. 4 and 5). London: Hogarth Press. (Original work published 1900)

Gay, P. (1988). *Freud: A life for our time.* New York: Norton.

Hall, C. S., & Lindzey, G. (1978). *Theories of personality* (3rd ed.). New York: John Wiley.

Horney, K. (1967). *Feminine psychology.* New York: Norton.

Khantzian, E. J. (1980). An ego/self theory of substance dependence: A contemporary psychoanalytic perspective. In D. J. Lettieri, M. Sayers, & H. W. Pearson (Eds.), *Theories on drug abuse: Selected contemporary perspectives* (DHHS Publication No. ADM 84-967). Washington, DC: U.S. Government Printing Office.

Khantzian, E. J., Halliday, K. S., & McAuliffe, W. E. (1990). *Addiction and the vulnerable self: Modified dynamic group therapy for substance abusers.* New York: Guilford Press.

Kinney, J., & Leaton, G. (1987). *Loosening the grip: A handbook of alcohol information.* (3rd ed.). St. Louis: Times Mirror/Mosby.

Wallace, J. (1978). Working with the preferred defense structure of the recovering alcoholic. In A. Zimberg, J. Wallace, & S. Blume (Eds.), *Practical approaches to alcoholism psychotherapy.* New York: Plenum Press.

Wurmser, L. (1974). Psychoanalytic considerations of the etiology of compulsive drug use. *Journal of the American Psychoanalytic Association, 22,* 820–843.

Wurmser, L. (1980). Drug use as a protective system. In D. J. Lettieri, M. Sayers, & H. W. Pearson, (Eds.), *Theories on drug abuse: Selected contemporary perspectives* (DHHS Publication No. ADM 84-967). Washington, DC: U.S. Government Printing Office.

Yalisove, D. L. (1989). Psychoanalytic approaches to alcoholism and addiction: Treatment and research. *Psychology of Addictive Behaviors, 3*(3), 107–113.

Zimberg, S. (1978). Principles of alcoholism psychotherapy. In S. Zimberg, J. Wallace, & S. B. Blume (Eds.), *Practical approaches to alcoholism psychotherapy.* New York: Plenum Press.

Zimberg, S., Wallace, J., & Blume, S. B. (Eds.). (1978). *Practical approaches to alcoholism psychotherapy.* New York: Plenum Press.

Conditioning Theory: A Behavioral Perspective on Substance Use, Abuse, and Dependence

The principal aims of "behaviorism" are to elucidate the conditions of human learning and to develop a technology for behavior change. Behaviorists believe that most or all human behavior is learned; this includes not only adaptive but also maladaptive behavior (e.g., addiction). One of the major premises, then, is that certain fundamental laws (known and unknown) govern the initiation, maintenance, and cessation of human behavior. Alcohol or drug use is considered a behavior that is subject to the same principles of learning as driving a car, typing a letter, or building a house.

Behavioral psychology, for the most part, restricts itself to the study of *overt* behavior—that is, behavior that is observable and measurable. There is a heavy emphasis on empirical evidence, as behaviorists are interested in building a true science of human behavior. For this reason, they are usually not interested in internal "mentalistic" constructs, such as mental illness, self-esteem, affective states, thoughts, values, personality structure (e.g., the ego), defense mechanisms, or the unconscious. These concepts cannot be directly observed or measured, and there is no way to prove or disprove their existence. It is thus believed that they are not appropriate subjects for scientific inquiry.

The most prominent behaviorist of the 20th century, B. F. Skinner, commented on how use of mentalistic constructs has distorted (in his view) our society's understanding of addiction and other problem behaviors. He did not believe that it is useful to describe persons as immoral, irresponsible, or diseased. According to Skinner (1975),

> When the control exercised by others is thus evaded or destroyed (by the individual), only the personal reinforcers are left. The individual turns to immediate gratification, possibly through sex or drugs. If he does not need to do much to find food, shelter, and safety, little behavior will be generated. His condition is then described by saying that he is suffering from a lack of values. As Maslow pointed out, valuelessness is variously described as anomie, amorality, anhedonia, rootlessness, emptiness, hopelessness, the lack of something to believe in and be devoted to. These terms all seem to refer to feelings or states of mind, but what are missing are effective reinforcers. Anomie and amorality refer to a lack of the continued reinforcers which induce people to observe rules. Anhedonia, rootlessness, emptiness, and hopelessness point to the absence of reinforcers of all kinds. . . . If people do not work, it is not because they are lazy or shiftless but because they are not paid enough or because either welfare or affluence has made economic reinforcers less effective. . . . If citizens are not law abiding, it is not because they are scofflaws or criminals but because law enforcement has grown lax. . . . If students do not study, it is not because they are not interested but because the standards have been lowered or because subjects taught are no longer relevant to a satisfactory life. (pp. 112–113)

Skinner (1975) noted that individuals do not choose to become addicted to chemicals. Rather, he believed that they are conditioned to engage in frequent drug-taking behavior by a society that is afraid to implement a scientific technology of behavior. In his view, individuals abuse drugs (or alcohol) because they have not been reinforced for engaging in other kinds of constructive behavior.

CONDITIONED BEHAVIOR

Learned behavior is usually classified according to whether it is the result of "respondent conditioning" or "operant conditioning." This distinction is an important one. However, the two types of conditioning do not represent different kinds of learning, but instead different types of behavior (McKim, 1986). Respondent behavior is under the control of a well-defined stimulus, whereas operant behavior appears voluntary and is not directly elicited by a stimulus situation. Most human behavior falls into the latter category.

Respondent Conditioning

Respondent conditioning is also known as "classical conditioning" or "Pavlovian conditioning." It was the first type of learning to be studied systematically, and was first investigated by the great Russian physiologist Ivan Pavlov. Respondent behavior is reflexive in the sense that it is under the control of well-defined environmental stimuli. Examples of respondent behavior include the following:

1. Blinking in response to a bright light.
2. Pulling one's hand away from a hot stove.
3. Salivating at the sight or smell of food.
4. Perspiring as the result of walking into a hot room.
5. Jerking one's leg forward when struck on the knee with a physician's hammer.

When a dog salivates at the sight of food, the salivation is considered respondent behavior, under the control of the stimulus of food. Pavlov found that if he paired the sight of food with a neutral stimulus like a ringing bell, the bell alone would eventually elicit the salivation. Thus, the bell became a conditioned stimulus able to elicit salivation—a very strange situation indeed! The respondent or Pavlovian conditioning model is diagrammed in Figure 4.1.

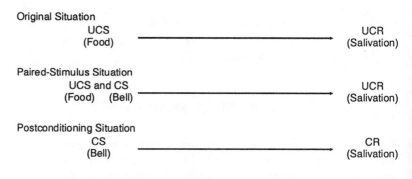

FIGURE 4.1. Model of respondent or Pavlovian conditioning.

Operant Conditioning

Operant behavior is different from respondent behavior in that operant behavior appears to be voluntary. In most cases, it does not seem to be directly elicited, or caused by, a specific stimulus in the environment. Furthermore, operant behavior is conditioned if it is followed by a reinforcer. In other words, operant behaviors are those that are maintained by events occurring after the behavior, not before it. If a behavior is followed by a reinforcer, the behavior will probably appear again. The subsequent change in rate of behavior is considered "learning."

A "reinforcer" is best defined as any event that increases the probability or rate of a behavior (Miller, 1980). Reinforcers can be any number of things. Some examples include alcohol, drugs, food, sex, verbal praise, money, a good grade, public recognition, and job promotion. Each person finds different things reinforcing. For example, some people (e.g., alcoholics) find alcohol to be a potent reinforcer, while others (e.g., recovering alcoholics) purposely avoid it as a result of past negative experiences. Furthermore, the potency of a reinforcer is determined by an individual's state of deprivation. A soldier who returns from 6 months of combat duty in a place where no beer was available is going to generate much more behavior to obtain a beer than a civilian who has ready access to alcohol.

The varying effectiveness of alcohol as a reinforcer is further illustrated by the ability of researchers to breed strains of alcohol-craving mice (McKim, 1986). Some strains show a strong fondness for alcohol; others demonstrate a dislike for the beverage. Alcohol-craving mice prefer alcohol to sugar water, and will occasionally drink to drunkenness. For these mice, alcohol is a potent reinforcer. They will learn new behaviors and engage in high rates of a behavior to continue to get alcohol; in other words, they will work for it. Among the mice that do not care for alcohol, the drink cannot be used as a contingency to train them. For this group, alcohol has little reinforcement value.

An important distinction in operant conditioning involves the difference between "positive reinforcement" and "negative reinforcement." In both situations, the rate or probability of a behavior increases. In addition, negative reinforcement is not punishment. A negative reinforcement procedure begins with an aversive stimulus; the behavior generated to remove the stimulus results in relief from the noxious stimulus. Thus, in a negative reinforcement procedure, relief is the reinforcer. The use of an alarm clock is a good example of negative reinforcement. The alarm sounds until one awakens in order to shut it off. The reinforcer in this case is silence, and the behavior change is reaching to turn off the alarm.

With addictive behavior, the classic example of negative reinforcement is withdrawal sickness. In alcoholic withdrawal, the symptoms include tremors, irritability, restlessness, anxiety, insomnia, and cravings. These symptoms are known by the alcoholic to disappear almost immediately upon taking a drink. Thus, drinking (in the case of chronic alcoholism with the presence of an abstinence syndrome) is reinforced by relief from the withdrawal symptoms. Notice that the reinforcer is not alcohol or withdrawal itself, but rather *relief* from withdrawal. In cases of alcoholism in which there is no withdrawal sickness (e.g., among teens, young adults, binge drinkers, etc.), drinking behavior is contingent on positive reinforcers, such as euphoria and enhanced sociability.

"Punishment" can be defined as any event that decreases the probability or rate of a behavior (Miller, 1980). Again, punishment and negative reinforcement have opposite effects: The former decreases behavior, whereas the latter increases it. Punishers can also be any number of things or events. They can include a "dirty" look, ignoring a comment, or even physical abuse. Obviously, people employ punishers quite often in their family, work, and social settings.

In regard to substance use and punishment, it is known that some people have particularly negative physical or psychological reactions to small amounts of alcohol or a drug. The examples of the person who becomes flushed, dizzy, and nauseated after one drink, and the person who becomes extremely paranoid and panicky after a couple of puffs on a joint of marijuana, illustrate this point. Such persons are essentially punished for substance use. The punisher (i.e., sickness or a paranoid panic attack) decreases the probability of future substance use. In cases such as these, there is little likelihood that substance dependencies will develop.

Generalization and Discrimination

Generalization and discrimination are two types of learning that are influenced by environmental stimuli, as well as by reinforcement. "Generalization" can be defined as the "tendency to perform a response in a new setting because of the setting's similarity to the one in which the response was learned, with the likelihood of the response's occurring being proportional to the degree of similarity between settings" (Mehr, 1988, p. 153). For example, let us imagine that a cocaine addict, 4 years into recovery, goes on a business trip to a distant city. After arriving at the airport, he heads to the subway to catch a train for a downtown meeting. While riding on the subway train, he experiences intense cravings for cocaine. The last time he can remember having such an intense desire for cocaine was when he used to snort the drug with his buddies while riding the trains in his hometown. He essentially generalized cocaine cravings (and use) to all subway trains.

By contrast, "discrimination" can be defined as the "learning of different responses to two or more similar but distinct stimuli because of the different consequences associated with each one" (Mehr, 1988, p. 153). The *failure* to discriminate contributes to many relapses during early recovery. For example, let us suppose that an addict is discharged from an inpatient treatment facility. He has many new friends that he has met through NA, and many old friends that he used to "get high" with. He insists that he can "hang out" with his old friends and not "pick up" or "slip." Unfortunately, he soon relapses, but gradually learns that his old friends represent a stimulus condition that he must avoid. This gradual recognition is the process of "discriminative learning." This learning process is also important for understanding the dynamics of controlled drinking—an issue to be discussed later in the chapter.

Extinction

Another conditioning principle is "extinction," which is the absence or removal of a reinforcer. With regard to substance abuse, abstinence and treatment represent extinction procedures. Relapse can be considered evidence of an *incomplete* extinction procedure. The sheer availability of alcohol and drugs, and their ever-present potential for producing euphoria, make complete extinction of drug-seeking behavior difficult. Thus, from a behavioral perspective, a return to drug use (i.e., relapse) is always a possibility.

INITIATION OF ALCOHOL AND DRUG USE

From a behavioristic perspective, the initiation of substance use is related to three factors: (1) availability, (2) lack of reinforcement for alternative behavior, and (3) lack of punishment for experimenting with alcohol or another drug. Obviously, use cannot begin if a substance is not available; this simple fact is the basis for the federal government's drug interdiction efforts. The second factor, lack of reinforcement, becomes operative when socially approved behavior (e.g., studying, working, attending church, family recreational activities) that could take the place of drug-using behaviors is not sufficiently rewarded. In such cases, individuals are likely to engage in drug-taking behavior, which is accompanied by more potent or alluring reinforcers. Third, and perhaps most important, many people who experiment with a substance do not receive *immediate* punishment. As a result of first use, few people get arrested, suffer an adverse physical reaction, lose a job, fail an exam, or receive harsh criticism from peers. The negative consequences of drug use are almost always delayed, sometimes for years or even decades (particularly with alcoholism and nicotine addiction). Not only are people unpunished immediately; they are usually quickly reinforced by euphoria and peer acceptance. Initiation, then, is the result of the combination of availability, reinforcers, and punishers in the social environment.

ADDICTION

McAuliffe and Gordon (1980) have offered the following behavioral definition of "addiction": an operantly conditioned response whose tendency becomes stronger as a function of the quality, number, and size of reinforcements that follows each drug ingestion. Each addict experiences his/her own set of multiple reinforcers. According to McAuliffe and Gordon (1980), there are three classes of reinforcers: (1) euphoria, (2) social variables, and (3) elimination of withdrawal sickness. The combination of these effects will vary for each individual and each type of drug. For example, elimination of withdrawal sickness may be a more potent reinforcer for the heroin addict than for the PCP addict. In addition, relief from withdrawal may be a stronger reinforcer for the physically dependent heroin addict than for one who is not physically dependent.

Euphoria is also important. For example, the euphoric consequence of cocaine ingestion may be more important to the maintenance of cocaine addiction than the euphoria that results from drinking alcohol. Furthermore, "peer acceptance," a social variable, may be a more potent reinforcer for the adolescent marijuana smoker than for the 40-year-old marijuana user. Thus, the specific combination of reinforcing effects is what "drives" each addiction.

For behaviorists, the inability to refrain from using a drug (i.e., loss of control) merely indicates that a sufficient history of reinforcement has probably been acquired to impel a high rate of use (McAuliffe & Gordon, 1980). Behaviorists do not believe that there is a single point at which an individual suddenly becomes "addicted." Rather, the word "addiction" is simply a term used to describe an operantly conditioned behavior that occurs at a relatively high rate. The individual's addiction develops gradually, and varies continually in response to drug-related contingencies. An "addict" is merely a person who engages in a high rate of drug use, and who has a sufficient history of reinforced drug taking to outweigh the more socially acceptable rewards of life (career accomplishments, family interests, marital sex, material possessions, etc.).

RELATIONSHIP BETWEEN ADDICTION AND PHYSICAL DEPENDENCE

For behaviorists, physical dependence on a drug is neither a necessary nor a sufficient condition for the development of an addiction (McAuliffe & Gordon, 1980). Physical dependence is simply a side effect of using certain classes of drugs at a high rate over a sufficient period of time. It merely sets the stage for experiencing withdrawal sickness and its relief. The relief is but one possible reinforcing effect that maintains addictive behavior. Euphoria and peer acceptance are equally potent, and in some cases, more potent, reinforcers. Again, this is especially true of drugs that do not produce physical dependence or do so only minimally (e.g., marijuana, hallucinogens, cocaine, etc.)

It may be readily apparent that some addictions are not driven by the reinforcing effects of relief from withdrawal sickness (e.g., addiction to marijuana). However, it should also be pointed out that physical dependence can exist in the absence of addiction. The most common example of this involves hospitalized patients recovering from surgery. Such patients are sometimes administered large doses of narcotic analgesics after surgery, over an extended period of time. When the patients are gradually weaned off the drug, they may experience some symptoms of withdrawal (e.g., irritability, diarrhea, headache, muscle ache, depression, etc.). However, because they are not "addicted," they typically do not engage in drug-seeking behavior or verbalize cravings for the drug. In fact, in many cases they do not even recognize the symptoms as those of withdrawal, but simply as those of recovery from surgery.

Even in heroin addiction, relief from withdrawal (i.e., physical dependence) is sometimes not an important reinforcing effect. McAuliffe and Gordon (1980) make note of three situations involving heroin addicts that illustrate the distinction between addiction and physical dependence:

1. Many heroin addicts who have been found to have no physical dependence on the drug claim they cannot stop using it, even though they want to, and are adamant about continuing their use despite the known risks.

2. Many compulsive, long-term heroin addicts go for months, sometimes even years, without ever interrupting their use long enough to experience withdrawal. This indicates that physical dependence (i.e., relief from withdrawal) is not the reinforcer driving their addictive behavior.

3. Many detoxified heroin addicts continue to report that they still feel addicted to the drug many months after last using it. They often continue to express strong desires for it.

CESSATION AND RELAPSE

From a behavioristic perspective, cessation of alcohol and drug abuse occurs when the punishers that follow ingestion become less temporally remote (McAuliffe & Gordon, 1980). The immediate severity of punishment effects gradually builds over months or years of abusing a drug. Typically, alcoholics and addicts will experience repeated brushes with the law, including perhaps longer and longer jail sentences; sources of money become scarce; jobs become harder to find and keep; family members and friends become increasingly hostile; medical problems worsen; and so on. As these contingencies become more closely linked in time to the chemical use, its rate will gradually, or in some cases abruptly, cease.

Behaviorists expect relapses to occur at relatively high rates among persons in early recovery, because drugs are widely available in our society, and because they always retain their ability to cause euphoria. Combined with these factors is the reality that many of the rewards (i.e., reinforcement) that come with abstinence and recovery are delayed. In fact, some abstinence-related reinforcers come only after months or years of sobriety. For example, to regain the trust and respect of family members and coworkers, addicts may have to maintain a year or more of abstinence. Some cocaine addicts have not been able to stabilize their financial affairs for years as a result of the debt they have incurred while using the drug. Drug dealers may not be able to make progress toward life or career goals because of jail time, or simply as a result of their convictions. Whenever reinforcers such as these are delayed to some distant point in the future, their effectiveness in maintaining behavior consistent with recovery is diminished. For these reasons, relapses are always a possibility, especially during early stages of recovery.

IMPORTANT BEHAVIORAL MODELS

Over the last 40 years, behavioral researchers have developed models to explain specific aspects of substance abuse and dependence. In this section, models pertaining to chronic administration, tolerance, cravings, and relapse are discussed.

The Tension Reduction Hypothesis

When alcoholics are asked, "Does drinking reduce tension and stress?," the overwhelming majority answer "yes." Stockwell (1985) found that 93% of a sample of 2,300 alcoholics in treatment reported that they drank to relax. Numerous other studies, using a variety of assessment methodologies, have arrived at similar conclusions for both nonproblem and problem drinkers (Brown, 1985; Masserman, Jacques, & Nicholson, 1945; Wanberg, 1969). Yet the "tension reduction hypothesis" (TRH) has been a long-standing source of controversy in the alcoholism field. There have been two principal reasons for this debate. First, the TRH deviates from some of the tenets of the disease model (e.g., loss of control), and has treatment implications (e.g., the possibility of controlled drinking) that are inconsistent with it (Langenbucher & Nathan, 1990). Second, the findings from studies of the TRH have inconsistently supported its validity (Cappell & Greeley, 1987).

The TRH relies on principles of operant conditioning. As a theory, it is rather simple, straightforward, and readily testable. Furthermore, it is consistent with both folklore and clinical observations. According to Langenbucher and Nathan (1990), "the theory presumes that alcoholic drinking is a product of escape learning; alcoholics drink because they have been negatively reinforced for drinking in the face of life stress" (p. 133). Essentially, the relief from stress (whether it be anxiety, depression, frustration, fear, etc.) maintains high levels of consumption. The relief from these negative emotional states is the reward provided by drinking.

The TRH model actually consists of two subhypotheses, which have been tested in a number of studies. These are as follows: (1) In the presence of stress, alcoholic drinking will increase; and (2) the stress of alcoholics will be relieved by drinking (Cappell & Greeley, 1987; Langenbucher & Nathan, 1990). Before the evidence for and against these subhypotheses is discussed, some of the early work in this area is examined.

According to a review of the TRH by Cappell and Greeley (1987), the pioneering alcoholism researcher of the 1940s, E. M. Jellinek, was among the first to link alcoholic drinking to tension reduction. Jellinek (1945) proposed that as modern society evolves, it becomes more complex and more difficult for the individual to cope with. As a result, "individuals are more likely to experience increases in frustration, anger, anxiety, and tension. Individual releases are sought. Since there is a substance which can give the desired relief, harassed man will want to take recourse to it" (Jellinek, 1945, p. 19). Jellinek was careful to avoid suggesting that all alcohol use is driven by a desire to find relief from tension; rather, he felt that this desire is one important motivation for drinking, especially for problem drinking. Jellinek's model is illustrated in Figure 4.2.

The subordination of the individual to society generates

TENSION

Tension is painful and demands

RELIEF

This demand creates

TWO PROBLEMS

PROBLEM	**PROBLEM**
of elimination or reduction of conditions that create tension	of finding a mode for relief of tension

FIGURE 4.2. Jellinek's schematic representation of the origin and consequences of tension. Adapted from Jellinek (1945) by Cappell and Greeley (1987). Copyright 1987 by The Guilford Press. Reprinted by permission.

Jellinek did not formally coin the phrase "tension reduction hypothesis," however. About a decade later, Conger (1956), in a seminal study on the relationship between alcohol use and tension, first used the term. Conger was an experimental psychologist who relied on laboratory data from animal studies. In the early 1950s, Conger made use of an approach–avoidance conflict procedure using rats (McKim, 1986). He trained his rats to run down an alley for food (the reward or reinforcer). As they began to eat, he would electrify the grid upon which they rested. Obviously, this produced conflict for the hungry rats! They were being reinforced and punished at the same time.

Over time, Conger (1951) adjusted both the food deprivation level (making the food a stronger or weaker reinforcer) and the electric shock level. Eventually, the rats "learned" to run part way down the alley, but not to touch the food. Conger found that when one group of rats was injected with alcohol, they would approach and eat the food almost immediately, despite the electric shock. By contrast, a group of rats that only received a placebo injection required many more trials before they would approach and eat the food on an electrified grid. In essence, the alcohol ameliorated the conflict between eating and receiving a shock. Conger (1951) concluded that these findings supported an important element of the TRH—that is, that alcohol mitigates aversive states such as fear or tension.

Since Conger's (1951) early work, numerous TRH studies have been conducted, and several comprehensive reviews of this body of research exist. Each one reaches slightly different conclusions about the validity of the TRH. The most recent review, by Langenbucher and Nathan (1990), indicates that empirical evidence generally supports the validity of the TRH. More specifically, the authors conclude that (1) there is a statistically significant positive correlation between a study's year of publication and its methodological quality; and (2) the greater the methodological adequacy of a study, the more strongly its findings support the TRH (Langenbucher & Nathan, 1990).

A 1987 review of TRH studies is somewhat more cautious in its assessment of the research. Cappell and Greeley (1987) observe that studies relying upon conflict procedures (e.g., Conger's work, described above) in both humans and animals "provide relatively consistent support for the TRH" (p. 44). However, these studies have not specified the exact elements of conflict that alcohol is able to ameliorate. Other work suggests that individuals under aversive stimuli (such as tension) respond in different ways when given alcohol. It is possible that biological differences among individuals make some much more responsive to the tension-dampening effects of alcohol than others. Furthermore, some studies have suggested that low or moderate amounts of alcohol may dampen responses to stress, whereas high amounts may actually exacerbate it. Finally, studies that have made use of social stressors (those most similar to the "natural" ones most alcoholics would experience) have been least likely to produce findings in support of the TRH. Cappell and Greeley (1987) conclude that the inconsistencies in the "social stressor" class of TRH studies are difficult to explain. However, it is possible that individuals interpret and respond to identical, stressful social situations (e.g., interpersonal conflict) in varied ways, with or without alcohol. Thus, the complexity of the relationship may be especially pronounced. Powers and Kutash (1985) have neatly summarized these findings in the following passage:

> Alcohol use does not cause the relief of stress, in that alcohol is neither a necessary nor a sufficient condition for that occurrence. Alcohol is not a necessary condition for stress relief, for very often stress relief occurs without the presence of alcohol. Alcohol is not a sufficient condition, for at times alcohol use results in an increase in stress or no change. Alcohol is best considered as one of many possible contributors to stress relief. Many interactive factors determine whether alcohol use results in a reduction of stress. The most prominent factors identified thus far include: expectations regarding alcohol's effects, pharmacological effects of alcohol at varying dosages, individual differences in the appraisal of stressors and in coping behaviors, and the entire constellation of stressors and stress responses experienced by the individual. (p. 471)

Blood Alcohol Discrimination

Many alcohol abuse prevention and early intervention programs promote the notion of "sensible" drinking. Controlled-drinking treatment programs for alcoholics essentially teach the same thing. That is, they attempt to arrange contingencies in such a way as to support moderate, nonproblematic consumption. Both types of programs have come under attack from government officials and some proponents of the disease model, who claim that approaches advocating "sensible" or "responsible" drinking are ineffective and dangerous (Harding, 1989). This would particularly be the case if humans were unable to discriminate between particular blood alcohol levels (BALs). In other words, if individuals (nonalcoholic or alcoholic) cannot reasonably estimate their BALs, then efforts aimed at teaching moderate drinking cannot rely on strategies using perceived intoxication as a cue to stop or slow one's drinking. A number of studies have examined this issue.

Silverstein, Nathan, and Taylor (1974) attempted to determine whether alcoholics could learn to identify cues linked with intoxication. Using four male alcoholic inpatients who had a strong desire to learn how to control their drinking, the researchers asked the subjects to estimate their BALs on the basis of internal cues. Essentially, they were instructed to link different feelings and sensations with differing BALs. The subjects were initially given no external (accurate) feedback about their performance. As the study progressed, the alcoholic subjects' ability to discriminate between BALs improved as they received more external feedback from the researchers. However, during subsequent training in which the external cues (feedback) were removed, the accuracy of their stimulations declined.

The results of Silverstein et al.'s (1974) study indicated that alcoholics could not use internal cues to discriminate between BALs. Subsequent research was conducted with nonalcoholic subjects to determine whether they could rely on internal cues to estimate their BALs, and if so, whether their estimation accuracy could be maintained by internal cues, external cues, or both, subsequent to training. The findings revealed that nonalcoholics were able to use both internal and external cues to estimate BALs. Thus, it appeared that nonalcoholics differed in an important way from alcoholics (Huber, Karlin, & Nathan, 1976).

Several subsequent studies that compared the relative ability of nonalcoholics and alcoholics to estimate their BALs obtained findings consistent with those of the early studies (Brick, 1990). These findings suggest that the differing levels of tolerance among the two groups account for the differences in ability to estimate BALs. Apparently, as a result of chronic, heavy alcohol use and the resultant increase in tolerance to the drug, alcoholics lose the ability to monitor their BALs via internal cues (i.e., feelings and sensations). It seems that chronic alcoholics receive weak, poorly defined, or perhaps nonexistent internal cues as a result of drinking low to moderate amounts of alcohol.

This inability to recognize BALs has important implications for alcoholics in controlled-drinking treatment programs. It suggests that alcoholics must rely exclusively on external cues, such as body weight and number of drinks, to determine their level of intoxication. Those who insist that they can tell when they have had "too much" are likely to be in error (and drunk). This also helps explain why problem drinkers (with high tolerance) will insist that they have not had too much to drink and are all right. To the outside observer, they demonstrate noticeable impairment (lack of coordination, slurring of speech, etc.), but internally they lack the cues that can provide this feedback.

These findings also suggest that prevention efforts advocating "responsible" drinking are possible as long as the targeted individuals possess normal alcohol tolerance. Unfortunately, many high school and traditional-age college students (the targets of responsible-drinking campaigns) may already demonstrate a high degree of tolerance to alcohol and have little motivation to monitor their drinking. This simply underscores the necessity of using diagnostic approaches to the prevention and early intervention of alcohol abuse among various subgroups of young people.

Behavioral Tolerance

In regard to alcohol and drug abuse, the term "tolerance" has been defined "either as the decreased effectiveness of a drug which results from the continued presence of the drug in the body, or, the necessity of increasing the dose of a drug in order to maintain its effectiveness after repeated administration" (McKim, 1986, p. 53). Alcoholics and addicts are typically described as having high tolerance for their substance of choice. Those unfamiliar with alcoholism are often surprised to learn that many alcoholics report drinking a quart or more of liquor a day.

Traditionally, tolerance has been thought to be the result of bodily adaption to the drug at the cellular level. That is, the cells of the body, after chronic exposure, adapt to or compensate for the presence of the drug. This compensation explains how alcoholics can drink a six-pack of beer and walk without an impaired gait or slur their speech.

Behavioral researchers have determined that learning also plays a very important role in the development of tolerance (Brick, 1990). It appears that both biological factors (i.e., cellular adaptation) and nonbiological factors create tolerance. Furthermore, it appears that behavioral tolerance is learned both by respondent (Pavlovian) conditioning and operant conditioning procedures. Shepard Siegel pioneered the Pavlovian model of tolerance (see Figure 4.3). Siegel (1982) hypothesized that drug tolerance is partially conditioned to the environment in which the drug is normally used. If a drug is administered in the presence of usual cues (i.e.,

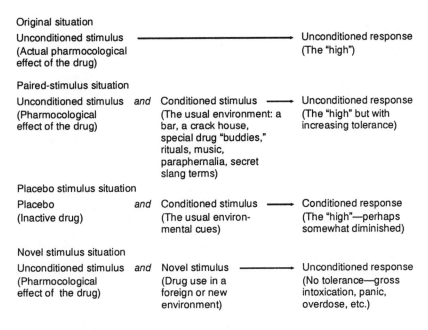

FIGURE 4.3. Pavlovian model of conditioned tolerance.

the normal environment), the drug effect will be somewhat diminished. In behavioristic jargon, "the drug effect is reduced by these anticipatory conditioned compensatory responses" (Brick, 1990, p. 178). Over time, as a drug is used repeatedly in the same environment, the diminishing effects increase in magnitude. This is the process of building tolerance.

As Figure 4.3 illustrates, after the unconditioned stimulus (pharmacological action of the drug) has been paired with the conditioned stimulus (the normal drug-using environment), placebo and novel stimulus conditions evoke distinctly different responses. Notice that in the placebo condition the usual environmental cues alone will elicit (at least for a period of time) the drug "high." Also notice that if a drug is used in a novel setting, much of the conditioned tolerance will be lost. In such cases, gross intoxication (alcohol), panic reactions (marijuana, PCP, LSD), and even overdose (heroin) may occur. McKim's (1986) description in Box 4.1 of an experiment by Siegel and his colleagues illustrates this point (see also Figure 4.4).

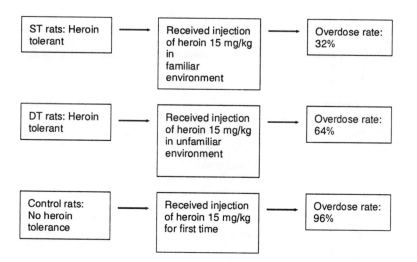

To some degree, drug tolerance is associated with the environment. Tolerance can disappear (to various degrees) if a drug is used in an unfamiliar environment.

FIGURE 4.4. A diagram of Siegel's rat experiment.

BOX 4.1. The Heroin Overdose Puzzle

One of the greatest risks of being a heroin addict is death from heroin overdose. Each year about one percent of all heroin addicts in the United States die from an overdose of heroin despite having developed a fantastic tolerance to the effects of the drug. In a non-tolerant person the estimated lethal dose of heroin may range from 200 to 500 mg, but addicts have tolerated doses as high as 1800 mg without even being sick (Brecher, 1972). No doubt, some overdoses are a result of mixing heroin with other drugs, but many appear to result from a sudden loss of tolerance. Addicts have been killed one day by a dose which was readily tolerated the day before. An explanation for this sudden loss of tolerance has been suggested by Shepard Siegel of McMaster University, and his associates, Riley Hinson, Marvin Krank, and Jane McCully.

Siegel reasoned that the tolerance to heroin was partially conditioned to the environment where the drug was normally administered. If the drug is consumed in a new setting, much of the conditioned tolerance will disappear and the addict will be more likely to overdose. To test this theory Siegel and associates ran the following experiment (Siegel, 1982).

Rats were given daily intravenous injections for 30 days. The injections were either a dextrose placebo or heroin and they were given in either the animal colony room or a different room where there was a constant white noise. The drug and the placebo were given on alternate days and the drug condition always corresponded with a particular environment so that for some rats, the heroin was always administered in the white noise room and the placebo was always given in the colony. For other rats the heroin was always given in the colony and the placebo was always given in the white noise room. Another group of rats served as a control: these were injected in different rooms on alternate dates, but were only injected with the dextrose and had no experience with heroin at all.

All rats were then injected with a large dose of heroin: 15.0 mg/kg. The rats in one group were given the heroin in the same room where they had previously been given heroin. (This was labeled the ST group.) The other rats, the DT group, were given the heroin in the room where they had previously been given the placebo.

Siegel found that 96 percent of the control group died, showing the lethal effect of the heroin in non-tolerant animals. Rats in the DT group who received heroin were partially tolerant, and only 64 percent died. Only 32 percent of the ST rats died, showing that the tolerance was even greater when the overdose test was done in the same environment where the drug previously had been administered.

Siegel suggested that one reason addicts suddenly lose their tolerance could be because they take the drug in a different or unusual environment like the rats in the DT group. Surveys of heroin addicts admitted to hospitals suffering from heroin overdose tend to support this conclusion. Many addicts report that they had taken the near-fatal dose in an unusual circumstance or that their normal pattern was different on that day (Siegel, 1982).

Note. From McKim (1986). Copyright 1986 by Prentice-Hall, Inc. Reprinted by permission.

The operant type of behavioral tolerance occurs in situations in which individuals learn, while intoxicated, to compensate for the deleterious effect of the drug. Animal research provides evidence of this learned tolerance. Campbell and Seiden (1973) trained rats to obtain food on a schedule that provided reinforcement for responding at a low rate (see Figure 4.5). The rats were injected with ampheta-

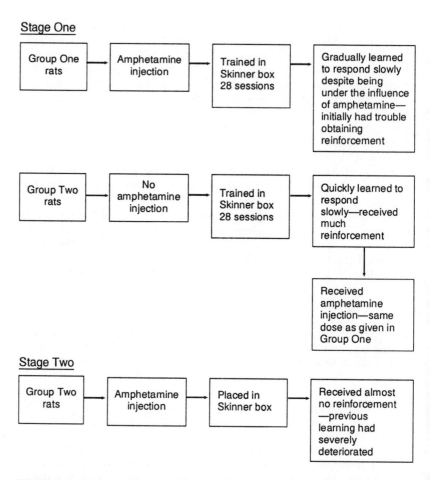

FIGURE 4.5. Tolerance via operant conditioning. This type of tolerance occurs in situations where subjects, while intoxicated, learn to compensate for the deleterious effect of a drug.

mine, which stimulated responding. Because of the schedule of reinforcement that the rats were on, this increased responding meant that they lost reinforcements. For 28 sessions, the researchers gave amphetamine to one group of rats and then immediately placed them in a "Skinner box," where they were continued on the "slow" reinforcement schedule. A second group of rats received the same 28 sessions; however, they received amphetamine injections *after* each training session.

During the course of the experiment, the rats that received amphetamine prior to their training sessions (i.e., Group One rats) were able to gradually obtain more and more reinforcements by learning to respond more slowly (see Figure 4.5). Essentially, they developed tolerance to the effects of amphetamine. The rats in the second group (i.e., those that had received amphetamine after their training sessions) were then pretreated with amphetamine and tested on the same schedule as before. These rats received very little reinforcement. They essentially had no tolerance in relation to the task of obtaining food, even though they had received the same amount of amphetamine during the course of the experiment. The only difference between the groups was the timing of the amphetamine injection (before or after training). This indicates that cellular adaptation had little to do with the development of tolerance in this case, since both groups received identical doses of amphetamine (Campbell & Seiden, 1973).

Among humans, these findings suggest that cellular adaptation does not, by itself, entirely account for tolerance. This may partially explain why intoxicated teens are much more likely to get into automobile accidents than equally intoxicated adults: The adult drinkers may have had many more years of "practice" at drunk driving than the young people. In other words, teens may not have learned how to compensate adequately for the effects of alcohol on driving.

CONTINGENCY CONTRACTING/BEHAVIORAL COUNSELING

The application of learning principles to the helping process is called "behavioral counseling," "behavior therapy," "behavior modification," "behavioral contracting," or "contingency contracting." This helping strategy has been used to establish and maintain controlled drinking; to encourage the adoption of recovery behaviors (e.g., taking an Antabuse tablet, attending AA each day, etc.); to decrease illicit drug use; and to manage residential treatment environments (see "Token Economies," below). Based upon the premise that alcohol and drug use (and addiction) are learned, the counselor's role is to assist clients in learning more effective ways of behaving so that clients reach *their* goals. According to Ullman and Krasner (1965), contingency contracting begins with the following sets of questions:

1. What behavior is maladaptive? Specifically, what behaviors should be increased or decreased?

2. What environmental contingencies currently maintain or support the behavior? That is, in this case, what are the rewards that maintain the chemical use? And what are the punishers associated with nonuse?

3. What environmental changes can be manipulated to alter the behavior?

In behavioral counseling, the development and maintenance of addiction are the same as the development and maintenance of any other behavior. This view has two important implications. First, chemical use is not inherently maladaptive; rather, it becomes inappropriate as the result of labels that significant others assign to it. For instance, an alcoholic is simply a person whose drinking behavior has adversely affected a family member, friend, or coworker. The second implication is that drinking or drug use is maintained because other, more adaptive behaviors are not reinforced or not possible. A typical example would include an alcoholic man in early recovery and his nonsupportive wife. As a result of several months of abstinence, the recovering father begins to demonstrate appropriate parenting behavior (e.g., he takes his son fishing, compliments his daughter's cooking), which his wife criticizes. The lack of reinforcement for these new behaviors soon leads him back to drinking.

According to Dustin and George (1973, p. 12), behavioral counseling is based on four assumptions about human nature and the change process. As applied to substance abusers, these assumptions are often questioned by laypeople and mental health professionals who feel that chemical dependence is driven by unique dynamics. The four assumptions of behavioral counseling are as follows:

1. Man is viewed as being neither intrinsically good nor bad, but as an experiencing organism who has potential for all kinds of behavior.
2. Man is able to conceptualize and control his own behavior.
3. Man is able to acquire new behaviors.
4. Man is able to influence others' behavior as well as to be influenced by others in his own behavior.

Three phases of contingency contracting have been identified by Dustin and George (1973). The first phase can be described as "problem specification." With emphathetic understanding, the counselor assists clients in identifying their problems in behavioral terms. For example, addicts who say that they are lonely and depressed may lack the kind of social skills necessary for meeting someone new. In teaching such skills, the counselor would help identify the necessary stimulus and reinforcing conditions for meeting someone new. The second phase consists of helping clients to "making a commitment to change." There are many barriers to achieving this, particularly with chemically dependent clients. Thus, at this phase many clients will drop out of counseling or treatment. The third phase is "specifying goals." Here it is important that the counselor work toward the clients' goals; the counselor should not impose goals on clients.

Controlled Drinking

It can be reasonably asserted that with a small portion of abusive drinkers (perhaps 15%), controlled drinking, managed by contingency contracting, is a viable alternative to abstinence (Miller, 1982). It should also be emphasized that controlled drinking is not an effort to encourage recovering alcoholics to "try drinking again." With selected candidates, it is one of many options at the onset of treatment.

Heather and Robertson (1983) have identified six possible advantages of a controlled-drinking strategy:

1. In our society, abstinence from alcohol is deviant behavior. This is unfortunate. However, the stigma and the label of "alcoholic" pose significant adjustment problems for some people.

2. Among some alcoholics, abstinence may lead to overwhelming states of anxiety or depression that are unlikely to be managed in other ways.

3. Sometimes, overall improvement in life functioning does not result from abstinence.

4. In some alcoholics, abstinence is associated with severe psychosocial problems that lead to frequent relapse.

5. Abstinence during treatment rules out the possibility for changes in drinking behavior.

6. The demand placed upon alcoholics to abstain deters many from seeking help until their problem is quite severe.

Miller and Hester (1980) have designed a model for controlled drinking based upon behavioral principles; it is called "behavioral self-control training" (BSCT). With selected candidates, Miller and Hester (1980) have demonstrated an effectiveness rate for BSCT of 60–80%. In a recent study, Harris and Miller (1990) reported that 78% of problem drinkers in a self-directed BSCT group and 63% of those in a therapist-directed BSCT group were rated as maintaining improvement 15 months after initiating treatment. The improved group consisted of abstainers (confirmed by collateral reports) and controlled drinkers. The criteria for being classified as "improved" included (1) on average, no more than 20 standard drinks weekly; (2) not exceeding BALs of .08 to .10 on any occasion (verified by collateral reports); and (3) for those who failed to meet the criteria for controlled drinking, succeeding in reducing their weekly alcohol intake by 30% or more (confirmed by collateral reports).

BSCT is comprised of the following components (Miller & Hester, 1980):

1. A functional analysis of the drinking behavior is conducted. Together, the client and the counselor determine specific and appropriate limits for alcohol consumption; these depend upon body weight and safety concerns. Typically, limits for consumption range from two drinks to perhaps four on one occasion.

2. The client monitors and records consumption.

3. Clients are trained to control the rate of their drinking.

4. Self-reinforcement procedures are created to maintain gains.

5. Emphasis is placed upon stimulus control training.

6. In place of alcohol, clients are taught a variety of coping skills for obtaining those outcomes they no longer derive from excessive alcohol use.

Numerous studies have demonstrated the effectiveness of BSCT in helping abusive drinkers to control their drinking. Unfortunately, it is probably not possible to apply BSCT to the broad spectrum of alcoholic clients who appear for treatment. In addition to not being appropriate for clients with certain medical conditions (discussed below), it may be ineffective for the large number of ambivalent or "unmotivated" clients (i.e., those who are more or less "forced" into treatment by employers, family members, the courts, etc.). Such clients often seek treatment to escape even more aversive sanctions, and frequently have little interest in learning to modify their drinking behavior. The limited appeal of BSCT among many abusive drinkers is highlighted by the fact that many controlled-drinking studies have found it difficult to recruit clients (Cameron & Spence, 1976; Robertson, Heather, Dzialdowski, Crawford, & Winton, 1986). Harris and Miller (1990) solicited clients in the Albuquerque, New Mexico metropolitan area for 6 months via the local news media. Despite the fact that the program was advertised as free of charge, they were able to recruit only 34 clients for their BSCT study.

It should be noted that even the proponents of controlled drinking do not believe that it is a viable strategy for most alcoholics (Miller, 1982). Good candidates are generally young, motivated clients who have no biomedical impairment from alcohol abuse. Lewis, Dana, and Blevins (1988, p. 153) have developed criteria for ruling out controlled-drinking candidates. Those who should not attempt it include the following:

1. clients with liver dysfunction, stomach problems, an ulcer, any other disease of the gastrointestinal tract
2. clients who have cardiac problems that would be adversely affected by alcohol
3. clients who have any physical illness or condition that would be negatively affected by alcohol
4. clients who have a diagnosis of alcohol idiosyncratic disorder intoxication (American Psychiatric Association, 1980, p. 132)
5. clients who are committed to abstinence
6. clients who have strong external demands for abstinence
7. female clients who are pregnant or considering pregnancy
8. clients who lose control of their behavior while drinking
9. clients who have been physically addicted to alcohol
10. clients using any medication or drug that is dangerous when combined with alcohol
11. clients who are abstaining from alcohol
12. those people with the following history: over 40, divorced and not in a supportive relationship, out of work, or with a family history of alcoholism
13. clients who have tried a competently administered moderation-oriented treatment and have failed

The Sobells' Controversy

In 1970–1971, Mark and Linda Sobell, two psychology graduate students, conducted an experiment at Patton State Hospital in California. The study compared the relative efficacy of two approaches to the treatment of alcoholism: abstinence and controlled drinking. The study, like many others conducted before and after it, found that controlled drinking (subjects were taught to modify their drinking via behavioral principles) was superior to abstinence on a variety of outcome variables.

In the July 9, 1982, issue of the prestigious journal *Science*, an article appeared that attacked the Sobells' study. The authors, Pendery, Maltzman, and West (1982), contended that the Sobells' research was severely flawed. Maltzman accused the Sobells of scientific fraud (Peele, 1983). The controversy was picked up by the national news media. Most news accounts portrayed the Sobells' work as dangerous, misguided, and of poor quality. According to Peele (1985), several of the media reports were made from the gravesites of controlled-drinking clients who had died after the study.

As Peele (1985) and others have subsequently pointed out, Pendery et al. (1982), in their investigation of the Sobells' research, conveniently ignored the outcomes among the abstinence treatment group. Although it was highlighted by Pendery et al. and the media that 4 out of 20 subjects in the controlled-drinking group had died in the years following the study, they neglected to add that 6 out of the 20 abstinence-treated subjects had died during the same period; 4 of these 6 were judged to have died of causes related to alcohol (Peele, 1983). Thus, there appeared to be no increased mortality risk associated with controlled drinking, compared to abstinence-oriented treatment.

Other respected proponents of the disease model added fuel to the controversy by somehow also overlooking the outcomes from the abstinence-treated group. For example, Sidney Cohen (1983) ignored the abstinence-treated group altogether in his review of the controversy. He stated that the key issue regarding the Sobells' work was this: "did the controlled drinking subjects control their drinking over time?" (p. 2). It is interesting that Cohen did not demand that the same scrutiny be applied to the abstinence-oriented treatment—namely, did the subjects in the abstinence program control *their* drinking over time?

A review of the Sobells' findings indicated that at last follow-up (19 to 24 months after inpatient treatment), the controlled-drinking group "functioned well," on average, for 160 of the past 183 days (Sobell & Sobell, 1986). By contrast, the group that had been trained to be abstinent had "functioned well," on average, for 80 days during the same time period. "Functioning well" was defined as using no alcohol or drinking less than the equivalent of 6 ounces of 86 proof alcohol on that day. The Pendery et al. (1982) group attempted to "explain away" these findings by suggesting that a number of the clients in the controlled-drinking group were not really alcoholic after all. According to them, the fact that they were able to moderate their drinking proved this to be true. This line of reasoning (i.e., assuming that some clients are not really alcoholic) would logically require abstinence-treated groups to be examined for nonalcoholism as well! It is possible that successful adherence to an abstinence-oriented program was also attributable to a false-positive diagnosis of alcoholism. Pendery et al. did not follow through on making such a recommendation.

The controversy raised by the debate between the Sobells and Pendery et al. led to the formation of an investigation committee commissioned by the Addiction Research Foundation. It consisted of professionals from law, medicine, psychology, and higher education administration. None of the committee members had links with the controversy. The committee examined eight allegations of research error or misconduct that were raised by the Pendery et al. group. The committee members sided with the Sobells on seven of the eight allegations. The eighth allegation referred to the Sobells' claim that they had been in contact with their subjects every 2 weeks; the committee members reported that they could find no evidence to support or refute their claim on this issue. The committee's findings were not widely reported in the media.

The Sobells' controversy highlights long-standing tensions that have existed between the "recovery movement" (i.e., AA, medicine, treatment programs, and many mental health professionals) and scientific investigators. Though well intentioned, many treatment providers have adopted rigid attitudes about effective clinical practice. Too often, the treatment field has taken the position that it knows "what works." There is little questioning about the effectiveness of the interventions employed. Furthermore, clinical decisions are often not data-based, or when data suggest different approaches they are ignored. Objective evidence, the cornerstone of scientific investigation and effective clinical practice, has been integrated into treatment regimens in far too few instances.

Contracting for the Initiation and Maintenance of Recovery Behaviors

In cases where abstinence has been chosen and initiated, certain behaviors are thought to be conducive to ongoing recovery. They may include the following:

1. Attending AA/NA meetings.
2. Calling one's sponsor.
3. Reading self-help literature (e.g., the AA "Big Book").
4. Getting to work on time.
5. Avoiding "slipping places."

6. Taking Antabuse as prescribed.
7. Socializing with fellow recovering addicts.
8. Practicing relaxation exercises or other coping skills.
9. Attending to one's family responsibilities.

Contingency contracting can be used to help clients initiate and maintain these behaviors and any others found to be conducive to recovery. Reinforcers and punishers are linked to the occurrence and absence of specified behaviors, as outlined in a written contract. Of course, the contract is not legally binding; however, both client and counselor should sign it, and the client should receive a photocopy. Again, it is not something that is forced upon a client, but something that counselor and client develop together.

Typically, contracts outline the rewards that clients give themselves if they engage in the specified behaviors. For example, if a client attends five AA meetings a week, he/she can go out for dinner on the weekend. If the client fails to make it to five meetings in a particular week, then he/she must forgo the restaurant outing. Likewise, a client may decide to "punish" himself/herself for neglecting to take Antabuse on a particular day. Such oversights can be self-penalized by arranging for donations (perhaps $5.00 or $10.00) to be given to a disliked political or religious organization.

There are a number of important principles involved in effective contingency contracting. Two of these are the temporal proximity of the reinforcer or punisher to the specified behavior, and the potency of the contingency (Miller, 1980). First, in brief, reinforcers and punishers are most effective when they occur immediately after the specified behavior; those that are delayed are generally less effective. Second, individuals differ considerably in regard to rewards and punishers. For example, ice cream may be a potent reinforcer for some recovering clients, but ineffective for others. Thus, effective contracts will rely on contingencies that have special significance for the particular client. Stitzer and Bigelow (1978) examined the desirability of reinforcers among a group of methadone maintenance patients ($n = 53$). Using a questionnaire, they found that the methadone "take-home" privilege was the most effective incentive available to methadone maintenance clinics. The second most effective reinforcer among this group was $30.00 per week, followed in descending order of desirability by $20.00 per week, opportunity to self-select methadone dose, fewer urinalyses, availability of a client representative/advocate, elimination of mandatory counseling, a monthly party, and finally the opportunity to play pool.

The Community Reinforcement Approach

Behavioral therapists have recognized that the application of contingency management procedures to isolated aspects of substance abuse
is a narrow approach. To enhance the effectiveness of behavioral
treatment, Hunt and Azrin (1973) and Azrin (1976) developed a
multicomponent treatment strategy that makes reinforcement in the
patient's community contingent on abstinence from alcohol and/or
drugs. A system of contingencies is created for four areas of a client's
life: vocational, recreational, social, and familial. As long as abstinence is maintained, the recovering client receives reinforcers in these
areas. Typically, the client's significant others are involved in these
contingency contracts, and his/her behavior may be shaped as well.
Hunt and Azrin (1973) compared a community reinforcement program to a standard hospital treatment program and found that the
former approach produced significantly better patient outcomes over
a 6-month period. Compared to patients in the standard hospital
program, those in the community reinforcement program spent less
time drinking alcohol, were less likely to be unemployed, and were
less likely to be readmitted for treatment. In a second study, Azrin
(1976) was able to replicate these findings using a 2-year follow-
up assessment.

Behavioral Treatment for Cocaine Dependence

A good illustration of behavioral treatment comes from a recent study
that combined contingency management procedures with the community reinforcement approach. It involved the treatment of cocaine addicts
in an outpatient setting (Higgins et al., 1991). The investigation compared the efficacy of behavioral treatment to that of a traditional Twelve-
Step drug counseling program. A total of 28 patients participated in
the study. The first 13 cocaine-dependent patients were offered the
behavioral treatment program; all 13 accepted it. The following 15
patients were offered the Twelve-Step drug counseling program. The
authors note that 3 of the 15 patients refused this program option.

The two treatment regimens were quite different, and the investigators describe each in detail. In the behavioral program, patients
and therapists jointly selected material reinforcers (Higgins et al.,
1991). The goal of the behavioral program was specifically to achieve
abstinence from cocaine. The program's contingencies pertained only
to cocaine use. Urine specimens were collected four times a week,

and patients were breathalyzed at these times as well; however, patients were not penalized for positive test results for drugs other than cocaine. The patients were informed of their urine test results immediately after providing their specimens.

The urine specimens testing negative for cocaine metabolites were rewarded with points that were recorded on vouchers and given to the patient (Higgins et al., 1991). Each point was worth 15 cents. Money was never given directly to patients; rather, they were used to make retail purchases in the community. Staff members actually made the purchases and gave the items to the patients. The first negative urine specimen earned 10 points (i.e., $1.50). The second specimen was worth 15 points ($2.25). The third one earned 20 points ($3.00). The value of each subsequent negative urine specimen increased by 5 points. Furthermore, to bolster the probability of continuous abstinence from cocaine, patients were rewarded with a $10.00 bonus each time they provided four consecutive negative urine specimens. Patients who remained continuously abstinent throughout the entire 12-week treatment program earned points worth $1,038.00, or $12.35 per day.

In cases where the patient tested positive for cocaine or failed to provide a specimen, the value of the vouchers dropped back to 10 points (i.e., $1.50). Items that had previously been purchased did not have to be returned. Higgins et al. (1991) report that the items purchased were "quite diverse and included ski-lift passes, fishing licenses, camera equipment, bicycle equipment, and continuing education materials" (p. 1220). In the program, counselors retained the right to veto purchases. Purchases were approved only if their use was consistent with treatment goals.

The community reinforcement procedures focused on four broad issues: (1) reciprocal relationship counseling, (2) identification of the antecedents and consequences of cocaine use, (3) employment counseling, and (4) development of recreational activities. These issues were addressed in twice-weekly 1-hour counseling sessions throughout the 12-week program. The emphasis appeared to be placed on the first issue, relationship counseling. Eight of the 13 patients in the behavioral program participated in reciprocal relationship counseling. This counseling was comprised of procedures "for instructing people how to negotiate for positive changes in their relationship" (p. 1220). The authors describe how this worked as follows:

> To integrate the community reinforcement approach and contingency management procedures, the patient's significant other was telephoned

immediately following each urinalysis test and informed of the results. If the specimen was negative for cocaine, the spouse, friends, or relative engaged in positive activities with the patients that had been agreed upon beforehand. If the result was positive for cocaine use, he or she refrained from the agreed upon positive activities but offered the patient assistance in dealing with difficulties in achieving abstinence. (Higgins et al., 1991, p. 1220)

The Twelve-Step drug treatment consisted of either twice-weekly 2-hour group therapy sessions or once-weekly group sessions combined with 1-hour individual therapy sessions (Higgins et al., 1991). In both formats, the Twelve Steps of NA were emphasized. The patients were informed that cocaine addiction was a treatable but incurable disease. They were required to attend at least one self-help meeting a week and to have a sponsor by the final week of treatment. The counseling sessions provided both supportive and confrontive therapy, as well as didactic lectures and videos on vital recovery topics. In the ninth week of treatment, attempts were made to involve family members in the treatment process. Finally, aftercare plans based on Twelve-Step principles were created in the latter weeks of treatment.

After 12 weeks, the two groups (i.e., behavioral treatment vs. Twelve-Step drug counseling) were compared on a variety of outcomes. Across all of these measures, the patients in the behavioral treatment showed better outcomes than those in the Twelve-Step group (Higgins et al., 1991). For example, 11 of the 13 patients in the behavioral treatment completed the 12-week program, compared to just 5 of 12 in the Twelve-Step treatment. In the behavioral treatment group, one patient dropped out at week 9 and returned to cocaine use, and the other one had to be admitted to an inpatient unit because of "bingeing." The seven unsuccessful patients in the Twelve-Step treatment terminated for the following reasons:

1. Terminated for lack of regular attendance.
2. Refused group counseling.
3. Refused to abstain from marijuana.
4. Did not return after being denied a prescription for antianxiety medication.
5. Following a relapse, entered inpatient rehabilitation.
6. Decided no longer needed treatment.
7. Murdered.

Patients in behavioral treatment were also more likely than those in the Twelve-Step treatment to have longer periods of continuous abstinence from cocaine (Higgins et al., 1991). Of 13 behavior therapy patients, 10 achieved 4-week periods of continuous abstinence; of the Twelve-Step patients, only 3 of 12 did the same. Furthermore, 6 of the behavioral therapy patients achieved 8-week periods of continuous abstinence, whereas none of the Twelve-Step patients accomplished the same. In the behavioral treatment group, 92% of all collected urine specimens were cocaine-free, whereas 78% were "clean" in the Twelve-Step group. This occurred even though many more urine specimens were collected from the behavioral treatment group ($n = 552$) than the Twelve-Step group ($n = 312$).

Interpretation of the Higgins et al. (1991) study has to be qualified by several limitations of the investigation. First, the sample of patients was small ($n = 25$), and all were Caucasian. Second, it is not clear how such a contrived system of contingencies would work over an extended period of time (6 months or longer). Third, the behavioral treatment focused narrowly on cocaine abstinence and did not address other drug and alcohol use. Fourth, it is difficult to imagine widespread public and/or government support for behavioral treatment programs that pay patients for not using illegal drugs.

With these limitations in mind, the Higgins et al. study (and other behavioral investigations like it) should cause us to reconsider some popularly held notions about the nature of substance dependence and how to treat it. First, the findings indicate that reinforcers can be found to compete with cocaine's intoxicating effects. The popular perception is that cocaine is so reinforcing that food, sex, and all other sources of reinforcement are given up by the addict; the Higgins et al. study shows that money can be an effective alternative reward. Second, the findings suggest that polydrug abusers need not be required to stop use of all drugs at the same time. Contrary to traditional drug treatment philosophy, perhaps it is possible, even preferable, to work on eliminating use of one drug at a time. Finally, the Higgins et al. study demonstrates how important incentives and anticipated benefits are in motivating clients to adopt and maintain abstinence. It appears that many clients drop out of traditional Twelve-Step programs in the early stages (i.e., the first 3 months) because they either do not receive or do not anticipate receiving significant rewards for staying in treatment. There is a vital need to provide incentives to those beginning treatment.

TOKEN ECONOMIES

Conditioning principles have been applied to entire residential treatment settings. Some therapeutic communities, for example, have employed token economies to shape their clients' behavior. According to Mehr (1988), "the token economy is a system for redesigning total environments to make them supportive of positive or socially desirable behaviors, and capable of extinguishing negative, maladaptive, or socially undesirable behaviors" (p. 163). As applied to chemically dependent populations, token economies encourage the adoption of behaviors that are associated with recovery.

The development of a token economy begins with the identification of "recovery behaviors" (as mentioned above). Sometimes, the behaviors are prioritized corresponding to differing levels of treatment progress. As clients master certain treatment goals (over weeks and months), they advance to the next level. The reward system is arranged such that clients receive immediate reinforcers (plastic tokens or paper chits) for daily behaviors (e.g., attending an AA meeting, cleaning up after lunch, etc.), and special privileges for advancement to a higher treatment level (e.g., visits home, their own room, etc.). The tokens are redeemable for material goods such as magazines, cigarettes, food, clothing, or a variety of other things. Advancement in treatment level is thought to signify important treatment gains. In addition, a system of fines is organized in which clients may lose tokens, or even be returned to a lower treatment level if they engage in certain behaviors that are inconsistent with recovery.

In Box 4.2, Pickens and Thompson (1984) describe a typical token (or point) economy that they established in a hospital-based drug treatment program.

BOX 4.2. A Point Economy in a Hospital-Based Treatment Program

In the ward-wide program, points are used as the medium for behavioral change. Throughout the 24-hr day, points are given to patients contingent on desired behavior and taken away contingent on maladaptive behavior. Point transactions are administered by all staff who normally work on the ward, including psychiatric nurses, occupational therapists, alcoholism and drug abuse counselors, and psychologists. All point transactions are recorded in a small booklet that each patient is issued daily.

Points are given to patients contingent on three classes of desired behavior: participating in activities considered to be therapeutically helpful to patients, participating in social activities, and grooming and personal care. Participating in therapeutic activities includes attending various classes that are offered on the ward several times each week. The classes are designed to help the patients in rational thinking about themselves, assertiveness, and problem solving, and to improve interpersonal skills and communication. Not only are points earned for attending such activities, but extra points may be earned for being on time and for the quality of participation in the activity. The points are given to patients individually at the end of each activity. At this time a staff person marks the points earned in the patients' point booklet and briefly describes how the quality of participation earned them extra points, or how they might improve their participation in the class to earn extra points in the future.

Other therapeutic activities that may earn points on the ward include work on the patient's individualized treatment plan. This plan is devised during the patient's first week of hospitalization. It includes a detailed description of problem behaviors to be changed, the desired behavior, the approach to be taken in changing the behavior, and how the behavioral change is to be "consequated," that is, what the prescribed consequences of the behavior will be. The plan is developed with the patient's cooperation, and is signed by both the patient and the primary staff person. It is considered a document of agreement between the patient and the staff, indicating goals and methods for behavioral change during the patient's stay on the ward.

Points are also given to patients for attendance and for degree of participation in other ward activities, such as planned outings to shopping centers, movies, or parks, as well as various work chores that must be performed on the ward (e.g., watering plants, preparing meals). Personal care activities that earn points include cleaning room, washing clothes, appropriate dress, and regular showers.

The availability of activities for earning points and the number of points to be earned by each activity are clearly defined in the patient's point booklet. However, points can also be given spontaneously by staff to a patient contingent on especially important therapeutic behavior, such as acting responsibly or being particularly helpful. On such occasions, the staff approaches the patient, tells the patient what they observed and liked about his or her behavior, and awards the special points.

As points are given to patients for healthy behavior, points are also taken away from patients for maladaptive behavior. Maladaptive behavior is defined as any behavior that is not in the patient's long-term best interest, regardless of whether it relates directly to drug use or not. Examples of maladaptive behavior would include verbal abuse, assault, theft, or not working on treatment plan. If a particular behavior has been a major problem for the patient in the past, that behavior is typically included in the patient's treatment plan. Otherwise, it is consequated as it occurs on the ward. The same procedure is used in point loss as in point gain. The staff person approaches the patient, tells the patient what was observed and what was inappropriate about the behavior, and then removes points for the behavior in the patient's point booklet.

Points earned by patients are exchangeable on the ward for a variety of goods and services. Points earned during a day are exchangeable for snack food and soft drinks, supplies, cigarettes, or personal care articles. Points not spent on a given day are placed in a savings account, from which the patient may purchase access to visitors, overnight passes, or weekend passes. The major use of points, however, goes towards purchase of the patient's daily privilege or responsibility level on the ward. With a low level of net point earnings, a patient may be able to purchase only the lowest privilege level on the ward—confined to ward. However, with higher levels of net point earnings, the patient may be able to purchase higher and higher privilege levels. At the highest privilege level, patients are able to purchase unlimited and unescorted privileges on the ward. The maximum privilege level obtainable by a patient is set by the staff and typically increases as a patient progresses through treatment.

Thus, the ward's point-economy program can be viewed primarily as a means for getting patients in contact with the therapeutic activities on the ward. Our patients typically attend most classes and participate actively in other ward activities. Though many of our patients are initially very disturbed, there is a low level of maladaptive behavior. While we tend to stress behavioral and cognitive–behavioral approaches in the therapeutic activities available to patients on the unit, the ward program could equally well be used with other treatment approaches.

The program appears to be well liked by both staff and patients. In a study of nursing staff attitudes toward behavior therapy, after working on the ward for one year, the nursing staff said that the behavior therapy approach was less superficial and less mechanistic than did nursing staff working on a more conventional psychiatry unit which emphasized interpretative individual and group psychotherapy (Thompson et al., 1980). While some patients may complain initially about the "mickey mouse" nature of the point program, most eventually report liking the program, especially as it provides immediate feedback of progress through treatment. The program seemingly works well with all types of patients. While many of our drug-dependent patients are alcoholics or polydrug abusers from lower socioeconomic levels, patients have also included physicians, psychologists, engineers, and other professionals.

Note. From Pickens and Thompson (1984).

EFFECTIVENESS OF BEHAVIORAL APPROACHES

An examination of the findings from behaviorally oriented studies of controlled drinking, contingency contracting with abstinence (individual treatment), and token economies indicates that operant conditioning can be an effective strategy for helping those with alcohol and drug problems. The strength of interventions based on operant principles is that they are grounded in science. Indeed, this is a principal concern of behaviorally oriented practitioners. Interest in behaviorally based interventions is likely to remain strong as long as public officials demand to know "what works." This emphasis on accountability, evidence, and outcomes is inherent to the behavior technology approach.

CRITICISMS OF BEHAVIORAL INTERVENTIONS

Despite the overwhelming evidence of the effectiveness of operant conditioning, there have been four long-standing criticisms of this approach (Franks, 1969). Each criticism mentioned by Franks could be applicable to the problem of chemical dependency.

1. Maladaptive behavior is symptomatic of underlying problems. Behavioral strategies only alter the client's behavior, and, as a result, are only superficial interventions.
2. Contingency contracting, token economies, and other behaviorally oriented strategies cannot, by their very nature, change the underlying causes of problem behavior (such as drug use).
3. The effects of behavioral approaches are usually not long-lasting because of their superficiality. When a client leaves treatment, the behavior (such as alcohol or drug use) will probably reappear.
4. Behavioral interventions often lead to symptom substitution; because the underlying cause remains, another behavior symptom

(e.g., gambling, overeating, compulsive work) will often appear in its place. This substitution phenomenon is evidence that deeper pathology exists.

In addition, it should be emphasized that many clients simply have no interest in applying operant procedures to the control of their drinking behavior, or to the maintenance of recovery-consistent behaviors. Many clients are resistant to the use of procedures such as contracting, for a variety of reasons. As a practical matter, this lack of appeal limits the utility of behavioral treatment strategies. This seems to be particularly the case in outpatient settings, where contingencies are difficult to monitor and control.

REVIEW QUESTIONS

1. What are some of the basic characteristics of behaviorism?

2. According to Skinner, who can be faulted for addiction and other problem behaviors?

3. How do respondent and operant conditioning differ?

4. What is the difference between positive reinforcement and negative reinforcement?

5. What is the difference between negative reinforcement and punishment?

6. What relevance do generalization and discrimination have for explaining relapse?

7. From a behavioristic perspective, what three factors predict initiation of substance use?

8. What are the three general classes of reinforcers in addiction? How do they vary across type of drug and characteristics of the user?

9. Why is physical dependence neither a necessary nor a sufficient condition for the development of an addiction?

10. When does cessation from substance abuse usually occur?

11. Why should relapse be expected among those in early recovery (in behavioral terms)?

12. What is the tension reduction hypothesis (TRH)? Do existing data support its validity?

13. How is tolerance related to one's ability to discriminate blood alcohol levels (BALs)?
14. What is meant by "behavioral tolerance"? How is it learned via respondent versus operant principles?
15. What are the assumptions of behavioral counseling? What are the three phases of it as described by Dustin and George?
16. What is behavioral self-control training (BSCT)?
17. What types of clients are good candidates for BSCT?
18. What was the Sobells' controversy about?
19. How can contingency contracting be used to maintain abstinence and to structure token economies?
20. What are some of the criticisms of the behavioral approaches to helping clients?

REFERENCES

American Psychiatric Association. (1980). *Diagnostic and statistical manual of mental disorders* (3rd ed.). Washington, DC: Author.
Azrin, N. H. (1976). Improvements in the community-reinforcement approach to alcoholism. *Behaviour Research and Therapy, 14,* 339–348.
Brecher, E. M., & The Editors of *Consumer Reports*. (1972). *Licit and illicit drugs.* Mount Vernon, NY: Consumers Union.
Brick, J. (1990). Learning and motivational factors in alcohol consumption. In W. M. Cox (Ed.), *Why people drink: Parameters of alcohol as a reinforcer.* New York: Gardner Press.
Brown, S. A. (1985). Expectancies versus background in the prediction of college drinking patterns. *Journal of Consulting and Clinical Psychology, 53*(1), 123–130.
Cameron, D., & Spence, M. T. (1976). Lessons from an out-patient controlled drinking group. *Journal of Alcoholism, 11,* 44–55.
Campbell, J. C., & Seiden, L. S. (1973). Performance influence on the development of tolerance to amphetamine. *Pharmacology, Biochemistry and Behavior, 1,* 703–708.
Cappell, H., & Greeley, J. (1987). Alcohol and tension reduction: An update on research and theory. In H. T. Blane & K. E. Leonard (Eds.), *Psychological theories of drinking and alcoholism.* New York: Guilford Press.
Cohen, S. (1983, January). The myth of controlled drinking by alcoholics. *Drug Abuse and Alcoholism Newsletter,* pp. 1–3.
Conger, J. J. (1951). The effects of alcohol on conflict and avoidance behavior. *Quarterly Journal of Studies on Alcohol, 12,* 1–29.

Conger, J. J. (1956). Alcoholism: Theory, problem, and challenge. II. Reinforcement theory and the dynamics of alcoholism. *Quarterly Journal of Studies on Alcohol, 13,* 296–305.

Dustin, R., & George, R. (1973). *Action counseling for behavior change.* New York: Intext Press.

Franks, C. (1969). *Behavior therapy: Appraisal and status.* New York: McGraw-Hill.

Harding, F. M. (1989). *Alcohol problems prevention/intervention programs.* Albany: New York State Division of Alcoholism and Alcohol Abuse.

Harris, K. B., & Miller, W. R. (1990). Behavioral self-control training for problem drinkers: Components of efficacy. *Psychology of Addictive Behaviors, 4*(2), 82–90.

Heather, N., & Robertson, I. (1983). *Controlled drinking.* London: Methuen.

Higgins, S. T., Delaney, D. D., Budney, A. J., Bickel, W. K., Hughes, J. R., Foerg, F., & Fenwick, J. W. (1991). A behavioral approach to achieving initial cocaine abstinence. *American Journal of Psychiatry, 148*(9), 1218–1224.

Huber, H., Karlin, R., & Nathan, P. E. (1976). Blood alcohol level discrimination by non-alcoholics: The role of internal and external cues. *Journal of Studies on Alcohol, 37,* 27–39.

Hunt, G. H., & Azrin, N. H. (1973). The community-reinforcement approach to alcoholism. *Behaviour Research and Therapy, 11,* 91–104.

Jellinek, E. M. (1945). The problem of alcohol. In Yale Studies on Alcohol (Ed.), *Alcohol, science, and society* (pp. 13–30). Westport, CT: Greenwood Press.

Langenbucher, J. W., & Nathan, P. E. (1990). The tension-reduction hypothesis: A reanalysis of some early crucial data. In W. M. Cox (Ed.), *Why people drink: Parameters of alcohol as a reinforcer.* New York: Gardner Press.

Lewis, J. A., Dana, R. Q., & Blevins, G. A. (1988). *Substance abuse counseling: An individualized approach.* Pacific Grove, CA: Brooks/Cole.

Masserman, J. H., Jacques, M. G., & Nicholson, M. R. (1945). Alcohol as a preventive of experimental neurosis. *Quarterly Journal of Studies on Alcohol, 6,* 281–299.

McAuliffe, W. E., & Gordon, R. A. (1980). Reinforcement and the combination of effects: Summary of a theory of opiate addiction. In D. J. Lettieri, M. Sayers, & H. Wallenstein-Pearson (Eds.), *Theories on drug abuse: Selected contemporary perspectives* (DHHS Publication No. ADM 84-967). Washington, DC: U.S. Government Printing Office.

McKim, W. A. (1986). *Drugs and behavior: An introduction to behavioral pharmacology.* Englewood Cliffs, NJ: Prentice: Hall.

Mehr, J. (1988). *Human services: Concepts and intervention strategies.* Boston: Allyn & Bacon.

Miller, L. K. (1980). *Principles of everyday behavior analysis.* Monterey, CA: Brooks/Cole.

Miller, W. R. (1982). Treating problem drinkers: What works. *The Behavior Therapist, 5,* 15–19.

Miller, W. R., & Hester, R. K. (1980). Treating the problem drinker. In W. R. Miller (Ed.), *The addictive behaviors: Treatment of alcoholism, drug abuse, smoking, and obesity*. Elmsford, NY: Pergamon Press.

Peele, S. (1983, April). Through a glass darkly. *Psychology Today*, pp. 38–42.

Peele, S. (1985). *The meaning of addiction: Compulsive experience and its interpretation*. Lexington, MA: D. C. Heath.

Pendery, M. L., Maltzman, I. M., & West, L. J. (1982). Controlled drinking by alcoholics?: New findings and reevaluation of a major affirmative study. *Science, 217*, 169–174.

Pickens, R. W., & Thompson, T. (1986). Behavioral treatment of drug dependence. In J. Grabowski, M. L. Stitzer, & J. E. Henningfield (Eds.), *Behavioral intervention techniques in drug abuse treatment* (DHHS Publication No. ADM 86-1281). Washington, DC: U.S. Government Printing Office.

Powers, R. J., & Kutash, I. L. (1985). Stress and alcohol. *International Journal of the Addictions, 20*, 461–482.

Robertson, I., Heather, N., Dzialdowski, A., Crawford, J., & Winton, M. (1986). A comparison of minimal versus intensive controlled drinking treatment interventions for problem drinkers. *British Journal of Clinical Psychology, 25*, 185–194.

Siegel, S. (1982). Drug dissociation in the nineteenth century. In F. C. Colpaert & J. L. Slangen (Eds.), *Drug discrimination: Applications in CNS pharmacology*. Amsterdam: Elsevier.

Silverstein, S. J., Nathan, P. E., & Taylor, H. A. (1974). Blood alcohol level estimation and controlled drinking by chronic alcoholics. *Behavior Therapy, 5*, 1–15.

Skinner, B. F. (1975). *Beyond freedom and dignity*. New York: Bantam.

Sobell, M. B., & Sobell, L. C. (1976). Second year treatment outcome of alcoholics treated by individualized behaviour therapy: Results. *Behaviour Research and Therapy, 14*, 195–215.

Stitzer, M., & Bigelow, G. (1978). Contingency management in a methadone maintenance program: Availability of reinforcers. *International Journal of the Addictions, 13*(5), 737–746.

Stockwell, T. (1985). Stress and alcohol. *Stress Medicine, 1*, 209–215.

Thompson, T., Labeck, L., & Zimmerman, R. (1980). Nursing staff adjustment as a function of psychiatric treatment modality. *Journal of Behavior Therapy and Experimental Psychiatry, 11*, 200–214.

Ullman, L. P., & Krasner, L. (1965). *Case studies in behavior modification*. New York: Holt, Rinehart & Winston.

Wanberg, K. W. (1969). Prevalence of symptoms found among excessive drinkers. *International Journal of the Addictions, 4*, 169–185.

A Social Learning Analysis of Substance Abuse

In this chapter, substance abuse is analyzed from a social learning theory (SLT) perspective. SLT is a cognitive–behavioral approach to understanding human behavior. "Cognitive" in this context refers to covert mental processes that are described by a number of diverse terms, including "thinking," "self-talk," "internal dialogue," "expectancies," "beliefs," "schemas," and so on. As a composite, these are referred to as "cognitive mediating variables." In SLT, these variables mediate the influence of external stimuli in the production of observable human behavior. Though cognitive, SLT, like operant conditioning, is a behaviorally oriented approach. SLT principles have been used to explain the initiation of substance use, as well as the maintenance of addictive behavior; they have also been used as a comprehensive strategy for the prevention of relapse.

THE PRINCIPLES OF SOCIAL LEARNING THEORY

Albert Bandura is recognized as the creator and leading proponent of SLT. This theory grew out of dissatisfaction with the deterministic views of human beings as expressed by both psychoanalysis and behaviorism. In the former, humans are considered to be under the control of the unconscious; the latter emphasizes control by external contingencies (i.e., rewards). In both of those theoretical systems, self-regulation plays no part. Bandura (1977) rejects this view and insists that humans can create and administer reinforcements (rewards and punishers) for themselves and to themselves. He describes it this way:

113

Social learning theory approaches the explanation of human behavior in terms of a continuous reciprocal interaction between cognitive, behavioral, and environmental determinants. Within the process of reciprocal determination lies the opportunity for people to influence their destiny as well as the limits of self-direction. This conception of human functioning then neither casts people into the role of powerless objects controlled by environmental forces nor free agents who can become whatever they choose. Both people and their environments are reciprocal determinants of each other. (1977, p. vii)

Note that Bandura indicates that self-direction is possible within limits. These limits vary by both person and environment. For example, a cocaine addict in early recovery who lives in a suburban neighborhood is probably going to have much more control over drug-taking behavior than a similar addict who lives in an inner-city, cocaine-ridden neighborhood.

Bandura's reasoning is apparent in the following passage:

If actions were determined solely by external rewards and punishments, people would behave like weathervanes, constantly shifting in different directions to conform to the momentary influences impinging upon them. They would act corruptly with unprincipled individuals and honorably with righteous ones, and liberally with libertarians and dogmatically with authoritarians. (1977, p. 128)

In SLT, the consequences of behavior (i.e., reinforcements and punishments) do not act automatically to shape behavior in a mechanistic manner. Rather, these external, environmental contingencies influence the acquisition and regulation of behavior. Internal cognitive processes are also important; they mediate the influence of environmental contingencies. Wilson (1988) states that cognitive processes are based on prior experience and serve to determine the following: (1) which environmental influences are attended to, (2) how these influences are perceived (e.g., as "good" or "bad"), (3) whether they will be remembered, and (4) how they may affect future behavior.

SLT stresses that individuals are actively involved in appraising environmental events. The acquisition and maintenance of behavior are not passive processes. Furthermore, Bandura (1977) maintains that the conditions for learning are facilitated by making rules and consequences known to potential participants. By observing the consequences of someone else's behavior, an individual can learn appropriate actions for particular situations. Bandura (1977) indicates that people create symbolic representations from these observations and rely on them to anticipate the future outcomes that will result from their own behavior. This cognitive process (i.e., symbolic representation) assists in generating motivation to initiate and sustain behavior.

Modeling

A central concept in SLT is that of "modeling," which is vicarious or observational learning. Wilson (1988) defines it in the following manner:

> In this form of learning people acquire new knowledge and behavior by observing other people and events, without engaging in the behavior themselves and without any direct consequences to themselves. Vicarious learning may occur when people watch what others ("models") do, or when they attend to the physical environment, to events, and to symbols such as words and pictures. (pp. 240–241)

Bandura (1977) has identified three types of effects on behavior that can result from observing a model:

1. *Observational learning effects.* These refer to behaviors acquired through observation of a model that did not previously exist in the individual's behavioral repertoire (e.g., smoking marijuana from a "bong").

2. *Inhibitory–disinhibitory effects.* These refer to increases or decreases in the intensity of a previously learned inhibition. Such behaviors usually result from observing a model's being rewarded or punished for some specific action. Thus a teenage boy may drink a beer—an action he had previously inhibited—when he observes an admired friend (i.e., a model) receive a reward for doing so. In this case, the "reward" may be any number of social consequences (e.g., other peers voice their approval; the admired friend becomes more sociable, funny, or easy to talk to; etc.).

3. *Response facilitation effects.* These refer to the appearance of behaviors that are not novel and were not previously inhibited. Examples of such behaviors are as follows: "People applaud when others clap; they look up when they see others gazing skyward; they adopt fads that others display; and in countless other situations their behavior is prompted and channeled by the actions of others" (Bandura, 1971, p. 6). The pace at which a small group of friends drink beer is another example of a response facilitation effect. In such a group,

drinking beer is not a new behavior and it is not inhibited, but the pace of an individual's drinking is influenced by that of the group. If the group is sipping slowly, then it is also likely that a particular individual will match that pace. Consider a wine-tasting event in which small amounts are consumed for taste and food is eaten to cleanse the mouth. In such cases, individuals rarely become drunk, since models of such behavior do not normally exist at such events. In contrast, consider a typical college fraternity party, in which models of heavy drinking abound. Again, SLT asserts that the models in both of these two drinking situations *facilitate* the pace of the group's drinking behavior. The models do not *cause* or *require* others to increase or decrease their drinking; they simply influence it.

Self-Regulation

Another central concept in SLT, and one of particular importance to the problem of substance use, is "self-regulation" (Abrams & Niaura, 1987). This refers to the capability of humans to regulate their own behavior via internal standards and self-evaluative assessments. The concept helps explain how human behavior can be maintained in the absence of external environmental rewards. In the process of self-regulation, humans make self-rewards (and self-punishments) contingent upon the achievement of some specific internal standard of performance. If a discrepancy develops between one's internal standards and one's behavioral performance, the individual will be motivated to change standards, behavior, or both. The internal standards are thought to be the result of one's history of modeling influences and differential reinforcement (Wilson, 1988).

In SLT, alcoholism and addiction are not thought to be conditions characterized by a lack of self-regulation, but rather forms of self-regulation that are deemed problematic by society (and possibly the family). In other words, the disease model's concept of "loss of control" is disputed by SLT. The alcoholic's or addict's lifestyle is seen as regulated (i.e., organized) around the consumption of alcohol or drugs. The person's behavior is not random or unpredictable; it is purposeful and goal-directed. The high degree of self-regulation is clear when consideration is given to the amount of time and effort needed (often daily) to obtain the drug, use the drug, conceal its use, interact with other users, and recover from its effects. Many chemically dependent persons manage such lifestyles for years, even while holding jobs and having families.

In this context, it should be noted that "self-regulation" does not imply "healthy." This is a value-laden term, which by definition is subjective. Furthermore, SLT maintains that in some cases addiction may be a means of coping (i.e., regulating the self) with internal performance standards that are too extreme or unrealistic. For example, an alcoholic may cope with long work hours by consuming many martinis. In other addicts, their evaluation of self is not "activated" by other persons' opinions of their substance use; that is, criticism from others has little impact on how they perceive themselves. Thus, they easily engage in behavior (alcohol/drug abuse) for which there is little external reward and perhaps much punishment (e.g., social/family ostracism, arrests, financial debt, health problems, etc.).

Reciprocal Determinism

In Bandura's (1977) view, person, behavior, and environment are continually engaged in a type of interaction called "reciprocal determinism." That is, each of the components is capable of changing the nature of the interaction at any time. Individuals are thought to be capable of reassessing their behavior, its impact on the environment, and the environment's impact on themselves and their behavior. In a given situation, one of the three components may gain momentary dominance. The relationship among these components is diagrammed in Figure 5.1. Notice that in Figure 5.1 an individual is not driven by internal forces alone, nor does he/she passively respond to external forces. Instead, a set of interlocking forces is involved. Wilson (1988) describes it this way:

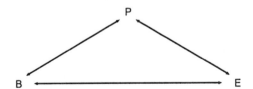

P = Person (cognitive mediating processes)
B = Behavior
E = Environment

FIGURE 5.1. Interactive schema of person, behavior, and environment.

... a person is both the agent and the object of environmental influence. Behavior is a function of interdependent factors. Thus, cognitions do not operate independently. In a complete analysis of the cognitive control of behavior, mediating processes must be tied to observable action. (pp. 242–243)

Using the concept of reciprocal determinism, White, Bates, and Johnson (1990) have integrated alcohol as a fourth component in the model. Figure 5.2 is a diagram that seeks to explain alcohol consumption from an SLT perspective. In this model, White et al. (1990) include perceived actions or "alcohol expectancies" in the alcohol domain. They note that it may be more appropriate to include these under the "person characteristics"; after all, they are cognitive variables. However, they feel that placing them within the alcohol domain emphasizes that many of the effects of alcohol, traditionally attributed to its pharmacological properties, are actually the result of socially mediated beliefs (White et al., 1990). (Alcohol expectancies are discussed in greater detail in a subsequent section of this chapter.)

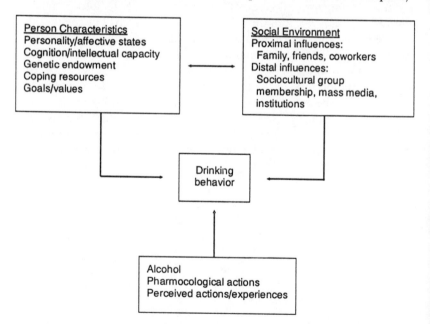

FIGURE 5.2. Interactive schema of person, environment, and drug variables affecting and affected by drinking behaviors. Adapted from White, Bates, and Johnson (1990). Copyright 1990 by Gardner Press, Inc. Adapted by permission.

Self-Efficacy

In SLT, the principle of "self-efficacy" is a unifying construct. Some writers even refer to it as a minitheory within the larger framework of SLT (Wilson, 1988). Self-efficacy has been defined as "a perception or judgement of one's capability to execute a particular course of action required to deal effectively with an impending situation" (Abrams & Niaura, 1987, p. 134). In addition, a distinction is made between "outcome expectations" and "efficacy expectations"; these two concepts can be thought of as components of self-efficacy. An outcome expectation is a person's estimate that a particular outcome will occur. In other words, an individual assesses the situation and the various factors involved in his/her own performance, and formulates an expectation of the probability that a specific course of action will lead to a particular outcome (Monte, 1980). Of particular relevance here are alcohol expectancies. Research has identified a set of anticipated outcomes that drinkers anticipate obtaining as a result of drinking (e.g., enhanced sociability, tension reduction, arousal with power, etc.). Such anticipated outcomes have been linked to various drinking practices (Goldman, Brown, & Christiansen, 1987).

An efficacy expectation is a person's belief that he/she can carry out the necessary course of action to obtain the anticipated outcome (Monte, 1980). Thus, an outcome expectation is knowledge of what to do, while an efficacy expectation is the belief (or doubt) that one can do it. Research has demonstrated that psychological treatments alter behavior to the extent that they affect efficacy expectations (Wilson, 1988). Procedures that enhance a person's sense of personal competence are likely to lead to improved functioning. According to Wilson (1988),

> . . . unless treatment creates strong expectations of efficacy, coping behaviors may be easily extinguished following the termination of therapy. The phenomenon of relapse is a problem for all methods of psychological treatment, including behavior therapy. Self-efficacy theory is a means of conceptualizing the relapse process and suggests procedures for facilitating the long-term maintenance of behavior change, especially in the addictive disorders. (p. 243)

According to Bandura (1977), efficacy expectations are based upon (and can be altered by) four sources of information. The most powerful influence is thought to be that of "performance accomplishments" in previous mastery situations. Past failure experiences will undermine efficacy beliefs, while success will boost them. The second source of efficacy expectations consists of "vicarious experiences"—that is, observation of others' success and failures. A third source is "verbal persuasion"; here, a person is told that he/she can master a task. This source has a relatively weak influence on efficacy expectations because it provides no personal experience of success or failure. The fourth and last source of efficacy expectations is the "emotional arousal" that stems from attempting a demanding task. The experience of anxiety is a powerful cue to people regarding their possibilities for success (or failure), and the amount of effort that they will have to exert to achieve mastery. High levels of anxiety and fear are likely to have a debilitating effect on a person's attempts at mastery.

Efficacy expectations are particularly important in relapse prevention. Addicts who doubt their ability to carry out tasks necessary for recovery are likely to relapse. Furthermore, the sources of efficacy expectations suggest specific relapse prevention strategies. Successful efforts will be those designed to ensure success (performance accomplishments) by first providing simple tasks and gradually building to more difficult ones. Successful efforts will also expose an addict to other successfully recovering addicts (vicarious experiences), and will teach ways to cope with negative affective states (emotional arousal). Lastly, the sources of efficacy expectations suggest that "verbal persuasion" (e.g., "I know you can do it") is an inadequate intervention.

ALCOHOL EXPECTANCY THEORY AND RESEARCH

The application of SLT to alcohol abuse and alcoholism has largely evolved from the concepts of "outcome expectations" and "efficacy expectations." The former concept has been used to predict and explain drinking behavior, whereas the latter plays a major role in relapse (and its prevention). This section provides a detailed discussion of alcohol outcome expectancies, or as they have more simply become known, "alcohol expectancies." To date, there has been no known research on illicit drug expectancies.

There is no widely accepted definition of the term "expectancy." Usually the term refers to a cognitive variable that intervenes between a stimulus and a response. This cognition is understood and described in a variety of ways ("information," "encodings," "schemas," "scripts," etc.). In alcohol expectancy theory (a minitheory within the SLT framework), "expectancy" is used to refer to the "anticipation of a systematic relationship between events or objects in some upcoming situation" (Goldman et al., 1987, p. 183). The concept implies an "if–then" relationship between a behavior and a desired outcome.

Many theories of alcohol use and abuse have focused on biological differences among individuals that make some people more susceptible to excessive consumption than others (Goodwin, 1990; Hunt, 1990). Other theories have scrutinized the pharmacological effects of ethanol itself (Hunt, 1990). Although it does not completely ignore the biomedical and pharmacological aspects of alcohol use and abuse, alcohol expectancy theory comes very close to doing so (Goldman et al., 1987). The theory asserts that drinking behavior is largely determined by the reinforcements an individual expects to obtain as a consequence of drinking.

Alcohol expectancies vary in strength from person to person; they are greatly influenced by one's family, peer group, and culture, and perhaps even by the mass media (e.g., alcohol advertising). Goldman et al. (1987) indicate that a lack of positive alcohol expectancies should lead one to abstain from alcohol, whereas heavy drinking can be predicted by a variety of strongly held expectancies. Thus, those drinkers who consume abusively may strongly expect alcohol to make them more relaxed, or more sexy, or possibly more aggressive. Moderate and light drinkers may hold weaker expectancies in these areas, or expect no positive outcomes in some of them.

The intriguing aspect of alcohol expectancy theory is that it is not necessary to assume that the outcomes of drinking (e.g., tension reduction, enhanced sexuality, aggression, etc.) are related to the pharmacological qualities of ethanol. According to Goldman et al. (1987),

> All this model requires is a belief in a relationship between stimuli and outcomes or between behaviors and outcomes. The model operates even if these beliefs are not based on reality. For example, if a person in a typical drinking environment believed they had consumed alcohol, they might produce covert and overt alcohol-related responses (which appear to observers as pharmacologic effects), not because the drug action of alcohol made them do it, but instead because they believed desired outcomes were available if they behaved in this way in this context. (p. 139)

The essence of alcohol expectancy theory, then, is that alcohol's ability to transform an individual's behavior is not attributable so much to the action of the drug as it is to the expectations of desired drinking outcomes.

Laboratory Research

Empirical support for the alcohol expectancy hypothesis comes from laboratory research utilizing placebo and balanced-placebo designs. In early laboratory research on alcohol use, placebo designs were used to control for the effects of expectancy. This was done for the most part as a control formality, following customary practice in pharmacological research (Goldman et al., 1987). It was not hoped that the placebo condition would produce effects similar to that of the actual condition.

One early placebo study tested the disease model's concept of loss of control (Merry, 1966). According to this concept (which has been discussed in detail in Chapter Two of this book), alcoholics experience intense, probably biologically induced cravings for alcohol after having consumed just a small amount; this intense need for alcohol (once consumed) leads to a loss of control over drinking behavior. Merry (1966) tested this hypothesis by administering alcohol to inpatient alcoholics without their knowledge. Each patient was given a fruit-flavored beverage each morning for about 2 weeks. The beverage was alternated every other day, such that the patients received either a totally nonalcoholic drink or one that contained 1 ounce of vodka. As a routine part of their treatment regimen, patients were asked to rate their level of alcohol craving later each day. There was no relationship between their ratings and the beverage consumed, indicating that the basis for alcohol cravings was not pharmacological. Other studies have yielded consistent findings.

In the 1970s, the placebo effects themselves increasingly became the focus of research. Investigators expanded the placebo design. They developed a balanced design that included four cells:

I. Told alcohol, given alcohol.
II. Told alcohol, given only tonic.
III. Told no alcohol, given alcohol.
IV. Told no alcohol, given only tonic.

In this balanced-placebo design, an "antiplacebo" condition (III) is added; this condition assesses alcohol effects in the absence of the usual drinking mindset (Goldman et al., 1987). This design is illustrated in Figure 5.3.

Using the balanced-placebo design, G. Alan Marlatt and his colleagues conducted pioneering research on the relationship between alcohol expectancies and drinking behavior. In one landmark study,

Subject actually receives

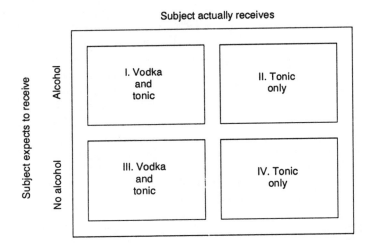

FIGURE 5.3. The balanced-placebo design. From Wilson (1988). Copyright 1988 by the Addiction Research Foundation. Reprinted by permission.

Marlatt, Demming, and Reid (1973) investigated the loss-of-control hypothesis by presenting separate groups of male alcoholics and social drinkers with a bogus alcohol taste-rating task. The subjects were told that the beverages were either vodka and tonic or tonic only. The actual beverage contents were systematically varied to be either consistent or inconsistent with the instructional set. It was found that both alcoholic and nonalcoholic men drank significantly more when they thought their drinks contained alcohol, regardless of the actual contents. This finding seriously challenges the disease model of alcoholism, which holds that alcoholic drinking is mediated by a physiological mechanism that can be triggered by the introduction of alcohol to the body. Rather, it appears that the subjects' beliefs (expectancies) about beverage content were the crucial factors in determining amount of alcohol consumed.

Survey Research

The results of survey research also provide strong support for the alcohol expectancy theory. Much of this survey work was initiated by Sandra Brown and her colleagues, who developed the Alcohol Expectancy Questionnaire (AEQ). This 90-item self-report questionnaire assesses whether alcohol, when consumed in moderate quantities, produces specific positive effects (Brown, Christiansen, & Goldman, 1987). The AEQ was derived from an initial pool of 216 verbatim statements collected from 125 people, who were interviewed individually and in groups. They ranged in age from 15 to 60; and their drinking behavior varied from total abstinence to chronic alcoholism. When the items were factor-analyzed, the following six alcohol expectancy factors emerged:

1. Global-positive change.
2. Sexual enhancement.
3. Physical and social pleasure.
4. Increased social assertiveness.
5. Relaxation and tension reduction.
6. Arousal with power.

These factors represent relatively distinct domains of anticipated drinking outcomes. The factors were subsequently used in a large number of survey research studies as variables to predict various drinking practices. In general, the research has consistently linked these expected consumption outcomes to actual use, abuse, and related problem behavior. For example, Brown, Creamer, and Stetson (1987) found that alcohol abusers expected more positive outcomes from drinking than did their nonabusing peers. Similarly, Critchlow (1987) found that heavy drinkers held stronger expectations of positive consequences of alcohol use than light drinkers, and that they generally evaluated all drinking outcomes more positively. Furthermore, Brown (1985) and I (Thombs, 1991) reported that alcohol expectancies were better predictors of heavy and problem drinking than a set of demographic variables.

Among young adolescents, alcohol expectancies have been shown to predict the onset of the initiation of drinking behavior 1 year later (Christiansen, Roehling, Smith, & Goldman, 1989). Among college students, one study found that problem drinkers expected more relaxation/tension reduction than did social drinkers, while the latter group expected more social enhancement (Brown, 1985). Another college student study found that the expectancy profile that distinguished female problem drinkers from female nonproblem drinkers was relatively distinct from the profile that separated these drinker types among males (Thombs, 1993). In this same study, the AEQ factor that had the strongest discriminating value among the women problem drinkers (and thus provided the clearest indication of what they sought through drinking) was arousal with power, whereas for the men it was physical and social pleasure (Thombs, 1993). Finally, one study examined cross-cultural differences in alcohol expectancies (Brown, Christiansen, & Goldman, 1987). A group of Irish (Dublin) adolescents was compared to a group of U.S. (Detroit) adolescents. The groups were matched by age and gender. Results indicated that there were no differences between the two groups on total AEQ scores. However, there were significant differences on subscale scores: The Irish teens expected more arousal and aggression and less sexual enhancement from drinking than the U.S. teens (Brown, Christiansen, & Goldman, 1987). Irish youth also had significantly lower expectations for enhanced social and cognitive-motor functioning compared to American youth.

RELAPSE

A "relapse" can be defined as an "uncontrolled return to drug or alcohol use following competent treatment" (Lewis, Dana, & Blevins, 1988, p. 193). It is probably the most significant issue in treating chemically dependent clients. It is often puzzling that individuals who seem to recognize the seriousness of their addiction, who appear committed to recovery, and who have gained some mastery over their drinking or drug-taking behavior often have tremendous difficulty in remaining abstinent.

Historically, views on relapse have tended to be moralistic. Such views still predominate in many segments of our society. Relapsed alcoholics or addicts are scorned: they are thought of as lazy, irresponsible, or possibly weak-willed. Essentially, they are viewed as having a defect of character. Unfortunately, such views, especially when held by legislators, government officials, and other key decision makers, impede progress in treatment approaches by depriving treatment and research centers of much-needed financial support.

Interestingly, the disease model of addiction has traditionally had little to say about relapse prevention. AA folklore, and especially its slogans, provide various messages of caution about "slippery places" and direct members to call their sponsors, but little is provided in the way of skills. Moreover, the disease model has not elaborated on the meaning of relapse. The loss-of-control concept in alcoholism has, in fact, been cited for inadvertently contributing to full-blown relapses (Lewis et al., 1988). The proposal that alcoholics cannot stop drinking once alcohol enters their bodies seems to establish an expectation that 1 drink must lead to 20. Thus, when many alcoholics do relapse, they often seem to go on extended binges.

The relative inattention directed to the problem has contributed to high relapse rates among abusers of all substances. For example, one prominent early study found that at 12 months following treatment about 62% of recovering alcoholics had relapsed, and about 80% of cigarette smokers and heroin addicts (Hunt, Barnett, & Branch, 1971). Ten years later, another research group reported that about 90% of all substance abusers surveyed relapsed within a year of treatment (Polich, Armor, & Braiker, 1981).

Such relapse rates are much higher than those often cited by treatment agencies themselves. Recent research indicates that typical follow-up procedures, which rely solely on client self-reports, may be inaccurate. A National Institute on Alcohol Abuse and Alcoholism (1990) review of this subject reveals:

> In one investigation of the validity of self-reports, Watson et al. (1984) found that barely half the variance in the alcoholics' self-reports corresponded to assessments of the alcoholics' drinking behavior made by collaterals (cohabiting friends or relatives). Comparison of collateral reports with alcoholics' self-reports suggested that alcoholics may have underestimated their alcohol use about three times as often as they overestimated it. (p. 273)

Furthermore, in a study relying on self-reports, collateral interviews, and blood and urine testing, it was found that the collaterals were three times more likely to report more drinking days than the patients were (Fuller, Lee, & Gordis, 1988). The researchers also found that only 65% of the recovering alcoholics who claimed continuous abstinence for 1 year had, in fact, been continuously abstinent. These findings underscore the severity of the relapse problem and should invite skepticism about treatment agencies that claim relapse rates of only 10–30%.

Stress as an Impetus for Relapse

Stress is frequently associated with relapse among recovering persons (Hunter & Salmone, 1986; Milkman, Weiner, & Sunderwith, 1984; Marlatt & Gordon, 1979). A review of the research literature indicates that it is the most frequently cited explanation for relapse (Milkman et al., 1984). For instance, of the 20 conditions that Hunter and Salmone (1986) describe as being associated with relapse, 12 are stress-related. One prominent study collected data on 137 relapse episodes reported by groups of alcoholics, cigarette smokers, and heroin addicts (Marlatt & Gordon, 1979). All subjects had completed treatment programs with complete abstinence as the goal. Results revealed that 76% of the relapses studied occurred in three contexts: (1) intrapersonal negative emotional states (37%), (2) social pressure (24%), and (3) interpersonal conflict (15%).

In general, it appears that relapsers evaluate more life situations as threatening than do nonrelapsers. Those who relapse seem to have greater difficulty in coping with unpleasant emotions, frustrating events, and unsatisfactory relations with others. In other words, they demonstrate low frustration tolerance (see below). The nonrelapsers seem to learn strategies for coping with the problems, while the relapsers do not. This seems to apply to the gamut of addictions. The cognitive dynamics appear similar in cigarette smoking, overeating, alcoholism, and heroin and cocaine addiction.

Hunter and Salmone (1986) note the role of self-evaluations in relapse in the following passage:

> Stress . . . can become a substantial problem when the feeling of stress underlies a perceived need to make up for lost time, as is frequently the case when a recovering alcoholic becomes a work addict. Impatience represents a lack of preparation for non-chemical coping and includes frustration experienced when one's goals have been set unachievably high. If one is unwilling to admit to mistakes in judgement, or in performance, one is left with two options: (1) being absolutely perfect, or (2) feeling totally worthless. The first of these is unrealistic; the second is a dangerously negative feeling about oneself. Recovering alcoholics cannot afford either of these extremes. (p. 24)

Thinking Patterns and Relapse

Obviously, all those in recovery who have a commitment to abstinence face stressful situations. In fact, stress can be viewed as a natural consequence of taking on the challenge of living drug-free. The key in determining whether recovery stress is facilitative or debilitative is the individual's interpretation of frustrating experiences—that is, how the person thinks about himself/herself, others, and the world. In this view, cognition, thinking, self-statements, internal dialogue, and so forth mediate stress. It is not so much stress itself (which is virtually a universal human experience) as the manner in which people evaluate it that is critical. As the ancient Stoic philosopher

Epictetus once said, "Men are disturbed not by things but by the views which they take of them."

The proponents of rational–emotive theory (a cognitive–behavioral approach quite consistent with SLT) have elaborated upon the thinking patterns and emotions of recovering alcoholics and addicts (Ellis, McInerney, Di Giuseppe, & Yeager, 1988). According to Ellis (1985), among the most basic and broadly experienced motivations for continuing with self-defeating behavior patterns are discomfort anxiety and low frustration tolerance; this is particularly true in addictive behaviors (Ellis et al., 1988). "Discomfort anxiety" is the emotion one experiences when anticipating an unpleasant or uncomfortable feeling. Ellis et al. (1988) write, "It is usually brought about by the irrational belief that pain, discomfort, or unpleasantness is unbearable, and that it cannot and must not be tolerated" (p. 25). Accompanying discomfort anxiety is "low frustration tolerance"—that is, the tendency to avoid situations or tasks that may be difficult or painful in some way.

These conditions are thought to be especially prominent in the covert cognitive functioning of the recovering addict. Rational–emotive theorists refer to this as the "abstinence/low-frustration-tolerance pattern" (Ellis et al., 1988). It stems from such dysfunctional beliefs as the following:

1. I cannot stand avoiding a drink.
2. I cannot function without a drink.
3. I am not strong enough to resist alcohol.
4. I cannot stand the deprivation of my desire for a drink.
5. I am a horribly deprived person if I cannot have a drink.
6. Life is too hard so I am entitled to have a drink.
7. To make up for my difficult life, I must have a drink.
8. I must have a drink or I can't go on.
9. I must not abstain when it's so enjoyable to imbibe.
10. I must not abstain when it is so painful to do so. (Ellis et al., 1988, p. 25)

These beliefs (and other similar ones) trigger the pattern as displayed in Figure 5.4.

Ellis et al. (1988) note that the reason addictive behavior is so easy to develop is that no alternative coping strategy (e.g., cognitive or behavioral) can reduce the discomfort anxiety as quickly and effortlessly as alcohol or drugs can. All other strategies require time to work, practice, and individual effort. During such a period, the addict is experiencing discomfort and susceptible to falling back into the habit of relying on chemicals.

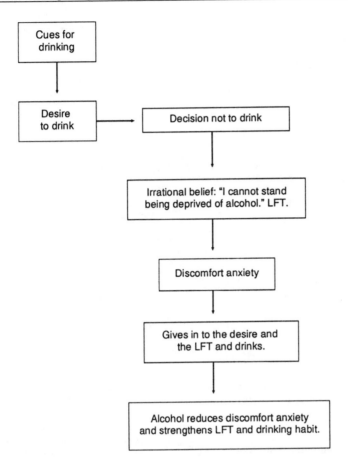

FIGURE 5.4. The abstinence/low-frustration-tolerance (LFT) pattern. Adapted from Ellis, McInerney, Di Giuseppe, and Yeager (1988). Copyright 1988 by Allyn and Bacon. Adapted by permission.

Described in Table 5.1 are five of the most common irrational beliefs associated with low frustration tolerance and relapse. Also listed are rational alternatives that a recovering person can use to dispute these irrational thoughts about the difficulties of recovery.

An Analysis of Relapse and Its Prevention

SLT offers a perspective on relapse that differs from the one put forth by the traditional disease model. According to Lewis et al. (1988),

TABLE 5.1. Self-Defeating Thinking That Might Lead to Relapse, and Some Model Rational Alternatives

Self-defeating thought	Rational alternative
1. This not drinking is just too hard. I can't stand not having what I want.	While not drinking is certainly difficult, I have stood it for some time now and one hour or one day at a time I can continue to stand it. I don't need everything I merely want, and while I may want a drink, I don't want all the problems that it will bring.
2. I need more excitement in my life. I'm so bored without seeing my friends I can't stand it anymore. I'll go visit my friends at the bar, but not take a drink.	Nobody ever died of boredom. While I certainly would like more excitement in my life right now, the price of associating with my friends might be drinking again. If I want to be less bored, I'd better find some other things to do.
3. Poor me. I must be so damn worthless to have to give up drinking when so many people can handle it. Nothing is going right for me, so what's the use? How could a drink make my life any worse?	Where is the evidence that I am worthless because I can't do "something that some other people can do"? I can't run a four-minute mile either. Does that prove I'm worthless? While things may not be great right now, it doesn't help to pity myself. It only makes me feel worse. I need to think through that drink I want. Remember the last drink? Did that make life better? Or did it lead to more and more drinks, which made a bad situation so much worse?
4. They shouldn't treat me this way. I'll show them who is boss, I'll fix them. I'll go get drunk and then they will be sorry.	I really hate it when I'm treated this way. I'd better learn to stick up for myself but punishing them may not be the way to do that. Besides, who am I really going to punish if I go out and get drunk?
5. I'm so upset and uptight. If I don't have a drink, I'll go crazy. I sure would rather be drunk than out of my mind.	A drink won't prevent me from going crazy. In fact, it may take me further down the road. Being uptight or upset can be best handled without a drink. People don't go crazy from not getting what they want.

Note. From Ellis et al. (1988). Copyright 1988 by Allyn and Bacon. Reprinted by permission.

"The social learning perspective . . . looks at a return to substance use as a learning experience that can be successfully used to bolster gains previously made in treatment" (p. 200). In fact, clients are taught to view "slips" in just this way. Relapse is not viewed as something that is "awful" or "terrible," and clients are not taught to fear it. Instead, they are encouraged to understand it as a response to environmental cues that constantly impinge on them. It is not evidence that they are incompetent, stupid, or worthless. Relapse provides clients with an opportunity to learn about their high-risk situations and to identify strategies that they can use to prevent them.

Much of the work done in relapse prevention has been carried out by Marlatt and Gordon (1985). They view relapse as the result of high-risk situations combined with the tendency to engage in self-defeating thinking. High-risk situations are those that may trigger a "slip"; they may include visiting a friend at a bar, attending a wedding reception, returning to an old neighborhood, or the like.

Marlatt and Gordon (1985) believe that self-defeating thinking emerges from lifestyle imbalances. These lifestyle imbalances occur when people's balance between external demands and their desire for pleasure and self-fulfillment is heavily weighted toward the former. In this imbalance, recovering clients feel pressure to "catch up" for lost time and thus feel deprived. As a result, they come to feel that they deserve indulgence and gratification. Cravings for their preferred substance appear, and they begin to think very positively about the immediate effects of the chemical. At the same time, they deny or selectively forget about all the negative consequences that go along with a reinitiation of use. There is often the tendency to rationalize the return to using (e.g., "I owe myself . . . ").

Apparently Irrelevant Decisions

In this process of covert cognitive change, recovering persons may find themselves in more and more high-risk situations prior to the first "slip." As this movement begins, they start making "apparently irrelevant decisions" (AIDs) (Marlatt & Gordon, 1985). According to Lewis et al. (1988):

> These AIDs are thought to be a product of rationalization ("What I'm doing is O.K") and denial ("This behavior is acceptable and has no relationship to relapse") that manifest themselves as certain choices that lead inevitably to a relapse. In this respect AIDs are best conceptualized as "minidecisions" that are made over time and that, when combined, lead the client closer and closer to the brink of the triggering high-risk situation. (p. 203)

Lewis et al.'s view of the role of AIDs and other cognitive antecedents of a relapse is illustrated in Figure 5.5.

Example of AIDs abound. Below is a list of typical ones as they apply to recovery from alcoholism:

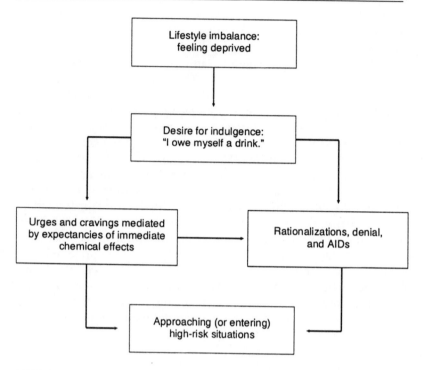

FIGURE 5.5. Covert (cognitive) antecedents of a relapse. Adapted from Lewis, Dana, and Blevins (1988). Copyright 1988 by Brooks/Cole Publishing Company. Adapted by permission.

1. A recovering alcoholic begins to purchase his cigarettes at liquor stores. He insists that the liquor stores are more conveniently located than other sales outlets.

2. A recovering alcoholic begins taking a new route home from work. She says she is bored with the old way. The new route is somewhat longer; it also has several liquor stores along the way.

3. A husband in early recovery begins to offer to run to the store for groceries. His wife is pleased. He regularly goes to the supermarket with a liquor store next door, even though it is further from home. He says that this market has better prices.

4. A recovering alcoholic goes to an old drinking buddy's house to borrow a hammer.

5. A recovering alcoholic offers to go alone on out-of-town business trips. Her supervisor says that it's not necessary that she always go, but the employee says she likes to get away.

6. A recovering alcoholic refuses to get rid of his liquor cabinet. He says he needs it when entertaining friends and relatives.

7. A recovering alcoholic transfers to a new job within the company. It is not a promotion, but it happens to have little direct supervision.

The Abstinence Violation Effect

In the SLT perspective, there is a significant difference between a "lapse" (or a "slip") and a full-blown relapse (Abrams & Niaura, 1987). A lapse is seen as a return to drinking that is brief, involves consuming a small quantity of alcohol, and has no other adverse consequences. By contrast, a relapse involves a return to heavy consumption, perhaps bingeing, and is accompanied by a host of emotional and physical complications. The aim of relapse prevention is to prevent lapses from turning into relapses (Abrams & Niaura, 1987).

The "abstinence violation effect" is the experience of intense shame, guilt, and embarrassment that frequently occurs following a lapse or a slip (Marlatt & Gordon, 1985). It increases the likelihood that a slip will turn into a full-blown relapse. Among those recovering persons who are committed to abstinence, the slip may be interpreted as evidence of personal inadequacy or incompetence. The person can be overwhelmed by intense self-directed negative emotion. One recovering alcoholic has told me that he remembers saying this to himself after he slipped:

> I can't believe I did this. I'm so stupid. What I've done is horrible. My wife will have no respect for me. This shows that I really am nothing but a no-good drunk—just a piece of shit. I might just as well keep drinking. It don't matter no more.

Early in treatment, prior to lapses, clients need to be educated about the meaning of slips and relapses. It is important that they not think of relapse as personal failure. This type of cognitive restructuring teaches them that a slip is only a mistake, not global evidence of a character flaw. Furthermore, it is helpful for the clients to attribute the slips to environmental cues, rather than to themselves. By doing this, they will place the focus properly on dealing effectively with the trigger situations. Such a focus will tend to build self-efficacy as the clients learn skills for coping with high-risk situations.

A Clinical Anecdote

To illustrate the potential power of this approach, I would like to
share a brief anecdote from my clinical practice. Don was a 32-year-
old client of above-average intelligence. Don recognized that he had
had a drinking problem for at least the previous 5 years. He sought
out help for the drinking problem on the advice of his primary care
physician, and was motivated to stop drinking because of physical
health problems. However, he expressed much frustration with his
past efforts (and failures) to stop drinking, which included AA and
intensive, psychoanalytically oriented therapy. He had numerous periods of abstinence (week- and month-long periods), but he always
returned to bingeing.

We quickly focused on the conditions and dynamics of Don's
relapses. For Don, a slip meant that he was monumental "fuck-up"
(his term). After each drinking episode he engaged in intense self-
downing, which only led to more heavy drinking. When I suggested
that his slips were only evidence of "fucking up" (my term), rather
than *being* a "fuck-up," tears came to his eyes and he reported feeling
as if an enormous weight had been lifted from his shoulders. He
quickly learned to reinterpret his slips as merely simple mistakes.

He soon reported that his need to resort to drinking had suddenly
diminished. Over the next few months, he slipped three more times,
but they were kept to a small number of drinks rather than full-
blown relapses. He was able to view them in an objective, dispassion-
ate manner; after a while, he was actually able to laugh at them, and
at himself. Don successfully terminated therapy after 4 months of
complete sobriety. Periodic telephone "booster" calls revealed that
he remained completely abstinent for an extended period of time. It
appeared that for Don, the key to overcoming relapse was to stop
linking his personal worth to whether he drank or abstained. He had
bought into the erroneous belief that he could only feel good about
himself when he abstained. When this connection was severed, the
act of drinking became less traumatic and had less emotional significance. As a result, he was able to attack the problem in a systematic
manner by focusing on the environmental cues (i.e., triggers).

SUMMARY

SLT provides a sound conceptual base for understanding the initiation
of substance use, as well for explaining the maintenance of abusive

intake and the occurrence of relapse. Furthermore, there exists substantial empirical evidence to support SLT-based explanations of initiation, maintenance, and relapse. A brief summary of these findings is in order.

The initiation of substance use can be adequately explained by the influence of modeling. Young people initiate substance use as a result of observing others. They imitate parents, peers, and media figures (i.e., celebrities).

Alcohol and drug abuse are self-regulated behaviors. The high degree of self-regulation is demonstrated by the time and effort that are required to maintain an alcohol or drug problem. Viewing such behavior as "out of control" is probably inaccurate in many cases.

The concept of "self-efficacy" is an extremely important one in assisting chemically dependent persons. Evidence suggests that a crucial determinant in whether treatment will be successful is the client's belief in his/her ability to master the various tasks of recovery. Without this belief, treatment is likely to fail. In addition, research indicates that self-efficacy is most likely to be enhanced by "performance accomplishments." Thus, it is imperative that clients initially be given small tasks at which success is virtually assured, before they attempt more difficult ones.

"Alcohol expectancies" are the anticipated outcomes of drinking. Evidence indicates that these beliefs are as important as, if not more important than, the pharmacological actions of ethanol in predicting drinking behavior. The beliefs that alcohol reduces tension and enhances social pleasure may be responsible for the maintenance of much abusive drinking. These outcomes do not arise entirely from the pharmacological effects of ethanol.

Relapse is often related to an inability to cope with environmental stressors. It often appears to result from negative emotional states, social pressure, and interpersonal conflicts, rather than being evidence of a character flaw. Effective relapse prevention strategies will anticipate these events by teaching clients specific coping skills tailored to their individual needs.

Lastly, SLT considers lapses (and even relapses) to be opportunities for learning. Instead of viewing them as events to be fearful of, and as evidence of treatment failure, treatment providers should assist clients in analyzing their high-risk situations and covert cognitive processes. Helping clients to think differently about the meaning of relapse can result in a reduction of the abstinence violation effect and thus in fewer subsequent full-blown relapses.

REVIEW QUESTIONS

1. As it relates to determinism, how does social learning theory (SLT) differ from both psychoanalysis and conditioning theory?

2. What role does cognition play in SLT?

3. How can alcohol/drug use be mediated by modeling?

4. In SLT, what is the significance of "self-regulation" and "reciprocal determinism"?

5. What is "self-efficacy"? How is it influenced?

6. What are "alcohol expectancies"?

7. How are placebo conditions use to study alcohol expectancies?

8. Has survey research been able to link expectancies to drinking outcomes?

9. How has relapse been viewed historically?

10. What are the relapse rates for different groups of addicts?

11. What is the most frequently cited explanation for relapse in the professional literature?

12. What are "discomfort anxiety" and "low frustration tolerance"? How do they lead to relapse?

13. What are some typical patterns that lead to relapse?

14. In SLT, how are recovering clients taught to view relapse?

15. What are "apparently irrevelant decisions" (AIDs)? How do they lead to relapses?

16. What is the "abstinence violation effect"?

REFERENCES

Abrams, D. B., & Niaura, R. S. (1987). Social learning theory. In H. T. Blane & K. E. Leonard (Eds.), *Psychological theories of drinking and alcoholism.* New York: Guilford Press.

Bandura, A. (1971). Analysis of modelling processes. In A. Bandura (Ed.), *Psychological modelling: Conflicting models.* Chicago: Aldine-Atherton.

Bandura, A. (1977). *Social learning theory.* Englewood Cliffs, NJ: Prentice-Hall.

Brown, S. A. (1985). Expectancies versus background in the prediction of college drinking patterns. *Journal of Consulting and Clinical Psychology, 53*(1), 123–130.

Brown, S. A., Christiansen, B. A., & Goldman, M. S. (1987). The Alcohol Expectancy Questionnaire: An instrument for the assessment of adolescent and adult alcohol expectancies. *Journal of Studies on Alcohol,* 48(5), 483–491.

Brown, S. A., Creamer, V. A., & Stetson, B. A. (1987). Adolescent alcohol expectancies as a function of personal and parental drinking patterns. *Journal of Abnormal Psychology, 96,* 177–121.

Christiansen, B. A., Roehling, P. V., Smith, G. T., & Goldman, M. S. (1989). Using alcohol expectancies to predict adolescent drinking behavior after one year. *Journal of Consulting and Clinical Psychology, 57*(1), 93–99.

Critchlow, B. (1987). Brief report: A utility analysis of drinking. *Addictive Behaviors, 12,* 269–273.

Ellis, A. (1985). *Overcoming resistance.* New York: Springer.

Ellis, A., McInerney, J. J., Di Giuseppe, R., & Yeager, R J. (1988). *Rational–emotive therapy with alcoholics and substance abusers.* Elmsford, NY: Pergamon Press.

Fuller, R. K., Lee, K. K., & Gordis, E. (1988). Validity of self-report in alcoholism research: Results of Veterans Administration Cooperative Study. *Alcoholism, 12*(2), 201–205.

Goldman, M. S., Brown, S. A., & Christiansen, B. A. (1987). Expectancy theory: Thinking about drinking. In H. T. Blane & K. E. Leonard (Eds.), *Psychological theories of drinking and alcoholism.* New York: Guilford Press.

Goodwin, D. W. (1990). Genetic determinants of reinforcements from alcohol. In W. M. Cox (Ed.), *Why people drink: Parameters of alcohol as a reinforcer.* New York: Gardner Press.

Hunt, W. A. (1990). Biochemical bases for the reinforcing effects of ethanol. In W. M. Cox (Ed.), *Why people drink: Parameters of alcohol as a reinforcer.* New York: Gardner Press.

Hunt, W. A. (1990). Brain mechanisms that underlie the reinforcing effects of ethanol. In W. M. Cox (Ed.), *Why people drink: Parameters of alcohol as a reinforcer.* New York: Gardner Press.

Hunt, W. A., Barnett, L. W., & Branch, L. G. (1971). Relapse rates in addictions programs. *Journal of Consulting and Clinical Psychology, 27,* 455–456.

Hunter, T. A., & Salmone, P. R. (1986). Dry drunk syndrome and alcoholic relapse. *Journal of Applied Rehabilitation Counseling, 18,* 22–25.

Lewis, J. A., Dana, R. Q., & Blevins, G. A. (1988). *Substance abuse counseling: An individualized approach.* Pacific Grove, CA: Brooks/Cole.

Marlatt, G. A., Demming, B., & Reid, J. B. (1973). Loss of control drinking in alcoholics: An experimental analogue. *Journal of Abnormal Psychology, 81,* 223–241.

Marlatt, G. A., & Gordon, J. R. (1979). Determinants of relapse: Implications for the maintenance of behavior change. In P. A. Davidson & S. M. Davidson (Eds.), *Behavioral medicine: Changing health lifestyles.* New York: Brunner/Mazel.

Marlatt, G. A., & Gordon, J. R. (Eds.). *Relapse prevention.* New York: Guilford Press.

Merry, J. (1966). The "loss of control" myth. *Lancet, i,* 1257–1258.

Milkman, H., Weiner, S. E., & Sunderwirth, S. (1984). Addiction relapse. *Addictive Behaviors, 3,* 119–134.

Monte, C. F. (1980). *Beneath the mask: An introduction to theories of personality.* New York: Holt, Rinehart & Winston.

National Institute on Alcohol Abuse and Alcoholism. (1990). *Alcohol and health: Seventh special report to the U.S. Congress* (DHHS Publication No. ADM 90-1656). Washington DC: U.S. Government Printing Office.

Polich, J. M., Armor, D. M., & Braiker, H. B., (1981). *The course of alcoholism: Four years after treatment.* New York: Wiley.

Thombs, D. L. (1991). Expectancies versus demographics in discriminating between college drinkers: Implications for alcohol abuse prevention. *Health Education Research, 6*(4), 491–495.

Thombs, D. L. (1993). The differentially discriminating properties of alcohol expectancies for female and male drinkers. *Journal of Counseling and Development, 71*(3), 321–325.

Watson, C. G., Tilleskjor, C., Hoodecheck-Schow, E. A., Pucel, J., & Jacobs, L. (1984). Do alcoholics give valid self-reports? *Journal of Studies on Alcohol, 45,* 344–348.

White, H. R., Bates, M. E., & Johnson, V. (1990). Social reinforcement and alcohol consumption. In W. M. Cox (Ed.), *Why people drink: Parameters of alcohol as a reinforcer.* New York: Gardner Press.

Wilson, G. T. (1988). Alcohol use and abuse: A social learning theory analysis. In C. D. Chaudron & D. A. Wilkinson (Eds.), *Theories on alcoholism.* Toronto: Addiction Research Foundation.

Family Systems Theory

Systems theory and family therapy have been linked with each other for several decades; however, the two are not synonymous. In "systems theory," the unit of analysis is the social system. Relatively little consideration is given to intrapsychic factors. The determinants of behavior are thought to be the "ongoing dynamics and demands of the key interpersonal system(s) within which the individual interacts" (Pearlman, 1988, p. 290). The emphasis is on social roles that are carried out within the context of the organizations to which one belongs. In this culture, the family is usually the dominant influence on behavior, though the workplace, the neighborhood community, and the church can also be considered influential systems.

"Family therapy" is a generic term given to professional services that help families improve their level of functioning. Family therapy does not necessarily rely on a systems framework. Some mental health professionals rely on traditional psychotherapeutic approaches (e.g., psychoanalytic or behavioral) to treat families. When a systems approach is taken, it is usually referred to as "family *systems* therapy."

KEY CONCEPTS

Social systems, such as families, are complex organizations that are hierarchical in nature. Their dynamics consist of stable, predictable patterns of relationships. Rules (which are often unspoken, but known to members) guide these relationship patterns. Whenever one element in the system is changed (e.g., an alcoholic family member stops drinking), all other elements are affected. The entire system attempts to compensate for the change. Thus, systems theory stresses the wholeness of the social unit, and the interdependence of all the members of the system is emphasized. Again, psychological factors are not usually scrutinized.

According to Steinglass (1978), the significance assigned to "wholeness" and interdependent relationships is that which distinguishes systems theory from most other perspectives on addiction.

Boundaries

In a family system (as well as other systems), there is organization. Several systems concepts are typically used to describe the nature of the organization. One such concept is referred to as "boundaries." Boundaries exist to

> . . . distinguish those elements contained within the system from other elements within the broader environment. Boundaries are significant within a system framework since they not only define membership within a given system or subsystem but also characterize the quality of the relationship between the system per se and its surrounding milieu. This latter property of a boundary is referred to as its permeability and describes the ease of exchange of information with other systems. (Pearlman, 1988, p. 290)

Boundaries have also been described as "rules of interaction" and "methods of functioning," which fall on a continuum from "very diffuse" to "very rigid"; in the middle of this continuum lie "clear" boundaries (see Figure 6.1). Within most family systems, boundaries

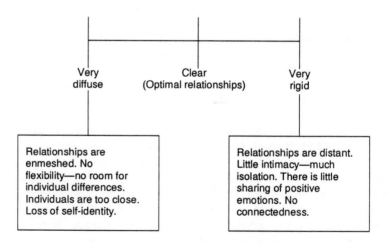

FIGURE 6.1. Family boundaries continuum.

lie at some point in the middle, though they may be closer to one extreme or the other. Optimally functioning family relationships are characterized by clear boundaries. That is, they allow for individuality, yet maintain intimacy; they are based on mutual respect; the members show genuine love and concern for one another without attempting to control one another; freedom and flexibility are evident; and communication patterns are clear and direct.

Where very diffuse boundaries exist, relationships are characterized by overinvolvement. There is no room for separateness or individual uniqueness; an overemphasis is placed upon sameness and unity (Lawson, Peterson, & Lawson, 1983). Families with very diffuse or enmeshed boundaries do not allow adolescents to pull away from the family. They discourage the development of exceptional or unique talents. Some adolescents may rebel against this "smothering" by abusing alcohol or drugs. When marital relationships are characterized by overinvolvement, the individuality of each spouse is "sacrificed" for the "sake of the marriage" (Lawson et al., 1983, p. 42).

In other chemically dependent families, boundaries may be very rigid or disengaged. Individual members of the family (particularly the alcoholic or addict) may be isolated, or, at other times, the entire family may be isolated from the community. According to Lawson et al. (1983, p. 42), alcoholic families have three rules:

1. "do not talk about the alcoholism,"
2. "do not confront drinking behavior," and
3. "protect and shelter the alcoholic so that things don't become worse."

Unfortunately, such rules enable an alcoholic or addict to keep drinking or using drugs, and inadvertently contribute to the progression of addictive behavior. A vicious cycle develops in which the isolation imposed by the three rules perpetuates the chemical abuse, and, in turn, the chemical abuse maintains the need for isolation (see Figure 6.2).

When one spouse is an alcoholic or addict, the marital relationship may be disengaged at a fixed distance. That is, the partners may remain married, but they lead relatively separate lives. The alcoholic or addict may work and spend much time with drinking or drug-using buddies, rather than at home. The nondependent spouse may carry the full parenting load and pursue other interests without the chemically dependent spouse. Children of these disengaged families typically feel rejected and unloved. They may develop emotional

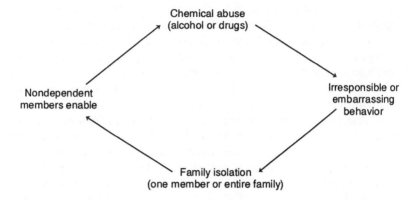

FIGURE 6.2. Reciprocal relationship between family isolation and chemical abuse.

problems or "act out." Either way, their maladaptive behavior represents a plea for help.

Subsystems and Hierarchies

"Subsystems" and "hierarchies" also contribute to the organization of the family system. There are several subsystems within the family. The original subsystem is the marital one. Within the marital subsystem, certain privileges, communication patterns, and behaviors are appropriate (e.g., financial decisions, career decisions, sexual relations, etc.). With the birth of the first child, a new subsystem (the parental subsystem) is created. Within this subsystem, the decisions about how to raise the children are made. This power rests with the parents; thus, a hierarchy appears in which parents have more power than the children. In chemically dependent families where the alcoholic or addict is a parent, the nondependent spouse typically assumes most of the parental power. The addicted spouse gives up or turns over power as a parent. This shift in role obligations places a heavy burden on the nondependent spouse and usually creates feelings of resentment. Sometimes a grandparent or older sibling may assume some parental power (as demonstrated by cooking meals, shopping, doing laundry, etc.); in this way, subsystem boundaries may become blurred.

A sibling subsystem also will evolve. Its complexity will depend upon the number of children, their age differences, their gender, and their common interests (Lawson et al., 1983). Sibling subsystems may distinguish the sons from the daughters, the oldest from the youngest, or the athletic from the nonathletic. In functional families, these subsystems will remain somewhat fluid and dynamic as time passes and the children mature. In dysfunctional families, the subsystems may remain static as the children are required to assume inappropriate roles, such as that of a parent. Allowing a child into the marital subsystem (e.g., incest) is another example in which subsystems are likely to remain static (Lawson et al., 1983).

Family Rules

Another characteristic of family organization pertains to the rules that govern interactions between and among members. Often these rules are implicit rather than explicit; however, most or all members somehow seem to know them. They define appropriate conduct within the family system. They function to provide order, stability, consistency, and predictability in family affairs. They also serve to restrict behavioral options (e.g., "incest is unacceptable"). Families usually have rules governing the manner in which different emotions are expressed. In some families anger is not allowed, whereas in others shouting is permissible. In some families affection is demonstrated with hugs and kisses, while in others physical contact is minimized.

Barnard (1981) has noted six areas in which families usually formulate rules:

1. To what extent, when, and how family members may comment on what they see, feel, and think.
2. Who can speak to whom and about what.
3. How a member can be different.
4. How sexuality can be expressed.
5. What it means to be male or female.
6. How a person can acquire self-worth, and how much self-worth is appropriate to possess.

In chemically dependent families, certain family rules are typical. For example, it is usually prohibited to talk openly about the substance abuse; this has been referred to as the "conspiracy of silence" (Deutsch, 1982). There often exists a "don't feel, don't trust, don't talk" rule in such families as well. A rule often found in alcoholic families is that "anger can only be expressed when the alcoholic is drinking" (Lawson, et al., 1983). The family's alcoholic sometimes operates according to this rule: "I am comfortable expressing my affection for you only after I have been drinking."

Causality in Family Systems

In systems theory, reciprocal rather than linear causality is emphasized. That is, relationships between and among variables or elements in systems include feedback loops. Simple cause-and-effect relationships are viewed as too reductionistic and as incapable of capturing the complexity of family interactions. Thus, behaviors that are stimulated by one element themselves become stimuli for other behaviors. Pearlman (1988) notes that most family therapists have first-hand knowledge of the reciprocal patterns in family relationship problems. As an example, the most common marital pattern in alcoholism is represented in Figure 6.3.

Homeostasis

"Homeostasis" has long been an important concept in systems theory (Pearlman, 1988). According to Stanton (1980), homeostasis in a

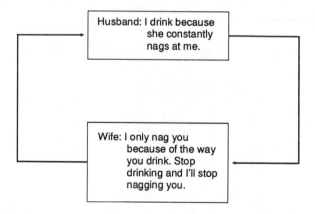

FIGURE 6.3. Reciprocal relationship between husband's abusive drinking and wife's nagging.

family with an alcoholic or addict is a pathological equilibrium in which the nondependent family members have an emotional investment in the chemically dependent member's maintaining his/her addiction. It explains "the family's tenacity in holding onto existing behavioral repertoires, resisting change, and exerting pressure to minimize or reverse change when it occurs" (Pearlman, 1988, p. 292). The abuse of alcohol or drugs plays a key part in maintaining the family balance. If the drinking or drug use is stopped (e.g., an attempt at recovery), the family is thrown out of balance. In order to regain it, nondependent family members will often (unconsciously) attempt to sabotage the member's recovery effort.

The sabotaging behavior of the nondependent members may take many forms. For example, let us suppose that a 40-year-old male alcoholic makes good progress in an aftercare program. After several months of abstinence and frequent AA attendance, his wife begins to complain bitterly that they never "go out" any more because he is always at "those" meetings. Her nagging eventually prompts him to relapse. She did not intend for him to slip, but her behavior has nevertheless had that result. Another example of sabotaging involves a husband of a female cocaine addict in early recovery. Upon her leaving inpatient rehabilitation, he agrees to care for the kids while she attends aftercare and NA meetings. After a few weeks, he protests that he feels too "tied down" and refuses to continue babysitting. She soon relapses. Other spouses have been known to complain that their recovering spouses are "not the same person"; often, they have ambivalent feelings about the behavioral and personality changes. They may feel that their mates are now too assertive, "kind of boring," or less sociable than when they were drinking or abusing drugs.

The newfound sobriety will not only throw the marital relationship into turmoil; the children are also affected. The following excerpt highlights typical reactions of children to a father in early recovery:

> Mother is not needed as the overly responsible martyr when Dad returns to take over running the household. Brother has no reason to stay away from home and must reevaluate his relationship with Dad. The family suddenly notices little sister's hyperactive mannerisms. (Lawson et al., 1983, p. 40)

From a systems point of view, the abusive drinking or drug use has adaptive consequences. That is, it functions to keep the family "in balance"—not a "healthy" balance, but a relatively stable one nevertheless. This pathological equilibrium is preferred over continual chaos and crisis. In essence, such families opt for low-level discomfort and "put up" with the substance abuse in order to avoid grappling with even more painful and sensitive issues.

Alcohol or drug abuse can stabilize a family (i.e., keep it in balance) in a number of ways. It can divert attention away from marital problems and allow angry or hurtful feelings to go unexpressed. For example, among married male alcoholics, abusive drinking is often a way to avoid intimacy with their wives. It establishes an emotional distance that can become fixed over time. Frequently, such men feel much ambivalence about their marriages and their children. They may love them, but at the same time may believe that their wives and kids are responsible for their lost opportunities. This may be particularly true of men who married and had children relatively young. The family is often seen as a financial and emotional burden, one which many men fear they will not be able to support. In such cases, men feel a loss of freedom, especially when the perceive themselves to be trapped in jobs that they dislike. Excessive drinking is one way to cope with these pressures. It serves as an analgesic for the family pain; it also prevents crises that could lead to family breakup if they were faced squarely.

Homeostatic mechanisms, such as drinking, regulate the amount of change to which a family can adapt at any one time. Change can occur in the family, but the need for balance slows it by relying on compensatory measures. In functional families, change is incorporated relatively easily via compensatory efforts that allow all members to get their needs met. If young Johnnie starts Little League baseball, for instance, Dad makes an effort to adjust his work schedule to get him to practice. However, in dysfunctional families, adaptation to the evolving needs of the members is more resistant and less fluid. All members are less likely to get their needs fulfilled.

Pearlman (1988) notes that these family regulatory processes are maintained by feedback loops, which can be points of intervention in family systems therapy. He states:

> Positive feedback loops introduce change into the system. Negative feedback loops, on the other hand, promote a steady state and diminish the impact of change that is introduced into the system. Negative feedback loops are, therefore, closely associated with a system's homeostatic tendencies, and have become an important focal point for the systems therapist in attempting to identify and ultimately overcome a family's seemingly inherent tendency to resist change. (p. 292)

It should be noted that dysfunctional families are not forever locked into maladaptive patterns of interaction. The concept of homeostasis only describes the *tendency* to regulate change; it does not describe an unalterable pattern of maladaptive interaction.

The Impact of One's Family of Origin

How are dysfunctional marriages and families created? Is the development of such a union predictable, or is it simply the result of choosing the wrong mate? Framo (1976) believes that individuals select mates in an attempt to fill voids they experienced in their own families of origin. This is an unconscious effort for the most part, and it involves bargaining: for example, "I will be your conscience if you act out my impulse" (Framo, 1976, p. 194). In this way, one spouse (typically the woman) will seek to control the other, while the other (typically the man) will express the rebellion that she dares not reveal (Lawson et al., 1983). This may partly explain why some women are attracted to men who engage in risky behavior (e.g., drinking abusively, using drugs, driving fast, fighting, etc.), and why such men often find restrained, traditional women desirable in turn.

Lawson et al. (1983) describe in the following passage how alcoholic marriages become increasingly problematic:

> The two personalities become dependent on each other and increasingly intertwined, making it difficult for either to leave regardless of the dysfunction of the relationship. Marital partners enmeshed in these relationships (based on the inability to function as an individual) can manifest dysfunctions leading to superficial relationships, emotional upheaval, and possible drinking behavior (if this drinking model was present in their family of origin). Often these marital partners reach out to each other for identity and fuse into a single entity in the marriage. To achieve some separateness the marital partners must set up emotional distance. One spouse may take the dominant position in the relationship with the remaining spouse adapting to the other and further losing identity. (p. 34)

A marital relationship usually consists of an "emotional pursuer" and an "emotional distancer" (Fogarty, 1976). In U.S. culture (and probably other Western cultures as well), the woman is the pursuer, and the man is the distancer. Typically, as the woman strives for intimacy, the man backs away. In healthy marriages, both individuals will at least occasionally be pursuers and thus will establish intimacy. In dysfunctional marriages, over time, a fixed emotional distance may occur; that is, neither spouse strives for emotional intimacy. Such is often the case when one spouse abuses alcohol or drugs (or when both do). This underinvolvement often leads the nonabusing spouse to become overinvolved with the children (when there are children). The nonabusing spouse may get some of their emotional needs met through the children. In addition, the children may become overly dependent on the nonabusing parent (typically the mother) because of the other parent's distance.

The Teen's Fear of Separation

Dysfunctional marital relationships can have deleterious effects on the teenage children of such unions. Adolescent alcohol or drug abuse is one of the negative consequences of problems between the parents. Stanton (1980) has explored the family dynamics that give rise to substance abuse among teens who are themselves children of alcoholics or addicts. He suggests that an overinvolvement with the nonabusing parent creates an intense "fear of separation." At the same time, the teen has normal developmental needs to begin separating from the family of origin. Thus, drug abuse becomes a way in which the teen demonstrates a "pseudoindividuation"—that is, a false independence from the family. The act of abusing drugs or alcohol represents rebellion and autonomy, but, according to Stanton (1980), it is only an "illusory independence." Such a teen establishes a link to the drug subculture (which outwardly suggests adulthood), but also maintains a foothold in the family.

Stanton (1980) cites his own research for evidence of pseudoindividuation among teens and young adults. He found that 66% of heroin addicts, for example, lived with or saw their mothers daily. This may not seem particularly unusual, until consideration is given to the fact that their average age was 28. Considering American cultural norms, this suggests prolonged overdependence upon their mothers. Thus, it appears that some young, unmarried addicts will vacillate between their families of origin and the drug subculture. They want to appear strong and independent, but they also fear separation from an overinvolved relationship with a parent.

Triads

Bowen (1976), Stanton (1980), and others maintain that dysfunctional families form triadic patterns of interaction, which contribute to the development of addiction in children. "Triads" are family sub-systems that consist of three members. Typically, this interactive pattern in a case of chemical dependence involves a young adult (or adolescent) addict and the parents. However, other triads can develop as well, especially in extended families. For example, a triadic subsystem may consist of a young adult male alcoholic, his wife, and his mother (with whom they reside).

In the most common triad, one parent is intensely involved with the addict, while the other parent is underinvolved and perhaps punitive. Usually the overinvolved parent is pampering and indulgent of the addicted child. This parent is usually of the opposite sex from the child; thus, the emotionally distant parent is often a father, the overinvolved parent is the mother, and the addict is male.

The triad forms as a means of protecting the marriage and the family. In essence, the triad serves a protective function: It helps maintain the family structure by distracting the parents from their own marital difficulties. The child's drug problem provides a focal point around which they can unify, instead of focusing on their own problems. The drug problem gives them a reason for remaining together. All their emotional energies are directed toward the child, rather than toward each other. Thus, the child's drug problem functions to suppress marital conflict.

Stanton (1980) asserts that it is no accident that alcohol or drug abuse typically begins in early or middle adolescence. Parents in a dysfunctional marriage may be threatened by the fact that their child is growing up. They may fear losing the child (to a girlfriend or boyfriend, to military service, to higher education or a career, to a move to a geographically distant area, etc.). This parental anxiety, according to Stanton (1980), stems from the deeper fear that they will have to face their relationship problems. They anticipate that the void in their marriage will no longer be filled by their child. Such parents often feel threatened and incapable of overcoming long-standing marital problems. They only see two options: (1) staying permanently in an unsatisfying relationship, or (2) divorce.

The Dance

Stanton (1980) has noted that triads become "stuck" in a chronic, repetitive pattern of interaction. He uses the metaphor of the "dance" to describe the process. This is more than simply a description; the "dance" metaphor explains, from a systems viewpoint, how relapse occurs. The dance consists of the various forms of repetitive, consistent, and predictable displays of behavior (Stanton, 1980). One of the steps in the dance is the act of abusing drugs or alcohol. Box 6.1 describes the experience of one 23-year-old polydrug addict who was engaged in a triadic relationship with his parents.

BOX 6.1. Billy and His Parents

For as long as Billy can remember, his parents argued. Sometimes their fights became violent, with many household items being broken. Billy began using drugs in his early teens; by his senior year in high school, he could be described as a drug addict. His drug use came to the attention of his parents because he was "busted" at school. Previously, they had been too involved with their own problems to notice.

Billy's parents reacted in distinctively different ways. His father was enraged and very condemning of Billy; he threatened him with all kinds of consequences. Mom, on the other hand, was very reassuring and protective. She attempted to shield him from his father and to make excuses for him. It appeared that his parents unconsciously welcomed the drug problem because it gave them relief from their own conflict. As a result, they focused much energy on disciplining Billy and helping him with his problem. They placed him in a drug rehabilitation program.

Upon Billy's discharge, he remained abstinent for several weeks. His parents were on their best behavior during this time. Gradually (and as a result of Billy's abstinence), Mom and Dad began to argue again. Their conflict resurfaced without Billy's "problem" to distract them. In turn, Billy relapsed. It was as if they were in a dance: When Mom and Dad's arguing flared up, so did Billy's drug abuse; when Billy's drug abuse subsided a bit as a result of their efforts and attention, Mom and Dad's arguing again resumed. They were right in step with each other.

This pattern continued for 5 years, with four attempts at inpatient rehabilitation. After his fourth discharge, Billy managed to obtain a good-paying job. He remained clean and sober, and he established a relationship with a woman he met through work. Everything was going well until his mother began to harangue him about not visiting and calling. One night she called him while she was drunk and accused him of not really caring for her, and not being appreciative of all of the things she and his father had done for him through the years.

In an aftercare group, Billy reported that he was "shaky" and anxious, and had suddenly begun having drug cravings. He had difficulty linking these symptoms to his conversation with his mother, though he felt her trying to "pull" him back home. Mom was threatened by Billy's increasing independence and maturity.

This story has a happy ending for Billy. He did not relapse, and is doing well in his job and marriage. Mom and Dad are now divorced.

The concept of the dance provides insight into the dynamics behind relapse. Stanton (1980) indicates that these dynamics often go unrecognized and that those who relapse are labeled "unmotivated" or perhaps "emotionally unstable." From a systems perspective, such assessments are superficial; they overlook the addict's enmeshment in the family system. Thus, effective relapse prevention should include intervention with the family, rather than just focusing narrowly on intrapsychic factors within the addict.

BOWEN'S FAMILY SYSTEMS THEORY

A relatively large number of family systems theories exist. Each one emphasizes different aspects of the family, though most share common elements as described above (Pearlman, 1988). Among the most prominent of these theories is the work of Murray Bowen. The Bowen theory is presented here as the prototypical family systems theory. It should be noted that this is not specifically a theory of addiction, but rather one of family dysfunction. Addiction is considered an example of dysfunction in the family unit.

Differentiation of Self

Bowen (1976) considers "differentiation of self" to be the central concept of his theory. This concept classifies people on a continuum. On one end of the continuum are people whose lives are extremely dominated by automatic emotional reaction. They are said to be "fused" (Bowen, 1976); that is, no differentiation exists between the emotional and the intellectual self. Emotion, at this extreme, completely dominates the self. According to Bowen (1976),

> These are people who are less flexible, less adaptable, and more emotionally dependent on those about them. They are easily stressed into dys-

function, and it is difficult for them to recover from dysfunction. They inherit a high percentage of all human problems. (p. 65)

On the other end of the continuum are those persons who are highly differentiated. That is, they possess a balance between emotional and intellectual responding, and these two processes are more clearly separated. Bowen (1976) maintains that complete differentiation of self is impossible. However, people whose emotional functioning and intellectual functioning are relatively well separated will be more autonomous, more flexible, and better able to cope with stress; they will also demonstrate more independence of emotions. In essence, they possess a high level of emotional maturity. Bowen (1976) states that "their life courses are more orderly and successful, and they are remarkably free of human problems" (pp. 65–66) (see Figure 6.4).

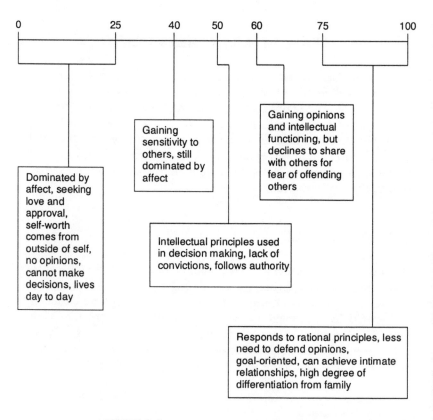

FIGURE 6.4. Bowen's scale of differentiation.

Of those persons on the low end of the continuum (scores = 0–25), Bowen (1976) writes:

> . . . the intellect is so flooded by emotionality that the total life course is determined by the emotional process and by what "feels right," rather than by beliefs or opinions. The intellect exists as an appendage of the feeling system. It may function reasonably well in mathematics or physics, or in impersonal areas, but on personal subjects its functioning is controlled by the emotions. (p. 66)

This insight may explain, at least partly, the resistance that many families (and individuals) demonstrate when offered help or therapeutic feedback. The assistance is usually principled; that is, it is formed from reason. It is rational. Thus, it is often rejected because of the overreliance on emotional functioning.

It should be noted here that Bowen does not discount the emotional dimension of human experience. He does not advocate human development that is cold, distant, or uncaring. Rather, he emphasizes that the poorly differentiated individual is "trapped within a feeling world" (1976, p. 67). They have no options in responding; they simply react in an automatic fashion. In contrast, a highly differentiated person can express emotion (both positive and negative) in appropriate, productive ways.

Poorly differentiated persons are "totally relationship oriented" (Bowen, 1976, p. 69). Most of their energy goes into pleasing others and keeping their relationships, especially with family members, in harmony. Conflict is avoided. Typically, these persons say "I feel . . ." when expressing their views. They are unable to form personal beliefs, and thus avoid saying "I think . . ." or "I believe . . ." (Bowen, 1976).

Persons with low levels of differentiation have other difficulties as well. They find it difficult to make plans and carry them out. Long-term goals are almost impossible to form for these individuals. They tend to live from day to day, and remain overly dependent on their parents well into adulthood. They are preoccupied with making others happy. Sometimes employers find such characteristics useful, so poorly differentiated individuals may remain in the same low-level positions for many years. Extremely low-functioning individuals in this group may be institutionalized and labeled "psychotic," "schizophrenic," or "mentally ill."

Bowen (1976) describes individuals whose level of differentiation is a bit higher (scores = 25–50) in the following passage:

> Lives are guided by the emotional system, but the life styles are more flexible than the lower levels of differentiation. The flexibility provides

a better view of the interplay between emotionality and intellect. When anxiety is low, functioning can resemble good levels of differentiation. When anxiety is high, functioning can resemble that of low levels of differentiation. Lives are relationship oriented, and major life energy goes to loving and being loved, and seeking approval from others. Feelings are more openly expressed than in lower level people. Life energy is directed more to what others think and to winning friends and approval than to goal-directed activity. Self-esteem is dependent on others. It can soar to heights with a compliment or be crushed by criticism. Success in school is oriented more to learning the system and to pleasing the teacher than to the primary goal of learning. . . . They may have enough free-functioning intellect to have mastered academic knowledge about impersonal things; they use this knowledge in the relationship system. However, intellect about personal matters is lacking, and their personal lives are in chaos. (pp. 70–71)

Bowen (1976) indicates that scores of 50–75 on his continuum represent moderate levels of self-differentiation. Among this group, the two systems, intellect and emotion, function cooperatively; neither system dominates the other. In particularly stressful situations, the intellectual system may be overwhelmed, but for the most part these individuals lead satisfying lives. The intellectual system learns that discipline is required to obtain long-term gains. Thus, persons in this group are capable to some degree of delaying gratification and planning for the future. They are also somewhat more able to think for themselves. They are aware of differences between thinking and feeling, and at least occasionally are able to state unpopular beliefs or opinions.

The highly differentiated person (scores = 75–100) is "more hypothetical, than real," according to Bowen (1976, p. 73). Few individuals reach such a level of development. Such persons are aware of the relationships around them, but they do not become mired in emotional "stuck-togetherness." They are aware of various response options available to them. They presumably choose how to act, instead of automatically reacting to a situation. Again, highly differentiated persons are not emotionally cold or distant; in fact, they welcome and express sincere, authentic emotion. However, they avoid the various insincere expressions of emotion that are often required by unwritten family rules or by social conventions.

Triangles

Whereas other family systems theorists have used the term "triad" (see earlier discussion), Bowen (1976) prefers "triangles." He attaches some special and unique meanings to the configuration that have not been emphasized by other writers. For example, his theory defines a triangle in the following way:

> [The triangle,] a three-person emotional configuration, is the molecule or the basic building block of any emotional system, whether it is in the family or any other group. The triangle is the smallest stable relationship system. A two-person system may be stable as long as it is calm, but when anxiety increases, it immediately involves the most vulnerable other person to become a triangle. When tension in the triangle is too great for the threesome, it involves others to become a series of interlocking triangles. (Bowen, 1976, p. 76)

A triangle is thought to consist of a comfortably close twosome and an uncomfortable outsider. In order to avoid separation, the partners in the twosome work to achieve closeness; often they are overinvolved with each other. The uncomfortable outsider seeks closeness to one of the twosome. These attempts at maneuvering have been described earlier in the chapter as the "dance." Bowen (1976) notes that the constant motion within the triangle results from moderate levels of tension in the twosome, which are felt by only one of them. The other is oblivious to the conflict in the pair. The "uncomfortable other" mediates or diverts some of the tension to himself/herself by engaging the twosome, and thus initiates a new equilibrium within the triangle.

During periods of great stress and tension, the "outsider" position is sought by each member of the triangle. In times of stress, this is the least uncomfortable position. Obviously, all three individuals cannot shift to the outside position. When such shifts are prevented, one of the twosome involves a new outsider, and a new triangle is formed. Bowen (1976) believes that these shifting dynamics will often result in all family members being "triangled" at different points in time. Furthermore, when all available family triangles have been exhausted, the family will typically seek to form triangles with people outside itself (e.g., members of the clergy, police officers, mental health professionals, social service agencies, school officials, etc.).

Bowen (1976) describes the typical triangle in the following passage:

> The best example of this is the father–mother–child triangle. Patterns vary, but one of the most common is basic tension between the parents, with the father's gaining the outside position—often being called passive, weak, and distant—leaving the conflict between the mother and

child. The mother—often called aggressive, dominating, and castrating—wins over the child, who moves another step toward chronic functional impairment. . . . Families replay the same triangular game over and over for years, as though the winner were in doubt, but the final result is always the same. Over the years the child accepts the always-lose outcome more easily, even to volunteering for this position. (pp. 76–77)

The Emotional System in the Nuclear Family

In each generation of a family, certain patterns of emotional functioning appear. These patterns, involving parents and children, are replicated from the mother's and father's separate families of origin. According to Bowen (1976), families transmit these patterns of emotional responding from generation to generation. These patterns are readily observable in most families.

Typically, the nuclear family begins with a marriage. Bowen (1976) maintains that individuals of similar levels of differentiation will be attracted to each other. The lower their level of differentiation, the more intense the emotional fusion in the marriage. In most marriages, one spouse becomes more dominant in decision making for the couple. The other spouse adapts to the arrangement. Bowen (1976) describes the fusion that occurs among most couples in the following passage:

> One [spouse] may assume the dominant role and force the other to be adaptive, or one [spouse] may assume the adaptive role and force the other to be dominant. Both may try for the dominant role, which results in conflict; or both may try for the adaptive role, which results in decision paralysis. The dominant one gains self at the expense of the more adaptive one, who loses self. More differentiated spouses have lesser degrees of fusion, and fewer of the complications. The dominant and adaptive positions are not directly related to the sex of the spouse. They are determined by the position that each had in their families of origin. From my experience, there are as many dominant females as males, and as many adaptive males as females. These characteristics played a major role in their original choice of each other as partners. (p. 79)

Spouses with relatively high degrees of differentiation make minor adjustments to cope with the anxiety that results from emotional fusion. Less differentiated spouses develop more problematic symptoms. Bowen (1976) describes four common manifestations of marital fusion:

1. Emotional distancing.
2. Marital conflict.
3. Dysfunction in one spouse.
4. Impairment of one or more children.

The first symptom, emotional distancing, occurs among couples of moderate levels of self-differentiation, as well as among those who are highly fused (and anxious about being so). It is extremely common among most couples, almost universal. Few couples want to maintain the degree of fusion that they experienced during their courtship and the early days of their marriage. The loss of self (adaptive role) and the burden of decision making (dominant role) exact too great an emotional cost over prolonged periods of time. Thus, emotional distancing occurs to various degrees in most marital relationships.

Marital conflict results when neither spouse is willing to "give in" to the other—that is, neither spouse is willing to assume the adaptive role. Bowen (1976) indicates that marital conflict does not involve the children. The spouses are intensely involved with each other, with occasional periods of emotional distancing.

Dysfunction in one spouse results when one spouse absorbs a large amount of undifferentiation into himself/herself while assuming the adaptive role (Bowen, 1976). In this situation, the dysfunctional spouse strains to adapt to the other over prolonged periods of time. There is a loss of self. The adaptive spouse develops such symptoms as physical illness, substance abuse, mental disorders, or irresponsible behavior. These disorders become chronic. Bowen (1976) notes that such marriages tend to be enduring, for this reason: "The underfunctioning one is grateful for the care and attention, and the overfunctioning one does not complain" (p. 81).

When the parents project their undifferentiation onto one or more of the children, they are likely to become emotionally impaired as well. According to Bowen (1976), the intensity of the parents' projection is related to two variables. The first variable has to do with the degree of emotional isolation of the family—that is, the degree to which the family is withdrawn from their extended family, their church, their community, and so on. The second variable pertains to the level of tension in the family: The greater the levels of anxiety (and isolation), the more pronounced the parental projection. Bowen

(1976) considers this process of projection to be fundamental to most human problems. As such, he more fully develops the concept by describing it as the "family projection process."

The Family Projection Process

The family projection process involves a father–mother–child triangle. The parents' undifferentiation is projected onto a child. Because the mother gives birth to the child and because she is usually the primary nurturer, Bowen (1976) believes that the process revolves around her emotional energy, which in turn originates in her family of origin. The family projection process can be the principal cause of a child's emotional impairment, or it can superimpose itself on a child's pre-existing illness (e.g., leukemia) or disability (e.g., Down's syndrome, spina bifida, muscular dystrophy). Bowen (1976) notes that "the process is so universal it is present to some degree in all families" (p. 81).

In Bowen's systems theory, the emotional energy arising from the parents' undifferentiation is expressed in one or more of the following ways:

1. Marital conflict.
2. Dysfunction in one spouse.
3. Projection to the children.

The undifferentiation is also absorbed in these three ways. Family members will typically shift the weight of the undifferentiation around so that no one member becomes too dysfunctional.

Thus, the children are sometimes projected onto in order to reduce marital conflict or spouse dysfunction. This homeostatic mechanism protects the marriage in the former case, and the adaptive spouse in the latter. According to Bowen (1976), "I have never seen a family in which there was not some projection to a child. Most families use a combination of all three mechanisms" (p. 82).

The projection to the children is not equally distributed. For various unconscious reasons (discussed below), the projection first focuses on one child. If the focus becomes too intense (i.e., if the child becomes too impaired), then it is often shifted to another child (a new father–mother–child triangle is created), and so forth. In this fashion, each child may become "triangulated" at some point in the life of the family.

It has been mentioned that the family projection process revolves around the mother's emotional energy. Bowen (1976) details the origins of this process in the following passage:

> The early thoughts about marriage and children are more prominent in the female than the male. They begin to take an orderly form before adolescence. A female who thinks primarily of the husband she will marry tends to have marriages in which she focuses most of her emotional energy on the husband, and he focuses on her, and symptoms tend to focus more in marital conflict and sickness in a spouse. Those females whose early thoughts and fantasies go more to the children they will have than the man they will marry, tend to become the mothers of impaired children. The process can be so intense in some women that the husband is incidental to the process. (p. 82)

Special children are selected for the family projection process. Bowen (1976) suggests that a variety of factors can be associated with a child's selection. They include the following possibilities:

1. A child conceived and/or born during a period of severe stress in the mother's life.
2. The first child.
3. An only child.
4. The oldest son or oldest daughter.
5. A child who is emotionally special to the mother.
6. A child who is perceived by the mother to be emotionally special to the father.
7. A child of one sex among several of the opposite sex.
8. A child with a defect.
9. A child who was troublesome or nonresponsive to the mother from infancy.

Bowen (1976) insists that mothers cannot have an "equal emotional investment in any two children," despite their protestations to the contrary (p. 83).

Once a child has been selected for projection, a father–mother–child triangle has been formed. Typically, the child perceives anxiety in the mother, and in turn responds anxiously. The mother labels the child's anxiety as a "problem," and becomes highly solicitous, sympathetic, and overprotective toward the child. Thus, the two become emotionally fused. Meanwhile, the more distant father passively supports this process. Over time, the child becomes increasingly demanding and dependent upon the mother. The child remains undifferentiated, just as the parents have been. In this way, families tend to transmit a level of differentiation from generation to generation.

Emotional Cutoff

The final concept in Bowen's theory to be presented here is "emotional cutoff." According to Bowen (1976), individuals with lower levels of differentiation have not separated emotionally from their parents. They have unresolved emotional attachments to their families of origin. "Emotional cutoff" describes the manner in which individuals separate from their parents. Some individuals separate by isolating themselves emotionally, though they continue to live close to their parents. Others may move to a geographically distant area, but remain emotionally dependent on their parents. Still others may sever all communication but remain affected by unresolved attachments. Bowen (1976) notes that many people will use a combination of these methods to "cut off."

The more intense the emotional cutoff, the greater the likelihood that an individual will bring the "unfinished business" from the family of origin into his/her present marriage and family. It is also likely that the children of such individuals will cut off in a similar fashion (Bowen, 1976). Again, parents tend to transmit their level of differentiation to their children.

The preceding discussion has provided a brief overview of the Bowen theory. The concepts provide a solid base for understanding substance abuse from a family systems perspective.

CODEPENDENCY

The concept of "codependency" (also called "coalcoholism" when alcoholism is involved) refers to an unhealthy pattern of relating to others that results from being closely involved with an alcoholic or addict (Subby & Friel, 1984). Codependency is a generic term. It has been defined in various ways, but all definitions describe unhealthy relationship patterns. The chemical abuser in a codependent's life is usually a husband, but it can also be wife, a parent, a close friend, a child, or a coworker.

Koffinke (1991) indicates that the codependent is overly focused on (i.e., overinvolved with) the substance abuser. Their relationship is enmeshed and problem-filled. The problems provide endless opportunities for the codependent to be preoccupied with the addict. Hypervigilance is the norm. For women who grew up in chemically dependent families, this behavior seems normal. In fact, some believe that women from such families learn codependent behavior early in life, and are thus attracted to chemically dependent mates (Koffinke, 1991). They also find it very difficult, if not impossible, to leave dysfunctional relationships.

As a result of this emotional enmeshment, the codependent tends to lose all sense of "self" or identity, and to become emotionally dependent upon the addict. The addict's mood dictates the codependent's mood. In a sense, the codependent becomes an appendage to the addict and the substance abuse.

The codependent often protects the alcoholic or addict from the natural consequences of substance abuse (Koffinke, 1991). Such behavior is referred to as "enabling." Examples include calling in sick to a dependent spouse's employer when the spouse has been out drinking or using drugs all night, or cleaning up after a spouse who has vomited during the night from too much alcohol. In addition, the codependent may purposely isolate himself/herself (and the family) from the extended family and friends, in order to keep the "family secret" and save the family from embarrassment. Unfortunately, this isolation removes opportunities to release feelings of anger, hurt, fear, and frustration (Koffinke, 1991).

Chief Characteristics

Several writers have identified chief characteristics of codependency. Below is a descriptive list of the psychological impairments codependents experience (Norwood, 1985):

1. *Poor self-esteem.* Codependents suffer from low self-esteem; that is, they feel little personal worth and think poorly of themselves. This has many sources. They themselves may have grown up in alcoholic families, or families in which chemical dependency was not an issue but physical or emotional abuse was present nevertheless. It is also possible that they grew up in homes in which the parents were overprotective and domineering.

2. *Need to be needed.* Many codependents hold the belief that their worth is dependent upon how well they take care of loved ones. In our culture, women are especially socialized to be nurturers, so it

may come easily for them. As a result, codependence may neglect their own emotional needs for security, love, and attention.

3. *Strong urge to change and control others.* Codependents usually develop the belief that they have the power to control the alcoholics or addicts, and therefore must use this power to change them (i.e., get them to cut down or stop their drinking/drug use). Norwood (1985) notes that many codependents learned this notion as children. They may have been instructed by their mothers to "leave dad alone when he is drinking, or you could upset him" (Norwood, 1985); such instructions teach them that they can control others. An overdeveloped sense of responsibility develops, in which the codependents come to believe almost grandiosely that they are at the center of the universe, and all-powerful in a very unhealthy sense. This may partly explain why some codependent women always seem to end up in dysfunctional relationships with addicted men, and why some women appear to take on unhealthy or impaired men as "social work projects."

4. *Willingness to suffer.* Norwood (1985) suggests that many codependents ask, "if I suffer for you, will you love me?" (p. 47). This is the tendency to become a martyr. It is as if some satisfaction or reward is gained from suffering. They may not be happy, but they can claim to be superior (i.e., morally, emotionally, or socially) to their impaired spouse (Norwood, 1985). They can also claim to be superior to others who desert the alcoholic/addict. Because many codependents grew up in chemically dependent families, they do not recognize that they are suffering emotionally. Depression and low self-worth have been experienced for so long that these conditions seem normal.

5. *Inability to see how they contribute to the chemical abuse.* Codependents are typically resistant to change. They become immobilized by their own sense of guilt. Leaving the alcoholic/addict is not an option, because they fear being overwhelmed by guilt feelings. These feelings make self-examination very painful; in fact, codependents may develop a great deal of secondary anxiety about feeling guilty. From a systems perspective, these beliefs and feelings preserve the family balance, but they blind the codependents from seeing their own role in maintaining the drinking or drugging.

I once worked with an alcoholic husband and his wife who exhibited this interaction pattern. In the first few years of marriage, the couple had two children. She then established a successful career as a personnel director of a large company. She allowed her husband to quit his job, presumably to stay home to care for the kids. He welcomed the opportunity because he could drink whenever he wanted to do so. His drinking gradually became more and more abusive. The wife came to believe that she was the cause of his drinking (i.e., "He feels inadequate because of my success" and "I refuse to have sex with him any more"). This self-blame caused her to feel quite guilty about her husband's alcoholism. When I encouraged the couple to talk about their relationship, she defensively remarked, "I thought this was a disease that he had." She subsequently made repeated, though subtle, attempts to sabotage his recovery. It appeared to be very threatening for her to talk aloud about the role she played in her husband's drinking.

6. *Difficulty in viewing the relationship problem with objectivity.* Frequently codependents are so guilt-ridden, frustrated, and angry that they can only see their relationship problems in moralistic terms. They have a strong tendency to blame either themselves or the alcoholic/addict. It is often difficult for a codependent to "frame up" the problem as one of faulty learning, distorted communication, or a disease. The counselor should attempt to help codependents stop blaming themselves, the alcoholic/addict, or others. Rather, the focus should be on solutions.

7. *Fear of change.* Typically, codependents fear and resist change. Again, from a systems perspective, codependents may have an emotional investment in the alcoholic's/addict's continued drinking/drug use. These are almost always unconscious desires. They may fear change (i.e., abstinence/recovery) because they (a) do not want assertive, sober loved ones; (b) may find something attractive, risky, or even sexy about the alcoholic's/addict's intoxicated behavior; (c) may be financially dependent on the substance abuser, and fear that divorce or other disruption would come with sobriety; (d) may want to avoid sexual relations, which would resume with sobriety; or (e) expect some family conflict or secret (e.g., incest) to emerge during sobriety.

Cognitive Distortions in Codependency

Certain maladaptive beliefs tend to be common among codependents. It would be appropriate to explore the extent to which each of the following beliefs prevail in codependent clients' self-talk. Helping them change debilitating internal dialogues will allow them to tend better to their own emotional needs. Some examples of dysfunctional thinking include the following:

1. I can't live without my mate (child, parent, etc.).
2. I must stay with my mate.

3. I should be able to change my mate.
4. I have the power to upset him/her.
5. I am worthless without him/her.
6. It is horrible when my mate is upset or drinking.
7. I can't stand his/her drinking.
8. My needs are less important than those of my mate.
9. My mate could not live without me.
10. It is better to stay in pain than to attempt change.
11. If I only behaved better, my mate would drink less.
12. My mate drinks because there is something wrong with me.
13. There is something terribly wrong with me, and I must hide it from others.
14. I do not deserve to have a satisfying, loving relationship.
15. Because of the way I was raised as a child, I cannot now change myself.
16. If my mate would stop drinking, our relationship would be perfect.
17. If I loved my mate more, he/she would drink less.

Beattie's Model of Codependency

In the popular self-help book entitled *Co-dependent No More* (1987), Beattie sketches a model of codependency. It consists of the following four dynamics:

1. Codependency is a process in which life becomes increasingly unmanageable.
2. The unmanageability occurs when the codependent is unable to detach (emotionally) from the alcoholic or addict.
3. The inability to detach (enmeshment) causes the codependent to become obsessed with controlling the addict's behavior.
4. The obsession leads the codependent to assume responsibility for events that are not actually under his/her control.

Furthermore, Beattie (1987) has identified six unspoken rules of co-dependency, all of which are linked to a lack of self-worth:

1. It's not OK for me to feel.
2. It's not OK for me to have problems.
3. It's not OK for me to have fun.
4. I'm not lovable.

5. I'm not good enough.
6. If people act bad or crazy, I'm to blame.

Enabling and Codependency

The issues of enabling and codependency are often intertwined within the same individuals. However, enabling behavior does occur among people who are not codependents. Enabling is a *behavior* that protects substance abusers from the undesirable consequences of their behavior. Enabling does not necessarily require an ongoing, established relationship. In contrast, codependency is a dysfunctional relationship pattern involving a chemically dependent partner.

The example of a police officer and a drunken driver may illustrate the distinction between the two concepts. A police officer can "enable" a drunken driver by simply not arresting him/her. The officer may want to get off work on time, or may simply want to avoid the hassle of an arrest and all the accompanying paperwork. In either case, the officer has no personal relationship with the impaired driver, and thus cannot be described as a "codependent." However, the officer behaves in an "enabling" manner.

In addition, many institutions and workplaces engage in enabling, without being codependent. Colleges and universities are good examples. At one Midwestern university, a large group of intoxicated students blockaded a street adjacent to campus, started large bonfires that led to several houses' burning down, and then bombarded firefighters with bricks and rocks upon their arrival on the scene. Police arrested dozens of students for their role in the incident. The district attorney's office declined to prosecute, however, saying that it was a disciplinary matter for the university to address. Unfortunately, the university likewise declined to become involved, saying that the incident occurred off campus and thus was not under its jurisdiction. Both the district attorney's office and the university thus became enablers of the student body's drinking problem!

Rewards Gained by Codependents

It is easy to understand why enabling occurs: The enabler is motivated out of a desire to avoid conflict. The problems created by the substance abuser are "smoothed over" and are not confronted. This is much less anxiety-provoking than challenging the alcoholic/addict, or applying some type of disciplinary sanction.

The rewards for staying in a codependent relationship are much less apparent. In fact, many inexperienced professionals are amazed at the amount of suffering codependents are willing to endure, and have a difficult time understanding why they do not simply leave the alcoholic/addict. Yet a deeper, more thoughtful examination reveals that codependents do attain rewards by staying in dysfunctional relationships. Codependents come to affirm their self-worth by "carrying the cross" of other persons' addiction (or other destructive behavior). They may quietly believe that because they suffer, they are special and important. This self-perception represents a misguided grandiosity, which is essentially a shield against feelings, personal inadequacy, and low self-esteem. Accordingly, professionals counseling codependents may find the advice presented in Box 6.2 useful for their clients.

BOX 6.2. Advice Commonly Given to the Codependent

1. Realize that you are in exceedingly difficult circumstances. Sometimes you may feel angry, frustrated, helpless, afraid, powerless, and enraged. Your loved one or friend may seem helpless and pathetic at certain times, and at other times stubborn and resistant. The person has come to have great power despite this seeming contradiction—and he/she doesn't even realize it. Naturally you feel confused and distraught.

2. Accept the fact that there are no quick or easy answers or cures to an alcohol/drug problem. Psychotherapists and physicians cannot work "magic." If your loved one/friend is to recover, then he/she must make changes in attitudes and behaviors. Also, the family must be willing to make some attitude and behavior changes to accommodate your loved one's new insights and growth.

3. Provide your loved one with support and encouragement, but also take care of yourself. Do not sacrifice yourself for your loved one/friend. You accomplish nothing except feeling emotionally drained and resentful. Make time for enjoyable activities and fun for the family—it sends an important message to the sufferer and gives the family/friends needed relief. Also, continue your interests and activities outside the family and encourage the person with the alcohol/drug problem to do the same.

---

4. Give up the concept of blaming. It is not useful or realistic to blame either yourself or the person with the alcohol/drug problem. No one is at fault. Guilt and blame are immobilizing and get in the way of recovery. However, it is important to recognize that recovery is the responsibility of the person with the alcohol/drug problem. It is equally important to recognize that you have responsibility to become aware of the ways you may be "enabling" (facilitating) or participating in the problem.

5. Encourage your loved one/friend to get into a Twelve-Step program (AA or NA) and/or supportive counseling. Do not hesitate out of fear that he/she will hate you or become increasingly ill. If the person is over 18, you need to admit that you have no control over whether he/she will or will not get help. Only he/she can choose to be helped. You do, however, have control over how you participate in the problems.

6. Don't be overprotective. For example, if the person is upset about school, relationships, or work, it is his/her responsibility to take care of the problem. Don't try to take care of the problem. Don't try to take care of it for him/her. Do not attempt to protect the person by giving him/her the power to avoid situations that may be distressing. Experiencing and dealing with uncomfortable and unpleasant feelings and situations is part of life and recovery.

7. Develop a dialogue with the person about issues other than drinking and drugging. Don't tie your caring to lectures about stopping the alcohol/drug use. Verbally and physically express honest love and affection to him/her. The person needs to feel appreciated for who he/she is, not for what he/she does.

8. Avoid attempts to control the person's use of alcohol/drugs. Such power struggles are "no-win" battles and will only reinforce an adversarial relationship. Also, he/she will be less able to perceive you as caring if you engage in such battles. Recovery from alcohol/drug dependence is his/her responsibility.

9. Constructive communications is very important. Do not make statements such as "You are ruining the whole family" or "Why are you doing this to us?" Instead, helpful comments may be such statements as "I am concerned about your drinking," "I'm frustrated with my inability to help you," or "I wish you would seek out professional help."

10. Participate in family therapy or an Al-Anon support group to work through your feelings during this emotionally charged period. Don't isolate yourself. A support group or psychotherapy can help you deal with yourself in relationship to the chemically dependent family member or friend. Recovery is a process. The

duration varies, depending upon the individual and the circumstances. Be kind to yourself.

Note. Adapted from a rehabilitation program handout. Author unknown.

Codependency and Adult Children of Alcoholics: Useful Concepts or Fads?

The two closely related concepts of "codependency" and "adult children of alcoholics" (ACOAs) have emerged from the self-help (popular) literature (Woititz, 1983). Only in recent years has there been much scientific scrutiny of these issues (Alterman, Searles, & Hall, 1989; Seefeldt & Lyon, 1992; Sher, 1991). Although the codependency/ACOA movement has maintained that codependents and ACOAs suffer from unique emotional patterns and problems, research to date has not supported their contention (Seefeldt & Lyon, 1992). For example, Alterman et al. (1989) found no differences between children of alcoholic fathers and control subjects on a variety of personality variables, mental health problems, and alcohol-related measures. The researchers warned against stereotyping ACOAs as necessarily having a special set of characterics or problems. A study by Seefeldt and Lyon (1992) reached essentially the same conclusion. They examined three groups: non-ACOAs ($n = 93$), ACOAs not in treatment ($n = 36$), and ACOAs in treatment ($n = 18$). Subjects were assessed on 11 different personality variables that Woititz (1983) describes as essential features of ACOAs. Seefeldt and Lyon (1992) found no significant differences among the three groups on any of the variables. In fact, the ability of the 11 variables to classify subjects correctly into the three groups was only slightly better than random assignment.

Researchers have attributed the popularity of the codependency/ ACOA movement to a tendency known as the "Barnum effect" (Goodman, 1987; Seefeldt & Lyon, 1992). Named after the huckster P. T. Barnum, this is "the tendency to interpret a description that applies to everyone as being particularly valid to one's self" (Seefeldt & Lyon, 1992, p. 588). It is argued that many descriptions of codependents and ACOAs are similiar to those used by fortune tellers and astrologers. At first they seem specific, but in reality they are actually quite vague and applicable to almost all persons. If future research does indeed confirm that a Barnum effect is in operation, it is likely that the "codependency" and "ACOA" concepts (at least in the forms described by some self-help authors) will fade in importance, similar to other "pop psychology" fads (primal scream, est, popularized metaphysics, transcendental meditation, etc.).

PARENTING STYLES THAT MAY PREDISPOSE CHILDREN TO ALCOHOLISM

Lawson et al. (1983) have identified four parenting styles that they believe make children vulnerable to developing alcohol problems in adolescence or later in life. These patterns were not derived from empirical research, but from the clinical practice of Lawson and his colleagues. The parenting styles assume that familial alcoholism results from family dynamics and learning. They do not include the possibility of genetic transmission of the disorder from parents to children. However, even with these limitations, the four patterns form a useful model for understanding how parenting practices can be linked to the development of alcoholism. (No such model has been developed to date for parenting styles that may predispose children to the use of illicit drugs.)

Alcoholic Parents

Children of alcoholics may learn alcoholic behavior by the process of modeling (Lawson et al., 1983). By observing an alcoholic parent, a child may learn that drinking is an acceptable way to cope with life's problems. Drinking becomes an option for the child who *covertly identifies* with the alcoholic parent. Although some children may reject alcoholic parents and grow up to be abstainers, other children, particularly boys of alcoholic fathers, may model themselves after the alcoholics. According to Lawson et al. (1983), it may be the only way they have to tell their fathers that they love them; other means of expressing affection may be unavailable. Lawson et al. (1983) refer to this dynamic as "See, I love you. I'm just like you." Daughters of alcoholic fathers may commit a similar "love act" by marrying alcoholic mates (Lawson et al., 1983). The message here is similar: "See, Daddy, I love you. I married someone just like you." Such women typically do not recognize their fathers' or husbands' drinking as pathological (Lawson et al., 1983).

Teetotaler Parents

Teetotaler parents not only do not drink, but also condemn those who do drink (Lawson et al., 1983). Teetotalers hold strong moral or religious beliefs that drinking is immoral or evil. Parents who hold such views tend to see the world in a dichotomous fashion (i.e., right or wrong, good or bad, black or white), and are generally very demanding of their children in regard to moral conduct. Lawson et al. (1983) note that children of such parents are likely to hear the words "should," "shouldn't," "must," and "must not" with great frequency.

Children raised in such an environment invariably find that they cannot abide by their parents' prohibitions. This leads them to rebel in a variety of ways. Of course, one common way for teens to rebel in U.S. society is to abuse alcohol. Lawson et al. (1983) claim that it is not unusual for an alcoholic parent (typically the father) to be married to a teetotaler (typically the mother). In such a situation, a child may be especially vulnerable to alcohol or drug abuse.

Overdemanding Parents

Overdemanding parents set unrealistic expectations for their children. Lawson et al. (1983) believe that these parents are often attempting to live vicariously through their children (Lawson et al., 1983). Because of some perceived inadequacy in themselves, they demand that their children achieve things that they failed to accomplish. Frequently, these parents are themselves successful, at least in the eyes of others. However, they may judge themselves to be only adequate or average, especially in regard to their careers. In many cases, these parents feel as though they should have done better in life (Lawson et al., 1983). They believe they had potential that was not realized. The difference between an overdemanding parent and a teetotaler parent is that the former has high expectations in regard to academics, sports, or some other type of performance achievement, while the latter has high expectations about moral conduct.

Children raised in achievement-oriented families are likely to compare themselves to their parents or their siblings. It is almost inevitable that most of these children will develop feelings of inadequacy as a result (Lawson et al., 1983). They may turn to alcohol or drugs in an effort to cope with these pressures. Substance abuse is a way of dealing with the fear of failure. For some youths, alcohol or drug abuse may also symbolize a rejection of their parents' values of achievement and productivity. Lawson et al. (1983) also note that many children of overdemanding parents will not become substance abusers, but will instead develop some other unhealthy behavior pattern (e.g., eating disorders, depression, anxiety disorders, compulsive gambling, etc.).

Overly Protective Parents

The final parenting style in the model is that of overly protective parents. Children of these parents are never allowed an opportunity to develop a sense of self-worth (Lawson et al., 1983). They typically view themselves in a negative way. According to Lawson et al. (1983), after a childhood and adolescence of being "taken care of," they do not adjust well to the challenges of young adulthood. Overly protective parents may raise their children this way in order to feel needed. By prolonging their children's dependency, these parents bolster their own sense of worth.

As adults, children of overly protective parents may find it difficult to establish careers or hold jobs, as well as to establish long-term intimate relationships. Furthermore, they may have poorly developed communication skills, appear passive, and have little confidence in their abilities (Lawson et al., 1983). These children often remain overly dependent on their parents through the third decade of life. Together, these characteristics predispose the individuals to substance abuse (Lawson et al., 1983).

CHILDREN OF ALCOHOLIC FAMILIES

Despite recent skepticism about the usefulness of the ACOA concept (see above), it is quite true that children growing up in alcoholic families often experience emotional difficulties. Charles Deutsch (1982), in his book *Broken Bottles, Broken Dreams*, describes what growing up in such a household is like from a child's point of view. He relies on extensive interviews with children from alcoholic homes. Deutsch (1982) pays particular attention to three conditions such children experience:

1. Inconsistency, insecurity, and fear.
2. Anger and hate.
3. Guilt and blame.

Each one is described in turn.

Inconsistency, Insecurity, and Fear

According to Deutsch (1982), inconsistency is the hallmark of most actively alcoholic parents. They demonstrate it both when intoxicated and when sober. They can change moods dramatically, swinging from being warm, caring, and jovial to angry and frustrated within minutes. Because the children do not know what to anticipate, they tend to be insecure. The lack of parental predictability breeds distrust and uncertainty. As a result, many children adopt the "don't feel, don't trust, don't talk" rule. As Deutsch (1982) reports one child saying, "we learned to walk on eggshells without cracking a single one" (p. 42).

Domestic violence is reported in many alcoholic homes. A child's insecurity and fear are heightened considerably when an alcoholic parent acts out in a violent way. Deutsch (1982) indicates that the target of the violence does not seem to matter. The alcoholic who only destroys property instills as much fear as the alcoholic who strikes family members. Interestingly, a child often reports that the nonalcoholic spouse is the more violent and feared parent. In such a case, the nonalcoholic spouse may be attempting to force the alcoholic to stop drinking, or may be ventilating pent-up anger and frustration about the drinking problem. Deutsch (1982) quotes one child as saying:

> "She tried to kill us, actually kill us. We all had our turns fighting her. Everybody used to say, 'ignore her,' but you can't ignore her when she comes after you with a knife, you know? One time she choked me, I mean, she was on top of me, choking me, and I would have died; I felt like I was dying. My father came in—this was really great—he had a cigarette in his mouth, he came in and my little sister was screaming—it was just me and my little sister at home. My mother had me and she was, I mean, I was blue, I thought I was dying, and my sister was standing there screaming. My father came in and threw the cigarette on the floor. And 'cause we were in my mother's bedroom, it started a fire and later our carpet had to be thrown out. My father came in and pulled my mother off me, and I just ran out of the house. When I came back five hours later, she told me, 'Now you're all right, you're all right.'" (p. 44)

Avoiding conflict becomes the primary concern of children in alcoholic homes. Children become preoccupied with not upsetting the alcoholic or violent parent. Conflict is avoided at all costs. One child quoted by Deutsch (1982) described it this way:

"There were things we all did just to placate him, like eating together whether we were hungry or not. We were scared a good deal of the time. One time, he demanded his dinner and my mother threw cereal boxes at him. I sat there thinking, 'now that was stupid, why the hell did you do that?' I wished she hadn't done it because I knew I'd have to keep him off her." (p. 44)

Anger and Hate

Though it may not be difficult to understand why children from such homes hate their parents, the children themselves often find these feelings unacceptable. Just as the alcoholics may deny a drinking problem, the children may deny hateful feelings toward their parents. The denial is unconscious; many of these children are simply unaware of these feelings. The "unacceptableness" stems from cultural norms that prohibit children from hating their parents.

The children's anger and hate may be directed at others or at themselves. It is not usually directed at the alcoholic parents, because that would be too dangerous. Deutsch (1982) quotes one 7-year-old boy as saying, "Yeah, sometimes I yell at my teddy bear and sometimes I yell at my teacher when I'm angry at my father. And I know she doesn't like it" (p. 46). Many of these children develop guilt feelings about hating their alcoholic parents. They are unaware that their thoughts and feelings, given the family circumstances, are normal. They feel especially guilty about fantasies they may have in which the alcoholics are killed, die, or just disappear. One adolescent girl confided to Deutsch (1982): "all the time, I used to lay in bed at night and plot how to kill her without getting caught and stuff. I was a mean kid" (p. 47).

Guilt and Blame

Young children are naturally egocentric. They tend to believe that they are the cause of all that goes on around them. Thus, they tend to blame themselves for their parents' problems; this is particularly true of parents' drinking problems. Alcoholic parents will often reinforce the children's self-blame with such rationalizations as these: "I'll stop drinking when you behave the way you're supposed to," "Why do you think I drink so much in the first place?", "You kids drive me to drink," or "I can't relax—you kids drive me crazy."

Nonalcoholic parents also teach these children to believe (falsely) that they cause their alcoholic parents to drink. Deutsch (1982) indicates that many children in alcoholic homes hear their nonalcoholic parents instruct them, "Please go with Daddy, it will make him happy," or "You have to be quiet today, Mom seems nervous." Implied in these instructions is the notion that the children have power over their parents' drinking—that they can increase it or decrease it through their actions. Deutsch (1982) believes that these children take this notion of personal power into adulthood. As adults, they continue to feel possessed of power and capable of controlling others. These needs to dominate and control others lead to dysfunctional adult relationships at home and work. As noted earlier, many such people refer to themselves today as ACOAs. At ACOA self-help meetings, power and control issues are often the focus of group discussion.

ROLE BEHAVIOR

At several points in this chapter, the chemically dependent family has been described as a closed social system. The family tends to isolate itself, its boundaries are rigid, and outside influences are not allowed to penetrate. This kind of closed, rigid system fosters tension. The tension is managed, in part, by each family member's adopting a specific, predictable role. The roles serve to divert attention away from the alcoholic/addict, or to reduce the family tension in total.

Family theory writers have created a variety of schemes for classifying the types of role behavior in the chemically dependent family. In the discussion below, one of the major classification schemes is presented. It includes the following:

1. The chemically dependent person.
2. The chief enabler.
3. The family hero.
4. The scapegoat.
5. The lost child.
6. The mascot.

In this scheme, the family is assumed to be a nuclear one, with two parents and four or more children. Also, because one of the parents is assumed to be chemically dependent, the scheme emphasizes the adaptive roles of the children in the family. Furthermore, it should be noted that while some chemically dependent families have members who clearly fall into a specific role, other families will have members who exhibit characteristics of more than one role; others will have members who shift from role to role as time passes; and in the life of some families certain roles will never appear. Thus, the roles are probably too "neat" for most chemically dependent families. However, for sake of discussion, each one is presented in its stereotypical form.

The Chemically Dependent Person

Within a family systems perspective, the chemically dependent member is not diseased but is playing a role, which is to act irresponsibly. This role has a homeostatic function. Typically, it serves to suppress more basic marital conflict, or to divert attention away from more threatening family issues.

An important aspect of the chemically dependent role is emotional detachment from the spouse and the children. One consequence of this distancing is the abandonment of parental power. The power is often assumed by the nondependent spouse and an older child (to be described below). The "first love" of the alcoholic or addict becomes the bottle or the drug. Over time, the self-administration of the substance becomes the central activity in this person's life; family life diminishes in importance.

The Chief Enabler

The second role is often referred to as the "chief enabler," or simply the "enabler." Often, numerous enablers exist in the family; however, the chief enabler is usually the nondependent spouse. Enabling, as discussed earlier, is a behavior that inadvertently supports the addiction process by helping an alcoholic or addict avoid the natural consequences of irresponsible behavior. Most addicts have at least one enabler in their lives, and many will have three, four, or more to keep them going.

From a family systems perspective, the chief enabler reduces tension in the family (i.e., maintains family balance) by "smoothing things over"—that is, making things right. The enabler often faces a dilemma: If he/she (more often she) does not bail the alcoholic/addict out of a bad, sometimes dangerous situation (e.g., a drunk husband alone at a bar), the substance abuser could do serious harm to self or others. A wife of an alcoholic once told me that she knew she was enabling her husband by picking him up from their snow-covered yard, but she stated that she had no choice, since otherwise he would have frozen to death.

In many cases, the chief enabler is unaware that the enabling behavior is contributing to the progression of the alcoholism or drug addiction. Enablers believe that they are simply being helpful, and acting to hold their families together. Though well-intended, their efforts often have destructive long-term consequences for their chemically dependent spouses (Deutsch, 1982).

The Family Hero

The role of the "family hero" is usually adopted by the oldest child. This role is also referred to as the "parental child," the "superstar," and the "goody two shoes" (Deutsch, 1982). This child attempts to do everything right. He/she is the family's high achiever, and as such appears quite ambitious and responsible. Given the family circumstances (i.e., a chemically dependent parent), the child is often admired for excelling under difficult conditions.

The family hero often takes on parental responsibilities that the chemically dependent parent gave up. He/she provides care for younger siblings by cooking for them, getting them ready for school, putting them to bed, doing laundry, and so on. The nondependent spouse (i.e., the chief enabler) usually does not have much time for these chores because his/her time is divided between working and caring for the alcoholic or addicted spouse.

Family heroes frequently do well in academic and athletic pursuits (Deutsch, 1982). They may be class presidents, honor students, starters on the basketball team, or the like. They are achievement-oriented and frequently develop well-respected professional careers. Deutsch (1982) suggests that many of them later become "workaholics." Some researchers even claim that family heroes are prone to "Type A" behavior as adults (Deutsch, 1982). This is a behavior pattern characterized by competitiveness, hostility, time urgency, and an obsession with work, among other features. Such individuals may be susceptible to stress-related disease (e.g., stomach ulcer, coronary heart disease).

The family hero reduces tension in the family simply by doing everything "right." The hero is the source of pride for the family, inspiring desperately needed hope and giving the family something to feel good about. The hero's accomplishments are distinctions around which the family members can rally and say to themselves, "We're not so bad after all."

The Scapegoat

The "scapegoat" role is often adopted by the second oldest child. The scapegoat can be viewed as the alter ego of the family hero (Deutsch, 1982). This child does very little right and is quite rebellious, perhaps even antisocial. Scapegoats may be involved in fights, theft, or other trouble at school or in the community; they are often labeled "juvenile delinquents." Male scapegoats may be violent, while female scapegoats may express themselves by running away or engaging in promiscuous sexual activity. Scapegoats of both genders most often abuse alcohol and drugs themselves.

A child in the scapegoat role seem to identify with the chemically dependent parent, not only in terms of substance abuse but in other ways as well (e.g., attitude toward authority, attitude toward the opposite sex, vocational interests, etc.). The scapegoat typically feels inferior to the family hero; still, the two of them are usually very close emotionally, despite the differences in their behavior. This special bond may continue throughout adulthood.

This child is referred to as the "scapegoat" because he/she is the object of the chemically dependent parent's misdirected frustration and rage. The child may be abused both emotionally and physically by this parent. This is especially true when the chemically dependent parent is the father and the scapegoat his son. In effect, the scapegoat becomes, in common parlance, "his father's son." That is, the son, filled with his father's anger and rage, adopts his father's self-destructive and antisocial tendencies. He models himself after his father despite hating him.

The scapegoat expresses the family's frustration and anger. The child in this role maintains family balance by directing some of the blame from the chemically dependent parent to himself/herself. This allows the chemically dependent parent to blame someone else for his/her own drinking and drugging. It also shields the chemically dependent parent from some of the blame and resentment that would have been directed at him/her; this process of diversion allows the addiction to progress further (Deutsch, 1982).

The Lost Child

Even in functional families, the middle children are thought to get less attention than their siblings, and seem less certain of their contribution to the family. This tendency is exacerbated in chemically dependent families (Deutsch, 1982). The "lost child" may be a middle child but may also be the youngest. The chief characteristic of the lost child is seeking to avoid conflict at all costs. Such children tend to feel powerless and are described as "very quiet," "emotionally disturbed," "depressed," "isolated," "withdrawn," and so on. These children tend to be forgotten, as they are very shy. They are followers, not leaders. They engage in much fantasy. If they stand out in school in any way, it is by virtue of poor attendance (Deutsch, 1982). If asked to do something they fear doing, they may pretend not to have heard the instructions or claim not to understand them (Deutsch, 1982). These behaviors point to a great deal of insecurity.

According to Deutsch (1982), the lost child is probably the most difficult child in a dysfunctional family to help. He/she may not have close friends or other systems outside the family for emotional support. Also, the child's behavior is usually not disruptive in school; hence, teachers and counselors do not identify him/her as needy.

As adults, lost children exhibit a variety of mental health problems. They may complain of anxiety and/or depression and obtain psychotherapy. They have difficulty with developmental transitions because they fear taking risks. Thus, they may put off making decisions about careers or where to live. They may also back out of intimate relationships once someone starts to get too close. According to Deutsch (1982), lost children may or may not abuse alcohol and drugs. If they do, their drug of choice is usually different from that used by their chemically dependent parents.

The lost child helps maintain balance in the family by simply disappearing—that is, by not requiring any attention. In essence, the youngster in this role supports the family equilibrium by causing no new problems and requiring minimal attention. In the extreme, the lost child will think, "if I killed myself, Mom and Dad would have one less thing to worry about" (Deutsch, 1982).

The Mascot

The last commonly described role is that of the "mascot." This role is also referred to as the "family clown," or simply the "clown." The youngest child in the family often adopts the role of the mascot. Everyone in the family likes the mascot and is comfortable with having him/her around. The family usually views the mascot as the most fragile and vulnerable; thus, he/she tends to be the object of protection. Deutsch (1982) notes that even the chemically dependent parent treats the mascot with kindness most of the time.

Mascots often act silly and make jokes, even at their own expense. The clownish behavior acts as a defense against feelings of anxiety and inadequacy. They often have a dire need for approval from others. As adults, they are very likeable but appear anxious. Deutsch (1982) believes that they may self-medicate with alcohol and/or tranquilizers.

The child in the mascot role helps maintain family homeostasis by bringing laughter and fun into the home. By "clowning around" and making jokes, he/she brightens the family atmosphere, becoming a counterbalance against the tension that is so prevalent and oppressive in dysfunctional families. The mascot may be the one family member that no one has a complaint about.

RESEARCH: FAMILY FACTORS ASSOCIATED WITH ADOLESCENT ALCOHOL AND DRUG USE

A large number of studies have examined the family factors that are linked with adolescent substance abuse. This brief literature review highlights some of the important findings from these studies.

It appears that family values are related to teenage substance abuse. Jessor and Jessor (1977) assessed mothers' religiosity, tolerance of deviance, and traditional beliefs. They found that adolescent problem behaviors, including abusive drinking and illegal drug abuse, were less prevalent in families in which the mothers were highly religious, conventional, and traditional. The teens with the greatest prevalence of problem behaviors (e.g., alcohol and drug abuse) had mothers whose ideology de-emphasized religion and traditional social values.

Several studies have linked adolescent substance abuse to single-parent families. For example, Burnside, Baer, McLaughlin, and Pokorny (1986) asked a large number of high school students about both their drinking practices and their family structure. The study found that teens in single-parent and stepparent families reported greater alcohol consumption than those in intact families. Furthermore, the parents in the nonintact families used more alcohol than the parents in the intact families, and the adolescents' alcohol use was positively correlated with that of their parents. The relative influence of nonintact family status versus parental alcohol use in predicting adolescent alcohol consumption was assessed as well; it was determined that nonintact status had an effect on teen drinking that was independent of parental alcohol use.

Family size, sibling spacing, and birth order are family structure variables that have been thought to be linked to the development of alcoholism. However, the findings in this area are equivocal at present. Barnes (1990), in a review of this literature, concludes that there is little evidence to support the notion that birth order influences alcoholism. The issue of sibling spacing has not been adequately addressed, either. Research findings regarding family size are somewhat clearer; it appears that a disproportionate number of alcoholics come from large families. Zucker (1976) has offered explanations for this relationship: Larger families may exhibit diluted socialization effects, more authoritarian discipline, looser parental controls, or greater sibling rivalries. Any one or a combination of these conditions may explain why a relatively large percentage of alcoholics come from larger families.

There exists convincing evidence that teenage drinking practices are linked with parental drinking behavior (Barnes, 1990). It appears that children and teens learn to drink (or not to drink) through the process of imitation. Young people tend to model their behavior (including drinking) after those that they observe, especially those they are close to. Kandel, Kessler, and Marguiles (1978), for instance, found that parents' use of hard liquor was a moderately good predictor of their adolescents' initiation to the use of hard liquor. In other words, the heavier the parental consumption, the earlier the teens began to use it. Data from a study by Harburg, Davis, and Caplan (1982) indicate that children tend to imitate their perception of their parents' drinking. Moreover, boys particularly imitate their perception of their fathers' drinking, as do girls with their mothers' drinking. However, when parental alcohol consumption was perceived to be extreme (i.e., unusual), imitation decreased; here, "extreme" meant either abstinence or heavy drinking by parents. This effect is consistent with that found by Barnes, Farrell, and Cairns (1986) in which abstaining parents had not only a high proportion of abstaining children, but also a high proportion of heavy-drinking children. It appears that children of abstaining parents lack adult role models for sensible drinking. Thus, if they do initiate alcohol use, they have a tendency to drink in a binge-like manner. The reason why this heavy-drinking subgroup initiates use in the first place (when another subgroup of children of abstaining parents abstain) is unclear at this point.

During the teenage years, it can be expected that the peer group will have more influence on adolescent behavior as the family (parental) influence diminishes somewhat. Numerous studies have examined the interaction between peer influences and family influences as they relate to teen drinking. For example, Barnes and Windle (1987) have collected data showing that adolescents who value peer opinions, as opposed to parental opinions, are at heightened risk for alcohol and drug abuse and for other problem behaviors. Kandel and Andrews (1987) found that parental closeness discouraged teen drug use and promoted the choice of non-drug-using friends. This finding is consistent with those of other studies, which have found that adolescents who are close to their parents are less likely to associate with deviant peers (Barnes, 1990). Similarly, Dishion and Loeber (1985) found that lack of parental monitoring had an indirect effect on teen substance abuse by increasing the probability that a teen would "hang out" with deviant peers.

According to Barnes (1990), one of the most neglected areas of research on the development of adolescent substance abuse is that of sibling influence. Though relatively few studies have been done, "siblings may constitute a potentially powerful combination of peer and family socialization agent" (Barnes, 1990, p. 151). In a sample of 9th- and 10th-grade students, Brook, Whiteman, Gordon, and Brenden (1983) investigated older brothers' influence on younger siblings' drug use. It was found that having an older brother who used marijuana had a significant effect on a younger sibling's substance use, even after nonfamily influence was controlled for. Needle et al. (1986) conducted a study in which information was obtained independently from both younger and older siblings. They found that the younger siblings' frequency of drug use was predicted by older siblings' and peers' substance use (each remained significant after the other variable was controlled for). In addition, older siblings, as well as peers, were sources of information about drugs and companions in the use of drugs with their younger siblings. Further research is needed in this area. Though this is not well substantiated at this point, it is not unreasonable to speculate that older siblings in the family may be a potent factor in determining whether younger siblings initiate the use of alcohol and drugs.

THE PROCESS OF FAMILY THERAPY

As indicated at the beginning of this chapter, "family therapy" is a generic term that describes professional services aimed at helping families. Family therapy may, or may not take a systems approach, depending, of course, on the theoretical orientation of the therapist. Rosenberg (1981–1982) has described the process of family therapy with a chemically dependent family, regardless of its theoretical bent. The phases of this process are described below.

Random Phase

In the initial stage of therapy, the family members will typically behave in an unstructured and hostile manner. There may be confusion as to why they are in therapy. In addition, there are few, if any, attempts to communicate about problems with each other or with the therapist. Essentially, the family members exhibit denial. They may recognize that there is an alcohol or drug problem within the family, but they are unaware that it has anything to do with interpersonal problems. It is seen only as an "alcohol problem" or "drug problem," and nothing more. In other words, it is understood in simplistic terms and not linked to more fundamental family conflict.

Recrimination Phase

In the recrimination phase, the family involves itself in accusations and counteraccusations (Rosenberg, 1981–1982). Family members try to engage the counselor in consensus rather than counseling; that is, they make repeated efforts to get the therapist to take sides. Frequently, members will resurrect "horror stories" from years past to convince the counselor who is right and who is wrong. In this phase, it is the task of the therapist to remain neutral. Typically, the family divides itself, with the nondependent members pitted against the alcoholic or addicted member(s). The natural tendency of the therapist is to ally himself/herself with the nondependent members. This is an impulse that must be resisted.

Policing Phase

In the next phase, the family begins to test the limits that the therapist has established for the therapy sessions. For example, certain members may miss sessions; the family may show up late for an appointment; they may make attempts to talk about the recent use of alcohol or drugs by a member (when they have been instructed not to for the time being); or a certain member may appear with alcohol on his/her breath. Rosenberg (1981–1982) indicates that a counselor who is unable to deal assertively with these behaviors will usually lose control of the direction of therapy. Furthermore, the therapist should understand that the "testing" is an effort by the family to avoid dealing with more sensitive, emotionally charged issues. By complaining about and challenging the rules, the family members can put off wrestling with conflict among themselves. Unless the therapist remains steadfast in enforcing the rules, the family progress will stop or become fixated in this phase.

Realization Phase

In the realization phase, therapeutic work or progress *begins* (Rosenberg, 1981–1982). All of the prior complaining and "testing" were simply posturings of sorts to set the stage for actual work. Ideally, the therapist and the chemically dependent member begin to develop a therapeutic relationship, and this same member begins to communicate more effectively with the other family members. A transition occurs in which therapy discussion becomes more focused on family problems and concerns, instead of on the rules of therapy. Another noteworthy shift is the family's efforts to identify solutions that address the needs of all members.

The task of the realization phase is to help family members develop a positive family image (i.e., "to feel better about us") and an expanded frame of reference (i.e., to be more adaptive and flexible in allowing everyone to get his/her needs met) (Rosenberg, 1981–1982). To accomplish this, the family will have to struggle through a hierarchy of negative feelings. According to Rosenberg (1981–1982), the family's struggle is analogous to climbing a flight of stairs. The therapist's role is to provide encouragement and to gently push the members through the traps of comfort, relief, and satisfaction that they will encounter during the struggle. Figure 6.5 illustrates this process.

The family moves through confusion, then anxiety, frustration, fear, anger, hostility, and resentment (Rosenberg, 1981–1982). The effective resolution of these emotions is opposed by such conditions as isolation, denial, resistance, and the desire to maintain the status

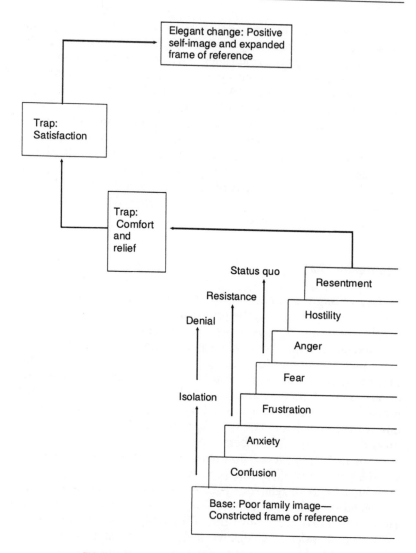

FIGURE 6.5. Family change and growth process.

quo. The combined force of these conditions works against the family's attempts to achieve "elegant change" (see Figure 6.5). They can be overcome with struggle and perseverance. Realistically, though, most families discontinue therapy before they achieve elegant change; many will terminate when they find some measure of relief or satisfaction. Though Rosenberg (1981–1982) identifies these as traps, this level of progress is often characterized by a significant decrease in substance abuse. Thus, therapists themselves can find satisfaction in helping chemically dependent families, even though the families may not resolve all interpersonal conflicts.

It should also be noted that some families will never get to the realization phase at all. That is, they will never begin doing any significant therapeutic work. Generally, these are families that have been dysfunctional and in disarray for many years. The children may be near or into adulthood and perceive their primary need as escaping rather than reuniting with their families of origin. Often the coping strategies and maladaptive roles are so rigidly defined that these seriously impaired families find therapy exceedingly difficult.

SUMMARY

It is imperative that substance abuse counselors be familiar with family systems concepts. As the primary social unit, the family exerts a powerful influence over an individual's drinking or drugging behavior. The systems emphasis on reciprocal causality is unique among theories of addictive behavior. It proposes that substance abuse is functional in a certain sense; that it is a manifestation of deeper conflict; and that it helps the individual to minimize, distract from, or cope with interpersonal problems. An understanding of these dynamics is necessary if a counselor is to be an effective helper.

A word of caution about family systems concepts is also in order. Put simply, there is not much empirical support for the efficacy of this approach (Collins, 1990). Relatively few well-designed studies have tested the effectiveness of family systems therapy. It has been shown to be as effective as individual treatment, but less effective than a behavioral treatment (McCrady, Moreau, Paolino, & Longabaugh, 1982; McCrady, Paolino, Longabaugh, & Rossi, 1979). O'Farrell, Cutter, and Floyd (1985) report that a brief family systems intervention is just as effective as more prolonged and intensive treatment. Collins (1990) concludes a review of this literature by stating that "while descriptions of systems approaches to treating alcoholic families abound, the body of methodologically sound empirical research on systems approaches is limited" (p. 296). Considering the reputation of family systems concepts, the discrepancy between their prominence and their empirically established validity is conspicuous.

REVIEW QUESTIONS

1. What are "boundaries," "subsystems," "hierarchies," "family rules," and "homeostasis"?

2. What is meant by "reciprocal causality"?

3. How does a person's family of origin affect the person's mate selection and manner of child rearing?

4. How does a teen's fear of separation contribute to his/her abusing drugs?

5. What are "triads"? How do they spur substance abuse?

6. What is the "dance"?

7. What does Bowen mean by "differentiation of self"? What are characteristics of poorly differentiated persons and highly differentiated persons?

8. What does Bowen mean by "triangles"?

9. How does Bowen describe the development of the emotional system in the nuclear family?

10. What are the four common manifestations of marital fusion?

11. What does Bowen mean by "family projection process"?

12. What does Bowen mean by "emotional cutoff"?

13. What is "codependency"? What are its chief characteristics? What are some of its cognitive distortions?

14. What four dynamics make up Beattie's model of codependency?

15. How are enabling and codependency distinguished from each other?

16. What rewards are gained in a codependent relationship?

17. What are the criticisms of the codependency and "adult children of alcoholics" (ACOAs) concepts?

18. What four parenting styles predispose children to alcoholism?

19. What three emotional conditions are prevalent in the lives of children living with alcoholic parents?

20. What are the six roles that typically develop in chemically dependent families? How does each reduce family tension?

21. What family factors are linked to adolescent substance abuse?

22. According to Rosenberg, what are the four phases of therapy with alcoholic families? Is Rosenberg optimistic about the family's attempts to achieve "elegant change"?

REFERENCES

Alterman, A. I., Searles, J. S., & Hall, J. G. (1989). Failure to find differences in drinking behavior as a function of familial risk for alcoholism: A replication. *Journal of Abnormal Psychology, 98*, 50–53.

Barnard, C. P. (1981). *Families, alcoholism, and therapy.* Springfield, IL: Charles C Thomas.

Barnes, G. M. (1990). Impact of the family on adolescent drinking patterns. In R. L. Collins, K. E. Leonard, B. A. Miller, & J. S. Searles (Eds.), *Alcohol and the family: Research and clinical perspectives.* New York: Guilford Press.

Barnes, G. M., Farrell, M. P., & Cairns, A. L. (1986). Parental socialization factors and adolescent drinking behaviors. *Journal of Marriage and the Family, 48*, 27–36.

Barnes, G. M., & Windle, M. (1987). Family factors in adolescent alcohol and drug abuse. *Pediatrician: International Journal of Child and Adolescent Health, 14*, 13–18.

Beattie, M. (1987). *Co-dependent no more.* Center City, MN: Hazelden.

Bowen, M. (1976). Theory in the practice of psychotherapy. In P. J. Guerin (Ed.), *Family therapy: Theory and practice.* New York: Gardner Press.

Brook, J. S., Whiteman, M., Gordon, A. S., & Brenden, C. (1983). Older brother's influence on younger sibling's drug use. *Journal of Psychology, 114*, 83–90.

Burnside, M. A., Baer, P. E., McLaughlin, R. J., & Pokorny, A. D. (1986). Alcohol use by adolescents in disrupted families. *Alcoholism: Clinical and Experimental Research, 10*, 274–278.

Collins, R. L. (1990). Family treatment of alcohol abuse: Behavioral and systems perspectives. In R. L. Collins, K. E. Leonard, B. A. Miller, & J. S. Searles (Eds.), *Alcohol and the family: Research and clinical perspectives.* New York: Guilford Press.

Deutsch, C. (1982). *Broken bottles, broken dreams: Understanding and helping the children of alcoholics.* New York: Teachers College Press.

Dishion, T. J., & Loeber, R. (1985). Adolescent marijuana and alcohol use: The role of parents and peers revisited. *American Journal of Drug and Alcohol Abuse, 11*, 11–25.

Fogarty, T. (1976). Marital crisis. In P. J. Guerin (Ed.), *Family therapy: Theory and practice.* New York: Gardner Press.

Framo, J. L. (1976). Family of origin as a therapeutic resource for adults in marital and family therapy: You can and should go home again. *Family Process, 15*, 193–209.

Goodman, R. W. (1987). Adult children of alcoholics. *Journal of Counseling and Development, 66,* 162–163.

Harburg, E., Davis, D. R., & Caplan, R. (1982). Parent and offspring alcohol use. *Journal of Studies on Alcohol, 43,* 497–516.

Jessor, R., & Jessor, S. L. (1977). *Problem behavior and psychosocial development: A longitudinal study of youth.* New York: Academic Press.

Kandel, D. B., & Andrews, K. (1987). Processes of adolescent socialization by parents and peers. *International Journal of the Addictions, 22,* 319–342.

Kandel, D. B., Kessler, R. C., & Marguiles, R. Z. (1978). Antecedents of adolescent initiation into stages of drug use: A developmental analysis. In D. B. Kandel (Ed.), *Longitudinal research on drug use.* Washington, DC: Hemisphere.

Koffinke, C. (1991). Family recovery issues and treatment resources. In D. C. Daley & M. S. Raskin (Eds.), *Treating the chemically dependent and their families.* Newbury Park, CA: Sage.

Lawson, G., Peterson, J. S., & Lawson, A. (1983). *Alcoholism and the family: A guide to treatment and prevention.* Rockville, MD: Aspen.

McCrady, B. S., Moreau, J., Paolino, T. J., & Longabaugh, R. (1982). Joint hospitalization and couples therapy for alcoholism: A four year follow-up. *Journal of Studies on Alcohol, 43,* 1244–1250.

McCrady, B. S., Paolino, T. J., Longabaugh, R., & Rossi, J. (1979). Effects of joint hospital admission and couples' treatment for hospitalized alcoholics: A pilot study. *Addictive Behaviors, 4,* 155–165.

Needle, R., McCubbin, H., Wilson, M., Reineck, R., Lazar, A., & Mederer, H. (1986). Interpersonal influences in adolescent drug use: The role of older siblings, parents, and peers. *International Journal of the Addictions, 21,* 739–766.

Norwood, R. (1985). *Women who love too much.* New York: Simon & Schuster.

O'Farrell, T. J., Cutter, H. S., & Floyd, F. J. (1985). Evaluating behavioral marital therapy for male alcoholics: Effects of marital adjustment and communication from before to after treatment. *Behavior Therapy, 16,* 147–167.

Pearlman, S. (1988). Systems theory and alcoholism. In C. D. Chaudron & D. A. Wilkinson (Eds.), *Theories on alcoholism.* Toronto: Addiction Research Foundation.

Rosenberg, D. N. (1981–1982). Holistic therapy with alcoholism families. *Alcohol, Health, and Research World, 6,* 30–32.

Seefeldt, R. W. & Lyon, M. A. (1992). Personality characteristics of adult children of alcoholics. *Journal of Counseling and Development, 70,* 588–593.

Sher, K. (1991). *Children of alcoholics: A critical appraisal of theory and research.* Chicago: University of Chicago Press.

Stanton, M. D. (1980). A family theory of drug abuse. In D. J. Lettieri, M. Sayers, & H. W. Pearson (Eds.), *Theories on drug abuse: Selected contemporary perspectives* (DHHS Publication No. ADM 84-967). Washington, DC: U.S. Government Printing Office.

Steinglass, P. (1978). The conceptualization of marriage from a systems theory perspective. In T. J. Paolino, Jr., & B. S. McCrady (Eds.), *Marriage and marital therapy.* New York: Brunner/Mazel.

Subby, R., & Friel, J. (1984). Co-dependency: A paradoxical dependency. In *Codependency: An emerging issue.* Hollywood, FL: Heath Communications.

Woititz, J. G. (1983). *Adult children of alcoholics.* Hollywood, FL: Heath Communications.

Zucker, R. (1976). Parental influences on the drinking patterns of their children. In M. Greenblatt & M. A. Schuckit (Eds.), *Alcoholism problems in women and children.* New York: Grune & Stratton.

Sociocultural Perspectives on Alcohol and Drug Abuse

Throughout this book, the origins of addictive behavior have been discussed. Previous chapters have explored theoretical viewpoints that account for social factors as they affect the individual (family theory stands as an exception). These theories have largely focused upon the "microenvironment"—that is, the physical and immediate social context of drug-taking behavior (McCarty, 1985). In contrast, this chapter emphasizes the "big picture," or the "macroenvironment" (Connors & Tarbox, 1985). Macroenvironment factors include government regulations, laws, and tax policy (on alcoholic beverages); organized crime networks; effects of urbanization; and social values, beliefs, and norms. Because one chapter cannot adequately address all of these issues, the discussion that follows is limited to the impact of social values, beliefs, and norms on substance use.

RESISTANCE TO CONSIDERING THE SOCIAL ORIGINS OF ALCOHOLISM

Research strongly supports the notion that alcoholism is linked to sociodemographic characteristics. For example, Vaillant and Milofsky (1982), in a 33-year prospective study of alcoholism, found that ethnicity and number of alcoholic relatives accounted for most of the variance in adult alcoholism. According to an earlier study by Cahalan (1970), heavy drinking was associated with age, sex, ethnicity, and social status. A recent federal government report indicates that among alcoholism treatment admissions, whites represent the majority of admissions (National Institute on Alcohol Abuse and Alcoholism [NIAAA], 1990). However, the proportions of black and Hispanic admissions were higher than their respective proportions in the U.S. population. In addition, Asian-Americans were significantly underrepresented among these admissions, and Native Americans were substantially overrepresented (NIAAA, 1990). It is also widely noted by researchers that Irish-Americans have relatively high rates of alcoholism, while Jewish-Americans have low rates (Heath, 1988). Such findings suggest that the roots of alcoholism are at least partially sociocultural in nature.

Unfortunately, the importance of social factors has often been discounted by the treatment community in the United States (Lawson, Peterson, & Lawson, 1983; Peele, 1988). For example, in a popular self-help book distributed to many patients in alcoholism treatment (*Under the Influence*, by Milam & Ketcham, 1983), it is asserted that the cause of alcoholism is strictly biological. Here is an excerpt from that book:

> In other words, while psychological, cultural, and social factors definitely influence the alcoholic's drinking patterns and behavior, they have no effect on whether or not he becomes alcoholic in the first place. Physiology, not psychology, determines whether one drinker will become addicted to alcohol and another will not. The alcoholic's enzymes, hormones, genes, and brain chemistry work together to create his abnormal and unfortunate reaction to alcohol. (Milam & Ketcham, 1983, pp. 34–35)

This view disregards the possibility that some alcoholics may have no physiological vulnerability at all, and others may only have a mild physiological susceptibility. In such cases, sociocultural (as well as psychological) factors are of great importance in determining alcoholism. The view expressed by Milam and Ketcham implies dangerously that those without this biological vulnerability can use alcohol with impunity.

It is interesting to note that sociocultural theorists do not necessarily rule out the possibility of important pharmacological, metabolic, hormonal, or genetic contributions to alcoholism (Heath, 1988). Yet many proponents of the disease model completely discount social and cultural origins of alcoholism (and possibly other addictions). This is unfortunate, because any comprehensive theory of alcoholism needs to account for the sociocultural variation in the disorder.

SOCIAL FACTORS AND DRUG ADDICTION

The causes of addiction to other drugs (cocaine, heroin, PCP, etc.) also stem from various social factors and conditions, as reflected by the demographic characteristics of addicts. For example, among a sample of cocaine addicts admitted to a Chicago hospital-based treatment program in 1984, males were overrepresented (69.2%), and the mean age of the group was 30.4 (National Institute on Drug Abuse [NIDA], 1987). Data from NIDA's Drug Abuse Warning Network (DAWN) reveal similar findings. In 1987, 49.4% of those patients who appeared at a DAWN emergency room site for cocaine-related reasons were between the ages of 20 and 29, while another 35.3% were between the ages of 30 and 39. About two-thirds of these cases were men, and about 55% were black (NIDA, 1988).

A similar profile emerges from an examination of DAWN data pertaining to heroin and PCP. In 1987, 52% of the heroin-related emergency room visits were patients between the ages of 30 and 39 (NIDA, 1988). About 69% of these cases were males, and about 50% were black. Heroin overdose deaths in the same year appeared to be heavily concentrated in three cities: Washington, D.C., Detroit, and particularly Los Angeles (NIDA, 1988). PCP overdose deaths were heavily concentrated in Washington, D.C., in 1987; in fact, 41% of all PCP-related deaths reported to the 27-city DAWN system that year occurred in Washington. In 1987, 74% of the PCP-related emergency room patients were male, 58% were between the ages of 20 and 29, and about 60% were black (NIDA, 1988). These statistics suggest that drug addiction differentially affects groups along racial, age, gender, and geographic lines. Young adults, minorities, males, and urban residents seem to be disproportionately vulnerable to drug dependencies. This vulnerability is probably a result of such pathological social conditions as poverty, racial discrimination, inadequate education, and lack of employment opportunities. The notion that these addictions are solely the result of a "disease" seems to ignore, or perhaps oversimplify, the contribution of sociological factors.

THE INFLUENCE OF CULTURE
ON DIAGNOSTIC DETERMINATIONS

From a sociological perspective, the problems of alcoholism and addiction have become "medicalized" (Schwartz & Kart, 1978); that is, because of its vested interests, the medical community has redefined the problem as one of "disease." According to sociologists, this labeling process functions as a means of social control (Schwartz & Kart, 1978). It gives credibility to physicians' efforts to control, manage, and supervise the care given to addicted persons. It makes legitimate such potentially lucrative endeavors as hospital admissions, insurance company billings, expansion of the patient pool, consulting fees, and so forth. It also serves to restrict the number and type of nonmedical treatment providers (e.g., professional counselors, psychologists, social workers, nurses, marriage and family counselors) who could independently provide care for substance-abusing clients. As a result, much of the treatment (both inpatient and outpatient) of such clients in the United States is carried out under physicians' supervision.

The alcoholism labeling process also functions to restrict alcohol consumption in the community. It defines, for the average citizen, appropriate and inappropriate drinking practices. For example, in our culture, conduct norms typically discourage obvious drunkenness, drinking before noon, drinking at work, impaired driving, and binge drinking. It is interesting to note that many of these popular, "man-on-the-street" notions of alcoholism have found their way into widely used "clinical" assessment instruments, such as the Michigan Alcoholism Screening Test (MAST).

When institutions or "experts" formally label problem behaviors, it is referred to as "diagnosis." To justify this labeling process, the helping professions have created elaborate sets of criteria based on clinical findings. One example of such a diagnostic criteria set is the *Diagnostic and Statistical Manual of Mental Disorders*, third edition, revised (DSM-III-R; American Psychiatric Association, 1987).

From a sociological perspective, diagnostic criteria for alcoholism are derived largely from cultural norms. Thus, those drinking practices that are considered "alcoholic" are those that deviate from socially acceptable standards. Alcoholism is considered social deviance rather than a medical problem. Sociologically, treatment is an effort to force the alcoholic to conform to socially "correct" standards of conduct.

The cultural foundations of alcoholism diagnoses have even been recognized by leading proponents of the disease model. For example, Vaillant (1990) has stated: "Normal drinking merges imperceptibly with pathological drinking. Culture and idiosyncratic viewpoints will always determine where the line is drawn" (p. 5). The sociocultural origins of diagnoses force us to consider certain possibilities. First, a diagnosis, as applied to a particular client, may not be very different from a personal opinion: It may be based not so much on scientific evidence as on the values and beliefs of the professional helper. The helper's own history, relative to his/her use of alcohol and drugs, clearly influences the opinion.

It is also possible that drinking that is considered "alcoholic" in one period of time or place may not be viewed similarly in another temporal or geographic context. Heath (1988) has noted that 150 years ago Americans consumed three times more alcohol (per capita) than they consume today. Clearly, the notion of what an alcoholic was then would have differed substantially from our conception today.

These cultural factors should also sensitize counselors as to the consequences, both positive and negative, of applying the diagnosis (i.e., label) of "alcoholism" or "drug addiction" to a particular client. In the best of cases, the diagnosis will motivate the client to adopt abstinence. However, a positive diagnosis may also lead to overly intrusive treatment (e.g., inpatient rather than outpatient or AA/NA), social stigma, estrangement from family members, loss of employment, feelings of worthlessness and humiliation, or even exacerbation of existing drinking problems. Obviously, the addiction diagnosis should be made with caution. One can legitimately question the value of making a positive diagnosis (even when one is clearly appropriate) if there is reason to believe that it will adversely affect a client.

FOUR SOCIOLOGICAL FUNCTIONS OF SUBSTANCE ABUSE

From a sociocultural vantage point, abuse of alcohol and drugs can be described as having four broad functions. One is the facilitation of social interaction. That is, the use of alcohol (and often illegal drugs as well) enhances social bonds. It makes communication involving self-disclosure easier. Interpersonal trust is strengthened, while barriers or guards are diminished. In addition, the intoxicated state and the attending rituals and jargon allow users the opportunity of a shared experience.

A second function is to provide a release from normal social obligations. Alcohol and drug abuse have been characterized as "time-out" periods (Heath, 1988). The purpose of intoxication is to permit people to withdraw from responsibilities that society normally expects teenagers and adults to carry out. In this view, addictive behavior is an effort to escape temporarily from the roles thrust upon individuals (parent, spouse, employee, student, etc.) Intoxication allows for a temporary respite from the stresses and strains inherent in these roles.

A third function of alcohol and drug abuse is to promote cohesion and solidarity among the members of a social or ethnic group. The use or nonuse of a drug can be viewed as a means of group identification. It also establishes group boundaries. That is, substance abuse serves as a social boundary marker, defining who "we" are and who "they" are. For example, Jews generally drink in moderation. It is part of their cultural tradition, one way in which they define themselves. They view drunkenness as a "vice of the Gentiles" (Heath, 1988).

A fourth function of substance abuse, from a sociocultural perspective, is the repudiation of middle-class or "establishment" values. A substance abuse subculture consists of abusers of a particular chemical who all hold similar antiestablishment values. In essence, members of drug subcultures "thumb their nose" at conventional mores and norms, particularly those related to morality and economic productivity. Lifestyles are characterized by hedonistic pursuits, spontaneity, and freedom from family responsibilities. This is a value structure at odds with that of working- or middle-class America.

Enhancing Social Facilitation

Illicit drug use (i.e., the use of cocaine, marijuana, heroin, and LSD) is often associated with motivations unrelated to increased sociability. These motivations are discussed in subsequent sections of this chapter. Alcohol, in contrast to the illegal substances, has a distinctive social function. Because its consumption is legal, alcohol is more closely associated with good times, parties, and fun with others.

The use of alcohol to facilitate social pleasure and interactions with others has been reported for thousands of years among most of the cultures of the world. For example, the Hammurabi Code, the earliest known legal code (promulgated circa 1758 B.C. in Babylon), contains laws governing the operation and management of drinking establishments (McKim, 1986). At another time, the Greek philosopher Plato expressed concern about the drinking of his countrymen, so he established rules for conduct at "symposia," which in reality were drinking parties. He directed that at each symposium a "master of the feast" must be present. This person was to be completely sober. His responsibilities included deciding how much water should be added to the wine and when to bring on the dancing girls (McKim, 1986). Plato observed:

> When a man drinks wine he begins to feel better pleased with himself and the more he drinks the more he is filled full of brave hopes, and conceit of his powers, and at last the string of his tongue is loosened, and fancying himself wise, he is brimming over with lawlessness and has no more fear or respect and is ready to do or say anything. (From Jowett's translation of Plato's *Laws*, i, 649b; Jowett, 1931, p. 28)

"Drinking" has been thoroughly integrated into mainstream American culture today. Alcoholic drinks have come to be known simply as a "drink." If a person invites a neighbor "to come over for a drink," it is usually recognized that alcohol is being offered. Alcohol consumption is expected behavior at various social, family, and business gatherings, both formal and informal. Though individuals are not usually directly pressured to take a drink in such gatherings, a subtle pressure to do so often exists. A blunt refusal often invites puzzlement, covert speculation, or even suspicion as to one's motives.

Frequently, refusing to drink is interpreted as passing on an opportunity to meet and talk in an informal way. This is particularly true in business or other work settings characterized by formal or professional relationships. In such settings, there is often a desire to escape from the restrictive confines of stiff or rigid professional roles. Drinking together is seen as the way to "loosen up."

Recent research with young people confirms that beliefs about the convivial nature of drinking are firmly established in adolescence. My colleagues and I (Beck, Summons, & Thombs, 1991) surveyed 1,698 high school students (grades 9–12) as to the social context of drunkenness and drunken driving. Two factors explained most of the variance in these two behaviors. A factor labeled "conviviality" emerged as most prevalent; between 40% and 50% of the students reported that they drink at least occasionally to be convivial. In this context, it appeared that alcohol was used as a means of having a good time. Drinking typically occurred at weekend parties where parents were absent. Purposeful intoxication appeared to be a common motivation. The second factor was identified as "negative symptom abatement," or drinking to reduce stress, tension, fatigue, or depression. Compared to "conviviality," this factor accounted for a larger amount of variance in drinking problems; however, only about 8% of the student sample could be classified as drinking to manage negative affect. Thus, it appeared that negative symptom abatement was more closely related to drunkenness and drunken driving, but that conviviality was the most common motivation for drinking of any type.

We (Beck et al., 1991) concluded that effective intervention strategies must target these different drinking contexts. Students who drink primarily for social enhancement may benefit most from nonalcoholic social and recreational functions, while those drinking to escape negative emotions need to be identified for referral to counseling. In either case, information in the form of "facts about alcohol" is not likely to meet the adolescents' social and emotional needs.

"Time Out" from Social Obligations

The Basic Hypothesis

The "time-out" hypothesis applies to both alcohol and drug abuse. It maintains that the abuse of intoxicants serves to release individuals temporarily from their ordinary social obligations. By becoming intoxicated, they are excused from their obligations as parents, spouses, students, employees, and so forth. MacAndrew and Edgerton (1969) came upon this notion by observing the fact that many cultures exhibit a certain flexibility in norms that allows for suspension of certain role obligations during times of drunkenness. They were careful to point out that the option of "time out" does not suspend all of the rules. In all cultures, certain behavior, even while intoxicated, is considered inexcusable; thus, intoxicated persons are viewed as less responsible rather than as totally unresponsible (Heath, 1988). According to MacAndrew and Edgerton (1969), "the option of drunken time-out affords people the opportunity to 'get it out of their systems' with a minimum of adverse consequences" (p. 169). Heath (1988) notes that the concept is more of a descriptive tool than an analytic one. However, he adds that it may be useful as an early sign of alcoholism. Young people who get intoxicated to avoid, or escape from, social role expectations may be susceptible to developing more serious drinking problems.

Achievement Anxiety Theory

The time-out hypothesis essentially describes "escapist drinking"—that is, drinking to escape role obligations of any sort. Misra (1980) has outlined a model that describes substance abuse as an effort to escape a specific class of role obligations. As Misra (1980) sees it, the substance abuser is attempting to evade the pressures placed upon him/her to achieve and produce (e.g., income). Blame, in Misra's model, is not placed upon the individual who abuses drugs, but rather on American culture and its obsession with materialism, financial success, and personal achievement.

Achievement anxiety theory maintains that drug abuse is a response to a "fear of failure" (Misra, 1980). It allows the abuser to withdraw from the pressures placed upon the individual to achieve. At the same time, substance abuse induces and maintains a sense of apathy toward standards of excellence that American culture defines as important. According to Misra (1980), one of the chief characteristics of technologically advanced countries, such as the United States, is anxiety about achievement. Obtaining or reaching socially prescribed goals can become a compulsion in itself (i.e., "workaholism"). Many Americans have a dire need to "be somebody." Such competitive conditions cause people to feel anxious, fearful, inadequate, and self-doubting. As a result of these modern pressures, many Americans, in Misra's view, are likely to rely on chemicals as a way to cope.

According to achievement anxiety theory, drugs are initially used to seek relief from the pressures of achievement and productivity (Misra, 1980). In effect, they provide a quick "chemical vacation" from the stresses of contemporary life. This conceptualization is nearly identical to that of "time out." However, Misra (1980) further develops the concept by noting that continued abuse of drugs tends to reduce the difference between "work life" and leisure-time activities. In essence, the chemical vacations gradually change from being infrequent, temporary respites to full-time pursuits (i.e., addiction).

In addiction, the primary goal becomes freedom from productivity. Misra (1980) has labeled this "antiachievement." In this state, relief from achievement anxiety is no longer the goal. Instead, the goal is to maintain a sense of apathy or even hostility toward recognized and socially prescribed standards of excellence. This is the work ethic in reverse. According to Misra (1980),

> ... drug abuse is, in a sense, a silent protest against the achieving society. It protects us from a sense of failure: "I may not be achieving what my neighbors and colleagues are, but I do attain a unique feeling of relaxed carelessness." Addictions form the nucleus of a subculture of people who all have the same feeling of nonachievement, and friendships evolve around this theme as efforts are made to create and maintain fellowship among the addicts. (p. 368)

In achievement anxiety theory, leisure, as pursued in technologically advanced countries like the United States, has a special relationship to substance abuse. Misra (1980) notes that Americans have to plan to relax. This is typified by those who arrange, well in advance, elaborate, action-packed vacations. Each day is planned out, including hectic travel itineraries. This situation is exacerbated by the fact that American holidays are relatively short in duration and rigidly defined.

Misra (1980) is critical of this approach to leisure. Doing "something" rather than "nothing" has become the hallmark of relaxation in the United States. As Americans creatively jam their leisure time with activity, they become as anxious about their vacations as they are about work. According to Misra (1980), people often come to believe that relaxation must be *achieved*, here and now. This sense of immediacy for relaxation encourages the adoption of time-saving techniques. Of course, substance abuse fills this perceived need. Alcohol or drug abuse becomes a quick, easy procedure for "getting away from it all" (Misra, 1980).

Promoting Group Solidarity/Establishing Social Boundaries

For hundreds of years, the use of alcohol and drugs has been an important feature of identification with one's ethnic or racial group. With the mainstreaming of various sociodemographic groups into American culture, drinking and drugging practices have served to promote solidarity and cohesion within groups (Heath, 1988). The use of substances also demarcates the boundaries between ethnic and racial groups. It is one source of identity. It solidifies a person's social identity and helps the person define himself/herself in reference to others. The use of alcohol or drugs also shapes the images that individuals want or expect others to have of them (Heath, 1988).

Anthropologists have identified numerous examples of how drinking or drug use has functioned to separate social groups and to promote cohesion within themselves. The American temperance movement (1827–1919) is one such example. During the 19th century, temperance groups were widespread in the United States. Initially, temperance groups sought to reduce the consumption of hard liquor and to promote drinking at home, as opposed to saloon drinking. This emphasis on temperance gradually gave way to one demanding abstinence. As could be expected, this led to quarrelsome disputes between "wets" and "drys," and eventually to Prohibition (1919–1933). However, the dispute actually represented deeper ethnic and social class conflict. According to Ray and Ksir (1990),

Prohibition was not just a matter of "wets" versus "drys," or a matter of political conviction or health concerns. Intricately interwoven with these factors was a middle-class, rural, Protestant, evangelical concern that the good and true life was being undermined by ethnic groups with a different religion and different standard of living and morality. One way to strike back at these groups was through Prohibition. (p. 154)

For those involved in the temperance movement, abstaining (vs. drinking) was a social boundary marker. It served to promote a self-righteous pride within movement workers, and was taken as proof that they were morally superior to those who did drink.

For the temperance movement, abstinence was the source of group identification. In other social/ethnic groups, drunkenness was and is the social boundary marker. Heath (1988), in a description of drunkenness among Native Americans, notes that "some Indians embrace the stereotype and use it as a way of asserting their ethnicity, differentiating themselves from others, and offending sensibilities of those whites who decry such behavior" (p. 269). Lurie (1971) has suggested that alcohol abuse by Native Americans is one of the last ways that they can strike back or rebel against white America. He refers to their drinking as "the world's oldest on-going protest demonstration" (p. 311).

Situated between the extreme conditions of abstinence and drunkenness are a variety of culturally distinct drinking practices. Again, these serve to facilitate group identification and boundary marking. One widely recognized example, as mentioned earlier, is the Jewish tradition of moderation (Heath, 1988). Alcohol plays a significant role in Jewish family rituals (Lawson, Peterson, & Lawson, 1983); however, excessive consumption, particularly drunkenness, is viewed as inexcusable behavior. Within the Jewish culture, conduct norms allow for frequent but sensible use. According to Glassner and Berg (1980), these beliefs and conduct norms "protect" Jews from developing problems with alcohol. The expression "*Schikker ist ein Goy*," a relatively well-known phrase in the Jewish community, means that drunkenness is a vice of Gentiles (Glassner & Berg, 1980). The Jewish tradition of moderation and sobriety reflects basic values emphasizing rationality and self-control (Keller, 1970). Thus, Jews perceive drunkenness as being irrational and "out of control."

Interestingly, Peele (1985) notes that Jews may express their compulsions by overeating rather than overdrinking. It has been pointed out that Jews refer to overeating as the Jewish version of alcoholism. Peele (1983) suggests: "What this quasi-joking reference meant is that Jews who have emotional and coping problems that lead to substance use that is harmful and degrading would be more likely to eat than to drink excessively" (p. 964). There is some evidence that Jews and members of other ethnic groups who drink less heavily also report greater problems with weight control (Peele, 1985). However, the evidence is probably best considered less than conclusive at this time.

It is generally accepted that Irish Catholics have relatively high rates of alcoholism (Lawson et al., 1983). For example, Vaillant (1983) found that Irish subjects in his sample were more likely to develop alcohol problems than those of other ethnic backgrounds; in fact, they were seven times more likely to be alcoholic than those of Mediterranean descent. In the same study, Irish subjects were found to be more likely to abstain in an effort to manage a drinking problem. Vaillant (1983) observed:

> It is consistent with Irish culture to see the use of alcohol in terms of black and white, good or evil, drunkenness or complete abstinence, while in Italian culture it is the distinction between moderate drinking and drunkenness that is most important. (p. 226)

It has been suggested that the Irish have distinctly ambivalent feelings about the use of alcohol (Lawson et al., 1983). Viewing alcohol use dichotomously, as either good or bad, eliminates the middle possibility—that is, moderate, sensible drinking.

Drinking has never been healthfully integrated into Irish family rituals (e.g., drinking at family wakes) or religious traditions (Lawson et al., 1983). Rather, in Irish tradition, drinking has been viewed as a means of coping with oppression and hard times. In the 19th century, the oppression was largely political in nature and came at the hands of the British. Poverty and famine were widespread, and many an Irishman turned to alcohol in an effort to cope (Bales, 1980). At this time, the terms "Irishman" and "drunkard" became synonymous (Bales, 1980).

What appears to have evolved in Irish culture is the shared belief that "alcohol is an effective way to deal with our hard times that so commonly befall us." Bales (1980) has proposed that cultures such as the Irish, which are characterized by suppression of aggression, guilt, and sexual feelings and which condone the use of alcohol to cope with these impulses, will probably have high rates of alcoholism. Alcohol use is seen by the Irish as their way of coping with personal distress. While on the one hand drinking is viewed as the "curse of the Irish," on the other it is seen as the quintessential Irish act, one embodying all that is "Irish." In a symbolic way, drunkenness connects the Irish to all of their similarly anguished ancestors. Though this may be an overly sentimental portrayal of Irish drinking customs, to some degree it captures the socially unifying aspects of drinking within the culture.

Illicit drugs have also been used to promote group identity and to establish ethnic boundaries. One frequently described example involves the Chinese laborers who were brought to the western United States in the last half of the 19th century to build the railroad system. Large numbers of Chinese were imported at this time to complete the arduous task of constructing new track; they brought with them their practice of opium smoking. Opium dens were created as places to spend their nonworking hours.

The practice of opium smoking never spread to other social groups. Local community leaders in many jurisdictions (who of course were Caucasian) passed legislation to forbid the practice. In general, most Americans viewed the use of opium by the Chinese with distaste and repugnance. Thus, for the white majority, opium smoking served as a significant social boundary. It was useful for the white community as a means of identifying who "we" (the good people) were, and who "they" (the Chinese, the bad people) were.

Furthermore, the drug experience (opium smoking) itself made apparent the distinctive value structures of the Chinese versus the white Americans. As noted by Ray and Ksir (1990),

> The opium smoking the Chinese brought to this country never became widely popular, although around the turn of the century about one fourth of the opium imported was smoking opium. Perhaps it was because the smoking itself occupies only about a minute and is then followed by a dreamlike reverie that may last 2 or 3 hours—hardly behavior that is conducive to a continuation of daily activities or consonant with the outward, active orientation of most Americans in that period. (p. 276)

Opium smoking was consistent with the Chinese emphasis on reflection and introspection. It was at odds with the American orientation toward productivity, action, and settling the West.

Today the abuse of illicit drugs, in the form of cocaine and PCP, serves much the same functions. During the 1980s, numerous public health indicators showed that illicit drug abuse was becoming increasingly concentrated among disadvantaged, minority-group, urban populations (NIDA, 1987; Thombs, 1989). For example, nationwide, blacks accounted for 24% of the PCP-related emergency room visits in 1976–1977. That figure more than doubled to 60.4% of such emergency room visits by 1987 (NIDA, 1988). Other evidence indicates that use of illicit drugs by white middle-class Americans was actually on the decline by the mid-1980s. In essence, the 1980s were a time of transition in which illicit drug use became an increasingly significant social boundary marker. Cultural perceptions of drug abusers shifted somewhat during this decade, as indicated by increased legal sanctions and the expansion of the number of prison beds. In many ways, the efforts by federal and state governments in the 1980s were reminiscent of the temperance movement of a century earlier. Both movements represent efforts by the dominant middle class to strike back at certain social groups perceived to be undermining the "American way of life."

Drug Subcultures: Repudiation of Middle-Class Values

The notion that addicts form clearly defined and separate subcultures has faded somewhat since the 1960s. Prior to that decade, illicit drug abuse was primarily concentrated among minority ghetto populations. Explaining illicit drug abuse within a subculture framework made a great deal of sense then. However, during the 1970s illicit drug abuse became more diffuse among social classes (Oetting & Beauvis, 1988). The availability and use of such substances as marijuana and heroin were not narrowly limited to lower socioeconomic groups, as they were in the 1950s. Thus, sociologists and anthropologists paid somewhat less attention to the subculture concept in the 1970s and 1980s.

There is still value to analyzing drug abuse within a subculture context, however. This is particularly true for examining substance abuse among teens and young adults. The framework offers insight into how substance abuse is initiated and maintained, and how drug subcultures are related to the youth culture, to the parent culture, and to broad American middle-class culture.

Definitions

Middle-class American culture is characterized by a broad set of rather diverse values and conduct norms for adults. It is essentially a parent culture that includes expectations for what youths can and cannot do. In general, parents expect youths to avoid tobacco, alcohol, and illicit drug use. This is reflected in laws that prohibit youths from purchasing cigarettes and alcohol before the ages of 18 and 21, respectively. To various degrees, the values and conduct norms of the parent culture are internalized by youths. Of course, the extent of this socialization varies from youth to youth, and across particular classes of values as well.

The youth culture defines what peers or friends expect each other to do or not to do (Gans, 1962). In attempts to influence youths, the parent culture competes with the youth culture. This competition is an ongoing, dynamic process. The parent culture usually attempts to defend traditional values, while the youth culture encourages experimentation with new or novel forms of expression.

According to Johnson (1980, p. 111), the youth culture emphasizes the following conduct norms:

1. The person must be loyal to friends and attempt to maintain group association.
2. Social interaction with the peer group should occur in locations where adult controls are relatively absent.
3. Within such peer groups, a veiled competition exists for status and prestige among group participants and leads to new forms of behavior or operating innovations.

"Youth culture" and "peer group" are closely related but distinct concepts. A young person's close circle of friends is his/her peer group. The term "youth culture" refers to a much broader influence—one that touches all peer groups via community, school, church, and media messages. The pervasive influence of the youth culture explains the great similarity among distant peer groups. This is particularly the case today with so many national media targeting youths (e.g., MTV).

A "subculture" consists of a culture within a larger culture (Johnson, 1980). It is characterized by values, conduct norms, social situations, and roles that are distinct from and often at odds with those of the middle class. The term "drug subculture" refers to these same components as they pertain to nonmedical drug use (Johnson, 1980).

Excluded from this conceptualization are the values and conduct norms associated with medical and most legal drug use. Thus, psychoactive drugs prescribed by a physician are not included, nor is use of over-the-counter medications or cigarettes. The moderate social use of alcohol is also excluded from a drug subculture analysis, because such drinking practices are clearly part of middle-class culture. However, in the subsequent discussion, the values and conduct norms of the alcohol *abuse* subculture are explored.

A relatively unique constellation of values define a subculture. According to Johnson (1980), "the most important elements of a subculture are its values and conduct norms. Values are here understood to be shared ideas about what the subgroup believes to be true or what is wants (desires) or ought to want" (p. 113). The most significant value of a drug subculture is the intention or desire to alter consciousness, or to get "high." This value (i.e., the wish to get high) is the organizing theme of all drug subcultures and their activities. The corresponding conduct norm is an expectation that all subculture participants will partake in the use of a drug, or at least express a desire to do so.

Within subcultures, certain behavior is expected of persons in particular social positions. These performances are referred to as "roles." In drug subcultures, there are three primary roles: seller, buyer, and user (Johnson, 1980). Performance of these roles is almost always illegal, so the execution of them is generally covert, or hidden from the public at large. Thus, the public is generally ignorant of the behavior needed to carry out the role of seller, buyer, or user (Johnson, 1980). This may, in part, explain the great fascination and curiosity nonsubculture members often express about these activities.

Also characteristic of drug subcultures are rituals involving highly valued objects. The objects are usually instruments for self-administration of drugs. For example, the heroin subculture favors the use of the hypodermic syringe, and incorporates it into rituals in which several addicts may share the same needle (e.g., in "shooting galleries"). The cocaine subculture has several ritualized practices, depending upon the route of administration. Objects include mirrors, spoons, special pipes, vials, and straws or rolled-up dollar bills for snorting. The marijuana subculture values such objects as "roach clips," water pipes, and rolling papers. These symbolic objects and drug rituals are rarely known outside the subculture, but are widely known within it. They serve to bolster group identity and solidarity.

By the time most illicit drug addicts have reached their mid-20s, they have developed a preference for one drug over others. This preference may simply be a function of their participation in a particular drug subculture. The addicts may have an elaborate set of reasons for why their drug is superior to others. Heavily influencing their attachment to one drug are their bonds and identification with their peer group. Johnson (1980) has noted that subculture participants tend to ignore great similarities in the behavior of drug addicts, and tend to emphasize the importance of differences that seem very small to outsiders. For example, many cocaine addicts "put down" PCP addicts; they believe that cocaine helps one think more clearly, while PCP just makes one "dumb." Alcoholics and heroin addicts take similar views of each other: Many alcoholics perceive heroin addicts as "low-lifes," while many heroin addicts view alcoholics as "wimps" and "crybabies."

Drug subcultures are dynamic. Historical, political, economic, and sociocultural factors influence their formation and dissolution. Some of these trends are predictable. Johnson (1980) has insightfully noted:

> When patterns of drug use are limited to low-income and low-status groups, societal reaction tends to be punitive, and government pursues a prohibitionist policy. When drug use becomes common in many segments of the youth population, public reaction is one of temporary alarm with later adjustment and easing of enforcement effects and legal punishments. (p. 115)

These trends and other dynamics indicate that drug subcultures are always changing; thus, any identification of the components of specific drug subcultures quickly becomes dated. Nonetheless, Johnson (1980) has identified key aspects of four drug subcultures (the alcohol, marijuana, polydrug, and heroin abuse subcultures) that still have relevance today. In addition, a preliminary attempt at identifying some key components of the crack cocaine subculture is made.

The Alcohol Abuse Subculture

Alcohol is a powerful mood-altering drug. Yet it is legally available and its use is widespread, even expected, in American middle-class culture. Alcohol is viewed as both a beverage and an intoxicant—one that is principally used to facilitate social interaction and relief from stress. There is significant social pressure in this society to drink, at least in moderation. Abstention from alcohol is considered almost as deviant as binge drinking.

In contrast to the sensible, "social" use of alcohol stands the alcohol *abuse* subculture. The conduct norms of this subculture expect participants to get "wasted," "totaled," "smashed," or "bombed." The emphasis is on excessive consumption. Alcohol is not used as a beverage, but as a drug; that is, drunkenness is intentional or purposely sought. Such drinking contrasts sharply with that of the larger middle class, where drunkenness is viewed with embarrassment and met with social disgrace. Many high school and college students become participants of the alcohol abuse subculture, though a sizable proportion seem to "mature out" of it as they assume full-time jobs, get married, and/or have children.

Certain reciprocity conduct norms exist in the alcohol abuse subculture. It is expected that participants will share in the pooling of money to buy relatively large quantities of alcohol (e.g., a case or keg of beer). There is the expectation that one member will buy drinks for other members, and that the favor will later be reciprocated. In some social groups, bottle passing is expected. In others, drinking games (e.g., "quarters," "pass out," others) and reliance on special paraphernalia (e.g., beer funnels, baseball caps designed to dispense beer) are encouraged. Again, these rituals and objects serve to promote group identity and solidarity. These social functions become very clear when one considers drinking within the context of college fraternities and sororities.

Participants of the alcohol abuse subculture are not always young people. Older adults may also be participants of this subculture. The middle class tends to label such adults "alcoholics." Their drinking may also be ritualized (e.g., three drinks before dinner, never drinking before noon, stopping at a bar each day after work, etc.). Elaborate liquor cabinets or even full-size bars may be set up at home. Large quantities of alcohol may be kept in reserve (e.g., a keg of beer on tap in the refrigerator, a dozen or more cases of beer bought at wholesale prices stored in the garage). Decorative mirrors, pictures, posters, clocks, ashtrays, and other "knick-knacks" from alcohol retailers may adorn their homes. Heavy drinking is clearly a central activity in their lives (Fingarette, 1988). That is, they organize their lives around the consumption of alcohol.

The Marijuana Abuse Subculture

During the 1970s, marijuana use became increasingly accepted in the United States (Johnson, 1980). However, the 1980s saw fewer and fewer young people experimenting with it or using it daily (Johnston, O'Malley, & Bachman, 1989). This reversal of trends, of a sort, suggests that the marijuana subculture of the 1990s may not resemble that of the 1970s. The nature of the values and conduct norms of this subculture today is not clear. However, a review of them as they existed 20 years ago provides a benchmark for considering this subculture in the 1990s.

The marijuana subculture of the 1970s generally expected its participants to smoke the drug relatively frequently—if not daily, then at least two or three times a week. The sharing of marijuana was promoted. Rock music lyrics reinforced this conduct norm (e.g., Bob Dylan emphasized in one song that "everybody must get stoned"). It should be understood, though, that the predominant values were not ones of aggression and pressure; rather, values emphasized peace, love, understanding, and social harmony. Yet a subtle form of peer pressure did exist within the subculture to use the drug.

Usually, no money was exchanged in the sharing of marijuana. Group participants were trusted to reciprocate at some future date. Those who bought relatively large amounts of "pot" were expected to share small amounts with friends, and to sell to friends at cost. There was an expectation that marijuana buyers and sellers were not supposed to turn large profits. Typically, buyers and sellers within this subculture were expected to socialize and smoke together. The business aspects of the transactions were de-emphasized.

Among the participants of the marijuana subculture, there was the naive but strong belief that marijuana use could correct many of the social ills of America. The middle class, particularly the parent culture, was perceived as obsessed with material things, as well as racist, sexist, corrupt, and hypocritical. Marijuana use was naively thought to be the single answer to all social problems. This conviction (among others) helped to forge the youth–parent culture conflict (i.e., the "generation gap") of the 1960s and 1970s.

The Polydrug Abuse Subculture

Johnson (1980) has identified a drug subculture characterized by polydrug abuse. The use of multiple substances, either simultaneously or on different occasions, is widely known by substance abuse counselors working in the field today. Among clients under the age of 40, dependence upon several drugs is common (e.g., alcohol and cocaine, alcohol and marijuana, cocaine and heroin). These patterns are especially common among teens and young adults in their early 20s.

According to Johnson (1980), the polydrug abuse subculture is an outgrowth of the marijuana subculture. One distinguishing conduct norm of this subculture is that participants are expected to use almost any chemical in an effort to alter consciousness. In addition to alcohol and marijuana, the use of cocaine, crack cocaine, tranquilizers, sedatives, narcotics, PCP, inhalants, amphetamine, hallucinogenic mushrooms, Ecstasy, and other designer drugs is encouraged. Conduct norms also require that members be willing to smoke and inhale (snort) a drug, as well as administer it orally. Usually, conduct norms do not expect participants to inject a drug; this is a boundary marker that distinguishes this group from the heroin abuse subculture. Polydrug abuse subculture participants frequently perceive self-administered injection as "going one step too far." They may be heard to say, "That [injection] is the one thing that I would never do."

Sharing is important in this subculture (Johnson, 1980). A participant who has pills is expected to share with someone who has cocaine, for example. In addition, particular drugs are more highly coveted than others; typically, crack cocaine is more highly valued than PCP (Thombs, 1989). Drug sellers (dealers) are not necessarily expected to socialize with buyers in the polydrug abuse subculture. Drug transactions are more formal, business-like exchanges.

The Heroin Injection Subculture

The heroin injection subculture expects participants (sometimes referred to as "junkies") to self-administer heroin via hypodermic injection (Johnson, 1980). Heroin can be inhaled or snorted, but in this subculture the conduct norms generally discourage these routes of administration. Heroin inhalation is more typical of the polydrug abuse subculture. Snorting (inhalation) is not thought by heroin subculture participants to provide the same "rush" as injection.

Conduct norms call for injections on a daily basis, usually two to five times (Johnson, 1980). It should be noted here that this schedule is maintained largely by role expectations of the subculture. Other theoretical perspectives emphasize the central importance of withdrawal sickness. However, drug subculture theory asserts that important social determinants are also involved in the maintenance of self-administered drug use.

Although heroin may be shared from time to time, there are very strong expectations that peers will reciprocate at a later time (Johnson, 1980). In addition, participants in this subculture are expected to carry out all three drug subculture roles: buyer, user, and seller (Johnson, 1980). Participants provide other participants with information ("connections") regarding where to secure more of the drug. Most participants of the heroin subculture were previously involved in the polydrug abuse subculture. They may continue their contacts with this network on a more limited basis.

The Crack Cocaine Subculture

The crack cocaine subculture emerged in the United States during the mid-1980s. According to data collected by the National Institute of Justice (NIJ) in 1987, crack use had become prevalent by this time in most major American cities (NIJ, 1988). Relatively large percentages of arrestees in various cities were found to test positive for cocaine. Another indication of the growth of this subculture (and the medical problems that participants tend to encounter) was the increase in the number of cocaine-related emergency room visits in the United States. Between 1983 and 1987, there was a 644% increase in the number of cocaine-related emergency visits reported by hospitals participating in the federally sponsored DAWN (NIDA, 1984, 1988). The percentage increase in such emergency room visits in some cities during this 4-year period was astounding. For example, between 1983 and 1987, cocaine-related emergency room visits increased 131% in Chicago, 874% in Detroit, 440% in Los Angeles, 398% in New York City, 2116% in Philadelphia, and 1208% in Washington, D.C. (NIDA, 1984, 1988).

A demographic profile of the typical crack cocaine subculture participant also emerged from data collected during this period. In 1987, 84.7% of the cocaine abusers who visited an emergency room in crisis were between the ages of 20 and 39 (NIDA, 1988). Only 6.8% were under the age of 20. About two-thirds of them were male. In terms of race, 55.1% of the cocaine abusers were black, 28.1% were white, and 9.0% were Hispanic (NIDA, 1988). It appears that the typical crack cocaine subculture participant is a young adult black male, probably from an impoverished urban neighborhood, who faces significant social and economic barriers to achieving middle-class status.

In the crack cocaine subculture, various conduct norms have developed. It is expected that participants will smoke the drug daily in a binge-like fashion over an 8-, 10-, 12-, or even 24-hour period (NIDA, 1987). The binge or "run" will stop when the addict has run out of money or is too exhausted to continue. The addict could also "fall out"—that is, have a seizure—and be taken to an emergency room. Obviously, participants place little value on their health, as judged by the variety and severity of medical complications that they encounter.

Sharing is typically not a conduct norm in this subculture; however, trading a commodity in exchange for crack is common. Participants may swap jewelry, stereos, guns, or even sex for crack. The exchange of sex is particularly true for female addicts, who may engage in prostitution for another "hit."

In many urban settings, crack subculture participants gather in a house where the drug can be used in private. Often the use of the house has been reserved entirely for this purpose. In these "crack houses," use of the drug typically goes on 24 hours a day. If the participants come under the scrutiny of police or neighborhood groups, they will probably move to another location. In essence, a crack house is the modern-day version of the "speakeasy" of the Prohibition era.

The distribution conduct norms of the crack subculture are highly secretive. This is hardly surprising, given the harsh legal sanctions that exist for cocaine sale and distribution. However, it appears that the business aspects of the transaction are emphasized. If sellers are cheated in a deal, conduct norms call for retaliation, often involving shootings. Violence and the threat of violence are pervasive in the subculture. In this way, the participants resemble the bootleggers (e.g., Al Capone) of the 1920s. Similar to gangsters of yesteryear, the sellers in this subculture are part of a structured hierarchy in which higher-level distributors attempt to shield themselves from arrest by relying on subordinates. Often, the subordinates or "runners" are young teens who are not subject to the same types of potential legal penalties as adults.

The emergence of the crack subculture in U.S. cities is the result of a confluence of social and economic forces. South American cocaine cartels have seized the opportunity to make fortunes by exporting the drug to this country. The well-intended interdiction effort of the federal government stops only a small percentage of the drug from entering the country. Even worse, these attempts to stem the tide have the unintended and indirect effect of organizing a subculture of disaffiliated American citizens. It is no accident that young adult black males predominate in this subculture. They represent one of the most powerless groups in America. Their access to the middle class is limited by a lack of social, educational, and economic opportunities. Given these imposed limitations (real and perceived), drug subculture involvement appears to be their alternative to the "American dream" of middle-class status.

IMPLICATIONS FOR COUNSELING

Sociocultural perspectives suggest that effective addictions treatment must address basic human values in the counseling process. Rokeach and Regan (1980) have pointed out that counseling is essentially "values therapy." They assert:

> Every counselor can be conceptualized as being in the business of administering value theory, and if a client's values remain altogether unaf-

fected by counseling it is doubtful that it can be said to have been successful. In short, the successful outcome of counseling can be formulated as always involving either a clarification or a change in specified value priorities and in value-related attitudes and behavior. (p. 576)

Substance Abuse Counseling and Values

The role of human values in counseling substance abusers has generally not been dealt with very well by the addictions treatment community. Though Step Six of AA's Twelve Steps refers to the need to remove "defects of character," the disease model has explained that the problems of alcoholism and addiction are not moral problems. The addict is seen as ill, not wicked. Presumably, character defects are problems that stem from holding destructive values; yet this moral dimension is removed when addiction is placed in the realm of disease. This contradiction is exacerbated by the AA emphasis on spirituality—again, presumably a values-laden approach.

Proponents of the disease model have frequently misunderstood sociological and anthropological perspectives on the role of human values in alcoholism and addiction. For example, Vaillant (1990) has suggested that social theories consider alcoholism to be "misbehavior" (p. 5). A more sophisticated view of sociocultural analyses would appreciate the objective nature of sociological and anthropological theory (Heath, 1988; Light & Keller, 1975). Obviously, sociologists and anthropologists are subject to personal biases and value judgments. However, as Light and Keller (1975) note, "For generations sociologists have labored under the eleventh commandment, 'Thou shalt not commit a value judgement' " (p. 36). Sociocultural analyses do not pass judgment on the "correctness" of addicts' values; instead, they serve as relatively impartial analyses of the social phenomena under scrutiny. If sociologists describe a drug subculture as placing a low priority on economic productivity, they are not insisting that addicts are "lazy." They are simply pointing out that their value structure emphasizes other pursuits, and that this structure deviates from that of the larger middle-class culture.

Many times the "resistance" demonstrated by chemically dependent clients in treatment reflects conflicts between their value structure and that necessary for recovery. Typically, there is a mismatch between the values imbedded in the disease model and those of a client (e.g., "Abstinence from all mood-altering chemicals is necessary"). The noncompliance of the client is usually described as "denial." From a sociocultural perspective, this may not be as much an unconscious defense as a refusal to adopt the values necessary for recovery. A client who indicates that he/she "cannot" attend 90 A.A. meetings in 90 days is revealing a preference for spontaneity over structure in organizing day-to-day life. A client who will not make a commitment to abstinence may be demonstrating a preference for short-term gratification and excitement over long-term gains (e.g., economic security, family stability) and improved health. Peele (1985), in particular, has noted that many addicts place relatively little value on their personal health. The old maxim, "Eat, drink, and be merry, for tomorrow we may die," seems to apply here.

Other addicts may balk at counselors' attempts to encourage introspection and self-analysis. This may reflect a value structure that elevates social relations, fun, and amusement over rational self-control and serious self-understanding. These conflicts are crucial issues to be uncovered, clarified, and discussed in counseling. Many, perhaps most, clients are unaware of their value priorities and of how these relate to their substance abuse. Though it may be painful, counselors should help clients bring these issues to the foreground of consciousness. They reveal sources of resistance, and possibly point toward suitable treatment goals. In working this way, counselors should maintain an objective attitude toward the clients' value structure.

The consequences of each client's value priorities should be explored. However, it should also be kept in mind that attempts at "bullying" a client into adopting values consistent with popular recovery models will often backfire. Changes in a client's values are likely to evolve slowly. Thus, when a counselor is faced with a client with a dysfunctional value orientation, patience is a much-needed resource.

Multidimensional Treatment

Sociocultural perspectives on addiction support the contention that treatment must be multidimensional in nature. This perspective illustrates that many of the factors that cause addiction and relapse are not "within" the individual (i.e., biological or psychological). As a result, effective treatment will have an impact in other domains of the addict's life. Successful interventions will alter a client's relationships to his/her family, peer group, workplace, and community. According to Galizio and Maisto (1985), these "psychosocial and environmental factors may be most critical in the determination of cessation and relapse" (p. 428).

For many clients in early recovery, their social system is not conducive to abstinence and other recovery-consistent behavior. Various social and environmental factors influence them to drink or use a drug. Mallams, Godley, Hall, and Meyers (1982) cogently describe these pressures in the case of alcohol abuse, and the needed alternative, in the following passage:

> Newly acquired social skills are subject to multiple environmental influences. For example, the physical environment (mass media, advertising, sensory cues for drinking) is structured to increase the likelihood of drinking, and drinking is associated with such social activities as conversation, recreation and dating. Under these environmental influences recovering alcoholics may not only lose existing support, but receive negative sanctions from former drinking associates. Finally, many recovering alcoholics do not have the personal resources (e.g., transportation, family, friends, employment) necessary to engage in new social situations. . . . An alternative approach is to create a new social system in the alcoholics' natural environment that provides wide varieties of social and recreational activities and reinforces the acquisition of appropriate social behaviors. (p. 1116)

Lewis, Dana, and Blevins (1988, p. 19) have identified nine possible treatment plan components that could address the harsh social (and possibly economic) realities of early recovery:

1. Job counseling: helping clients find permanent, full-time, well-paying jobs that would interfere with a return to drinking.
2. Marital counseling: providing counseling for all married couples and arranging "synthetic families" for unmarried alcoholics
3. Resocialization and recreation: arranging alcohol-free social and recreational activities in addition to making Alcoholics Anonymous referrals
4. Problem-prevention rehearsal: teaching clients how to handle situations that might otherwise lead to drinking
5. Early warning system: providing a mail-in Happiness Scale to be used by clients
6. Disulfram: developing positive, supportive mechanisms for clients to use Antabuse for impulse control
7. Group counseling: providing supportive mechanisms that can develop into social or recreational groups after release
8. Buddy procedure: selecting recovering peer advisors to work closely with each client

9. Contracting: using written contracts to formalize the agreements be-
    tween counselors and clients regarding the program's procedures
    and the client's responsibilities

These nine intervention strategies underscore how closely intertwined chemical use (and nonuse) is with the addict's relationships
to family, worksite, and peer groups. The drug or alcohol problem
cannot be neatly separated from other spheres of the addict's life.
They are inseparably entangled with the social experience. Substance
abuse counselors should keep in mind that they are treating *peo-*
ple—that is, social beings, not "drug problems."

LIMITATIONS

There are two major limitations of the sociocultural perspective. First,
the concepts in this view are considered elusive or too abstract by
some professionals. The concepts of social boundary markers, subcultures, conduct norms, "time out," and so on are sometimes seen as
too intellectual, or perhaps useless because they cannot be readily
measured or observed. Critics have occasionally charged that sociocultural theorists are the sideline observers of the "war on drugs."
They provide grand conceptualizations, but are reluctant to get directly involved in the problem (i.e., provide direct services).

The second limitation pertains to the relative inability of substance abuse counselors (and treatment programs) to significantly
alter the social, cultural, and environmental factors that cause addiction and relapse. In this vein, sociocultural theory may be viewed as
interesting, but of little practical value because these variables cannot
be directly manipulated. Substance abuse counselors can do little to
alter drinking customs among certain ethnic groups, for example.
This lack of practicality is likely to prevent sociocultural perspectives
from gaining more prominent status among theories of addictive
behavior.

REVIEW QUESTIONS

1. What are the sociodemographic variables that are linked to
    alcoholism?
2. How has the treatment community in the United States viewed
    sociocultural perspectives on addiction?

3. What are the sociodemographic variables that are linked to illicit drug addictions?

4. What is meant by the "medicalization" of addiction?

5. How do cultural factors influence diagnostic determinations?

6. What are the four basic sociological functions of substance abuse? How do they support substance abuse?

7. What is a "drug subculture"? How is it distinct from middle-class culture?

8. What particular values and conduct norms characterize a drug subculture?

9. What are some of the unique aspects of the alcohol abuse subculture, the marijuana abuse subculture, the polydrug abuse subculture, the heroin injection subculture, and the crack cocaine subculture?

10. How should values be dealt with in substance abuse counseling?

11. What is meant by "multidimensional" treatment?

12. What are the two major limitations of the sociocultural perspective as it pertains to substance abuse counseling?

REFERENCES

American Psychiatric Association. (1987). *Diagnostic and statistical manual of mental disorders* (3rd ed., rev.). Washington, DC: Author.

Bales, F. (1980). Cultural differences in roles of alcoholism. In D. Ward (Ed.), *Alcoholism: Introduction to theory and treatment*. Dubuque, IA: Kendall/Hunt.

Beck, K. H., Summons, T. G., & Thombs, D. L. (1991). A factor analytic study of social context of drinking in a high school population. *Psychology of Addictive Behaviors, 5*(2), 66–77.

Cahalan, D. (1970). *Problem drinkers: A national survey*. San Francisco: Jossey-Bass.

Connors, G. R., & Tarbox, A. R. (1985). Macroenvironmental factors as determinants of substance use and abuse. In M. Galizio & S. A. Maisto (Eds.), *Determinants of substance abuse: Biological, psychological, and environmental factors*. New York: Plenum Press.

Fingarette, H. (1988). *Heavy drinking: The myth of alcoholism as a disease*. Berkeley: University of California Press.

Galizio, M., & Maisto, S. A. (1985). Toward a biopsychosocial theory of substance abuse. In M. Galizio & S. A. Maisto (Eds.), *Determinants of substance abuse: Biological, psychological, and environmental factors*. New York: Plenum Press.

Gans, H. J. (1962). *The urban villagers*. New York: Free Press.

Glassner, B., & Berg, B. (1980). How Jews avoid drinking problems. *American Sociological Review, 45*, 647–664.

Heath, D. B. (1988). Emerging anthropological theory and models of alcohol use and alcoholism. In C. D. Chaudron & D. A. Wilkinson (Eds.), *Theories on alcoholism*. Toronto: Addiction Research Foundation.

Heath, D. B. (1990). Anthropological and sociocultural perspectives on alcohol as a reinforcer. In W. M. Cox (Ed.), *Why people drink: Parameters of alcohol as a reinforcer*. New York: Gardner Press.

Johnson, B. D. (1980). Toward a theory of drug subcultures. In D. J. Lettieri, M. Bayers, & H. W. Pearson (Eds.), *Theories on drug abuse: Selected contemporary perspectives* (DHHS Publication No. ADM 84-967). Washington, DC: U.S. Government Printing Office.

Johnston, L. D., O'Malley, P. M., & Bachman, J. G. (1989). *Drug use, drinking, and smoking: National survey results from high school, college, and young adult populations* (DHHS Publication No. ADM 89-1638). Washington, DC: U.S. Government Printing Office.

Jowett, B. (Trans.). (1931). *The dialogues of Plato* (3rd ed., Vol. 5). London: Oxford University Press.

Keller, M. (1970). The great Jewish drink mystery. *British Journal of Addictions, 64*, 287–295.

Lawson, G., Peterson, J. S., & Lawson, A. (1983). *Alcoholism and the family: A guide to treatment and prevention*. Rockville, MD: Aspen.

Lewis, J. A., Dana, R. Q., & Blevins, G. A. (1988). Substance abuse counseling: An individualized approach. Pacific Grove, CA: Brooks/Cole.

Light, D., & Keller, S. (1975). *Sociology*. New York: Knopf.

Lurie, N. (1971). The World's oldest on-going protest demonstration: North American Indian drinking patterns. *Pacific Historical Review, 40*, 311–332.

MacAndrew, C., & Edgerton, R. B. (1969). *Drunken comportment: A social explanation*. Chicago: Adline.

Mallams, J. H., Godley, M. D., Hall, G. M., & Meyers, R. J. (1982). A social-systems approach to resocializing alcoholics in the community. *Journal of Studies on Alcohol, 43*, 1115–1123.

McCarty, D. (1985). Environmental factors in substance abuse: The microsetting. In M. Galizio & S. A. Maisto (Eds.), *Determinants of substance abuse: Biological, psychological, and environmental factors*. New York: Plenum Press.

McKim, W. A. (1986). *Drugs and behavior: An Introduction to behavioral pharmacology*. Englewood Cliffs, NJ: Prentice-Hall.

Milam, J. R., & Ketcham, K. (1983). *Under the influence*. New York: Bantam.

Misra, R. K. (1980). Achievement, anxiety, and addiction. In D. J. Lettieri, M. Sayers, & H. W. Pearson (Eds.), *Theories on drug abuse: Selected contemporary perspectives* (DHHS Publication No. ADM 84-967). Washington, DC: U.S. Government Printing Office.

National Institute on Alcohol Abuse and Alcoholism (NIAAA). (1990). *Alcohol and health: Seventh special report to the U.S. Congress* (DHHS Publication No. ADM 90-1656). Washington, DC: U.S. Government Printing Office.

National Institute on Drug Abuse (NIDA). (1984). *Data from the Drug Abuse Warning Network, Series I, No. 3* (DHHS Publication No. ADM 84-1353). Washington, DC: U.S. Government Printing Office.

National Institute on Drug Abuse (NIDA). (1987). *Drug abuse and drug abuse research*. (DHHS Publication No. ADM 87-1486). Washington, DC: U.S. Government Printing Office.

National Institute on Drug Abuse (NIDA). (1988). *Data from the Drug Abuse Warning Network, Series I, No. 7* (DHHS Publication No. ADM 88-1584). Washington, DC: U.S. Government Printing Office.

National Institute of Justice (NIJ). (1988, January). *Drug use forecasting (DUF)*. Washington, DC: U.S. Department of Justice.

Oetting, E. R., & Beauvis, F. (1988). Common elements in youth drug abuse: Peer clusters and other psychosocial factors. In S. Peele (Ed.), *Visions of addiction: Major contemporary perspectives on addiction and alcoholism*. Lexington, MA: Lexington Books.

Peele, S. (1983). Is alcoholism different from other substance abuse? *American Psychologist, 38,* 963–964.

Peele, S. (1985). *The meaning of addiction: Compulsive experience and its interpretation*. Lexington, MA: D. C. Heath.

Peele, S. (Ed.). (1988). *Visions of addiction: Major contemporary perspectives on addiction and alcoholism*. Lexington, MA: Lexington Books.

Ray, O., & Ksir, C. (1990). *Drugs, society, and human behavior*. St. Louis: Times Mirror/Mosby.

Rokeach, M., & Regan, J. F. (1980). The role of values in the counseling situation. *Personnel and Guidance Journal, 58,* 576–582.

Schwartz, H. D., & Kart, C. S. (1978). *Dominant issues in medical sociology*. Reading, MA: Addison-Wesley.

Thombs, D. L. (1989). A review of PCP abuse trends and perceptions. *Public Health Reports. 104*(4), 325–328.

Vaillant, G. E. (1983). *The natural history of alcoholism*. Cambridge, MA: Harvard University Press.

Vaillant, G. E. (1990). We should retain the disease concept of alcoholism. *Harvard Medical School Mental Health Letter, 6*(9), 4–6.

Vaillant, G. E., & Milofsky, E. S. (1982). The etiology of alcoholism: A prospective viewpoint. *American Psychologist, 37*(5), 494–503.

Implications for Clinical Practice

In this volume, contemporary theories of addictive behavior and supporting research in each area have been reviewed and critiqued in depth. Each perspective has offered concepts that are critical to effective clinical practice. In particular, these concepts can be used to direct the design of individual treatment plans. All too often lip service has been paid to the notion of individualized treatment planning, but very little actual implementation of the practice takes place, or the tailoring of treatment goals for individuals has occurred only within narrow parameters. It is my hope that the contents of this book suggest an expanded range of possible paths to recovery. Let us briefly review the major contributions of each theoretical position and their importance for counseling practice.

DISEASE MODEL

The importance of the disease model stems from the fact that it removes alcoholism and other addictions from the realm of sin. Without this shift, there would be no basis for offering treatment. Punishment, including incarceration, would be perceived by most of society as the only means of addressing the problem. Aside from making treatment possible, the disease model has also been a "good fit" for many clients in recovery. Often the subjective experience of addiction feels like being "sick"; moreover, as in other chronic diseases, professional intervention is necessary for effective treatment of severe addictive disorders. The model is a particularly good fit for those who have progressively deteriorated, and those who have biomedical ("disease") complications.

PSYCHOANALYTIC MODEL

Though the psychoanalytic framework is not widely used by practitioners today, psychoanalytic formulations provide keen insights into the dynamics of compulsive drug use. First and foremost, this perspective emphasizes the role of unconscious forces in the maintenance of addictive behavior. Defense mechanisms, such as denial and rationalization, certainly have to be accounted for in the treatment-planning work done with many clients in early recovery. The theory informs us that these defense mechanisms are linked with weakened ego strength. That is, many clients in early recovery lack strong internal controls, and will benefit from strong external support and encouragement. This is particularly true of the early recovery period.

Psychoanalytic theory also forcefully points out that actions of the compulsive drug user are only symptoms of deeper disturbances of personality. Many chemically dependent clients abuse substances to satisfy a psychological hunger for stimulation. When a person relies almost entirely on external stimuli (i.e., drugs and alcohol), the ego remains weak, and nondrug coping strategies remain poorly developed or nonexistent. This suggests that treatment planning must include strategies for enhancing such capabilities as delaying immediate gratification, organizing daily activities, making plans, prioritizing wants and needs, and setting long-term goals. In addition, treatment plans should perhaps help clients identify less destructive (i.e., alcohol- or drug-free) means of satisfying intense needs for external stimulation. For example, among high-sensation-seeking clients, exciting outdoor sports, music, computer games, or other activities may temporarily fill internal voids. Though such efforts may only serve to distract the clients from deeper issues, they can help to solidify a period of drug-free time.

CONDITIONING THEORY

Reward is the core concept in the conditioning approach. This theory and body of research remind us that the self-administration of drugs is goal-directed behavior. The behavior is driven by the anticipated, predictable euphoria or change in consciousness that follows self-administration. This principle readily explains why smoking crack or injecting heroin tends to evolve rapidly into a compulsive pattern. The euphoria is obtained within seconds of administering the drugs.

The immediacy of the reinforcement derived from drug use is essential to understanding addiction.

The conditioning model, with its emphasis on reward, also explains why recovery is difficult for most clients and why relapse is common. By the time most chemically dependent clients reach treatment, the self-administration of drugs is often the only source of pleasure in their lives. Either family, social, or recreational activities have been given up, or the drug us has been incorporated into them. In either case, a client usually finds the period of early recovery to be one of deprivation. The old rewards (i.e., reinforcers) have been removed, but the alcoholic or addict knows they are still readily available. Thus, "slips" or full-blown relapses always remain a possibility; this is especially true of the first year of abstinence.

Strategic treatment planning should include activities that help clients identify nonchemical rewards, and then make use of them to maintain gains made in recovery. This is not an easy task for the counselor. Sometimes clients have limited experience with recreational activities, hobbies, or other enjoyable pursuits. However, if enjoyable alternatives to the chemical experience can be found and used, clients may be able to build a stable recovery relatively quickly and without enormous struggle.

SOCIAL LEARNING THEORY

Social learning theory provides us with a framework for understanding the cognitive dynamics of addictive behavior. It should be understood that social learning explanations are entirely consistent with the conditioning model of drug self-administration. However, social learning theory goes further by elaborating on the unobservable cognitive processes that accompany reinforcement from drug use. For example, the construct of "alcohol expectancy" shows that alcoholic drinking is linked to a variety of strongly held *anticipated* outcomes, in contrast to more moderate drinking, where these expectancies are more weakly held. Thus, the behavior of drinking is contingent only on those rewards that are expected or anticipated to occur. This cognitive element is the defining aspect of the social learning approach to addiction.

Social learning theory has also been used to identify strategies for relapse prevention. Of particular importance here is the concept of "self-efficacy," which is defined as a judgment of one's ability to carry out some course of action. As applied to recovery, this is (roughly) the client's confidence in his/her ability to perform those tasks deemed necessary in treatment (i.e., refrain from substance use, attend counseling sessions and Twelve-Step programs, take Antabuse as prescribed, etc.). Clients with little self-efficacy will be likely to relapse. Those with strong self-efficacy, on the other hand, are likely to be successful at recovery efforts.

Strategies have been identified to bolster clients' self-efficacy; they involve the teaching of skills. An important concept in this skill-building approach to relapse prevention is the "abstinence violation effect," or the tendency of clients committed to recovery to exaggerate the significance of a "slip." Clients often engage in intense self-downing after an initial drink or use of a drug; as a result of the self-condemnation, they continue to abuse substances, rather than just limiting their use to a "slip."

To prevent clients from engaging in the abstinence violation effect, counselors should help clients prepare to encounter high-risk situations. In addition to educating clients about the meaning of "lapse" and "relapse," counselors should teach skills that will enable the clients to identify the "triggers" for cravings (e.g., the smell of a burning match, a beer commercial on television, etc.). The enhancement of self-efficacy through skill building is the cornerstone of this approach to relapse prevention.

FAMILY SYSTEMS THEORY

Family systems theory views addiction as role behavior which serves to *prevent* the breakup of the family unit. The chemically dependent role is seen to be just one of a variety of adaptive roles that family members adopt in order to maintain an unhealthy balance. This pathological equilibrium is preferable to family disintegration; thus, other family members unconsciously work to maintain the addict in his/ her role. The alternative would be squarely facing the sensitive, emotionally charged problems within the unit. However, this is often avoided because of a sense of hopelessness, and the fear that if the family were actually to wrestle with the core issues it would break up.

The systems perspective requires that the counselor account for family dynamics in the treatment planning process. Whenever possible, the client's family members must be included in the treatment process, and when appropriate, they should be treated concurrently with the identified patient. It is particularly useful to explore the family patterns of enabling that may have developed, and to discuss the adjustments that will be necessary in recovery. Family systems theorists maintain that relapse, especially recurrent relapse, is often the result of the family's being left out of the treatment process. In such cases, inadvertent sabotaging of the recovering member may occur because the family still has a need for a grossly dysfunctional role figure (i.e., the alcoholic or addict). In effect, relapses allow the nondependent family members to avoid dealing with more serious, fundamental problems within the unit.

SOCIOCULTURAL PERSPECTIVES

Of the models reviewed in this volume, sociocultural perspectives probably have the least applicability to the clinical practice of substance abuse counseling. They do indicate that values are important to address in the counseling process. However, beyond that, it is difficult to imagine how practitioners can alter the structure of communities and drug subcultures, or reshape cultural, ethnic, and racial traditions in the United States. Yet the sociological perspective is probably more important than any other model in identifying what needs to be done to *prevent* addiction in our society. Clearly, from a "macro" point of view, alcoholism and addiction are manifest symptoms of much deeper social pathology. In order to prevent addiction problems, basic issues of social and economic justice need to be addressed; only then will there be significant, long-term declines in alcohol and drug abuse. Substance abuse counselors can work collectively toward these goals. Through their respective professional organizations, political action can become one of the many roles performed by addiction practitioners.

TOWARD AN INTEGRATED APPROACH TO RELAPSE PREVENTION

It is frequently stated that alcoholism and other drug dependencies are "biopsychosocial" in nature. This term is usually not well defined. A unified model that integrates pharmacological, physiological, psychological, and social determinants to explain chemical dependence has yet to be developed. As the contents of this volume suggest, the creation of a unified model that encompasses many diverse concepts will be difficult. One reason for this is that addiction cannot be easily characterized; it does not follow a limited number of patterns. Peele

(1985) notes this diversity by observing that addiction reflects much of the variety that is seen in other forms of human behavior.

Though a biopsychosocial model of the etiology of chemical dependence has not yet evolved, it appears that a consensus may be emerging in regard to strategies for the prevention of relapse (*Harvard Mental Health Letter*, 1992; McCrady, 1991). The four areas of agreement are as follows:

1. Enhancement of clients' self-efficacy (through skill building).
2. Use of incentives (to create and maintain motivation).
3. Holistic treatment packages (to address clients' lifestyles).
4. Patient–treatment matching (to individualize treatment strategies).

There appears to be "room" within each of the theoretical positions discussed in this book to make use of these four strategies. Let us briefly examine the importance of each strategy.

Relapse prevention strategies that seek to bolster clients' self-efficacy show great promise (Annis & Davis, 1991). Homework assignments that challenge but do not overwhelm clients have been found to be very helpful in teaching skills to cope with environmental "triggers." In turn, the successful completion of these tasks leads to a sense of mastery. The clients gain hope and greater confidence in their ability to help themselves. The skills that have been found to be most important to preventing "slips" include identification of cravings, anticipation of high-risk situations, rehearsal of alternative responses to use when faced with a trigger, and practicing new behaviors in increasingly difficult situations (Annis & Davis, 1991).

It is often noted that many clients in treatment lack the motivation to remain abstinent from alcohol/drugs. Programs that provide positive incentives to do so will be helpful to these unmotivated clients. Traditional treatment programs have relied, for the most part, on punishers (i.e., negative consequences) to warn clients against a return to substance use. The use of rewards to build sobriety or drug-free time has unfortunately been overlooked in many instances. Such efforts would go a long way toward changing the grim, punitive environment that exists in some treatment facilities.

Holistic treatment packages are increasingly being recognized as necessary for good treatment outcomes (McCrady, 1991). By "holistic," it is meant that treatment must address issues in a client's life other than just the use of alcohol and/or drugs. A narrow focus limited to maintaining abstinence may leave the client vulnerable to relapse.

A holistic package may include marital/family counseling, employ-ment counseling, assertion training, social skills training, literacy classes, and other elements.

Finally, it appears that treatment should be tailored to a client's individual needs. Treatment programs have not always emphasized patient–treatment matching. It is important that programs make a stronger effort to institute this strategy. Studies suggest that it leads to improved client outcomes (Woody, McLellan, Alterman, & O'Brien, 1991). For example, it has been found that level of client psychopa-thology affects the relationship between treatment and outcome (McLellan, Childress, Griffith, & Woody, 1984). In a comparison of methadone maintenance and a therapeutic community, it was found that those with greater psychological disturbance fared better in the former treatment. Those with higher levels of psychopathology who were treated in a therapeutic community showed not merely a lack of progress, but a worsening of their status (McLellan et al., 1984). Though much more research is needed in this area, it appears that client characteristics (i.e., type of substance abuse, psychiatric status, gender, age, employment history, marital status, etc.) are particularly important in choosing treatment strategies.

Implementation of these four strategies poses a great challenge to substance abuse counselors. Lack of resources, heavy caseloads, and administrative obstacles are difficult barriers to overcome. We are obli-gated to struggle for the improvement of alcoholism and drug depen-dence treatment. Not only do we owe it to our clients, but we must also convince the public and elected officials that treatment can "work."

REVIEW QUESTIONS

1. What are some of the implications of each model of addiction for individualized treatment planning?
2. What four strategies are being recognized as essential components of effective relapse prevention?

REFERENCES

Annis, H. M., & Davis, C. S. (1991). Relapse prevention. *Alcohol, Health, and Research World, 15*(3), 204–212.
Harvard Mental Health Letter. (1992). Addiction—Part II. *Harvard Mental Health Letter, 9*(5), 1–4.

McCrady, B. S. (1991). Promising but underutilized treatment approaches. *Alcohol, Health, and Research World, 15*(3), 215–218.

McLellan, A. T., Childress, A. R., Griffith, J., & Woody, G. E. (1984). The psychiatrically severe drug abuse patient: Methadone maintenance or therapeutic community? *American Journal of Drug and Alcohol Abuse, 10*(1), 77–95.

Peele, S. (1985). *The meaning of addiction: Compulsive experience and its interpretation.* Lexington, MA: D. C. Heath.

Woody, G. E., McLellan, A. T., Alterman, A. A., & O'Brien, C. P. (1991). Encouraging collaboration between research and clinical practice in alcohol and other drug abuse treatment. *Alcohol, Health, and Research World, 15*(3), 221–227.

Index

Abstinence (*see also*
    Controlled drinking)
    and chronic disease belief, 41, 42
    collateral interviews in assessment
        of, 126
    contingency contracting for, 99,
        100, 101–104
    disadvantages, 95
    family homeostasis
        disruption, 145
    and personality change, 145
    psychoanalytic treatment
        approach, 65
    reinforcement of, 82, 83
"Abstinence/low-frustration-
    tolerance pattern," 128
"Abstinence violation effect,"
    133, 222
Abstaining parents, 180, 181
Acetaldehyde, 34, 35
Achievement anxiety theory,
    197–199
Achievement-oriented families,
    170, 171
Addiction
    behavioral definition, 80, 81
    physical dependence relationship,
        81, 82
Addiction as sin position, 1–3
    advantages and disadvantages, 2, 3
    practitioners' understanding of,
        6, 7
"Addictive search," 61, 69
Adolescent beliefs, drinking,
    196, 197

Adolescent substance abuse
    family factors, 148,
        179–181
    peer group influences, 181
Adoption studies, 24–29
Adult children of alcoholics,
    168, 169
"Adventitious entrance," 61, 69
"Affect defense" theory, 62, 63,
    69, 71
Age factors
    in drug addiction, 192
    in spontaneous remission, 40, 41
Age of onset, alcoholism, 32, 33
Alcohol
    behavioral tolerance to, 88–93
    as reinforcer, 77
Alcohol abuse subculture, 206, 207
Alcohol-craving mice, 77
Alcohol expectancies, 120–125
    balanced-placebo study, 122, 123
    cross-cultural studies, 125
    laboratory research, 122, 123
    survey research, 123–125
    theoretical aspects, 120, 121
    treatment implications, 221, 222
Alcohol Expectancy Questionnaire,
    123, 124
Alcohol industry, vested interests, 4
Alcoholics Anonymous
    chronic disease belief, 41, 42
    disease model conceptualization,
        20, 21
    loss of control belief, 36, 37
    and value conflicts, 212, 213